"The awful loss of innocent lives that occurred on September 11, 2001, was but the first tragedy of what has become known simply as '9/11.' The loss of civil liberties occasioned by the government's reaction to those terrorist attacks is a further tragedy of huge proportion that affects all Americans. More than most who have studied 9/11 and its effects on our society and our legal system, Anthony Romero understands that the slippery slope on which our country now finds itself began not on September 11, 2001, but decades earlier, even before the start of World War II. He also understands that the government programs and policies that have given us warrantless surveillance of Americans, the use of secret evidence, endless detention of those suspected of terrorist acts, and so much more, constitute assaults on all of us, not just those detained in military brigs. *In Defense of Our America* presents a fascinating compendium of real stories of real people who have suffered real harm as a result of the assault on the Bill of Rights since 9/11. These real-life stories draw on American history to drive home the point that must not be lost on all of us: unless we all stand together and fight against this attack on our civil liberties, the next victim could very well be us."

— BOB BARR
FORMER CONGRESSMAN (R GA-7), 1995–2003

"A brave, powerful book from one of freedom's most courageous defenders. These stories remind us how real—how personal—the threats to our Constitutional rights really are—and of the duty that we all have to protect them in times of trouble. Woven through these riveting chapters is a strong reminder: democracy is the best security."

— ELI PARISER
EXECUTIVE DIRECTOR, MOVEON.ORG POLITICAL ACTION

"These remarkable stories are told with an astute understanding of how ordinary people chose to fight for their rights in extraordinary times. *In Defense of Our America* is a great read—informative, intimate, disturbing, and, ultimately, profoundly inspiring."

— CECILE RICHARDS
PRESIDENT, PLANNED PARENTHOOD FEDERATION OF AMERICA

"This is a powerful book that makes abstract concepts about rights and liberties compellingly real. There is only one problem with this book— once you start reading it you can't put it down."

— JOHN W. DEAN
FORMER NIXON WHITE HOUSE COUNSEL

"These powerful stories bear witness to the crisis of conscience in American society: we as a nation purport to stand for freedom while looking away from the willful destruction of individual liberties, the further erosion of a national ethos of fairness and justice, and the shredding of our Bill of Rights. Hearing the voices of victims of torture and bigotry reminds us that we must never be complacent or complicit to human suffering in this or any age. Don't look away. Be inspired. Be outraged. Get busy."

— DERRICK BELL
VISITING PROFESSOR, NEW YORK UNIVERSITY SCHOOL OF LAW
AUTHOR, *ETHICAL AMBITION* AND *FACES AT THE BOTTOM OF THE WELL*

"These are powerfully written stories of ordinary Americans struggling to protect our freedom from governmental oppression in crisis times. It reminds us of the continuing importance of individual acts of courage and of the work of the American Civil Liberties Union."

— MARY FRANCES BERRY
CHAIRPERSON, U.S. COMMISSION ON CIVIL RIGHTS, 1993–2004

"*In Defense of Our America* is not just a book of fascinating stories. It is a collection of parables, snatched from the headlines, whose lessons we ignore at our collective peril."

— ELLIS COSE
AUTHOR, *BONE TO PICK*, *THE ENVY OF THE WORLD*,
AND *THE RAGE OF A PRIVILEGED CLASS*

"Anthony D. Romero makes the abstract issues of civil liberties hit home in an immediate and visceral way."

— LARRY FLYNT
PUBLISHER, *HUSTLER* MAGAZINE

"As a conservative, I don't like many of the clients the ACLU represents and consider some of what their attorneys do more political than it ought to be, but anyone who cherishes the freedoms the founders sought to guarantee through the constitution and Bill of Rights should recognize the importance of an organization that believes those documents mean what they say and are willing to fight anyone who doesn't. This book tells the story of those struggles, and Romero understands that a concern for civil liberties crosses the political spectrum.

"Those in government who abuse power usually believe they do so 'for our own good.' The ACLU is there to remind them and the rest of us as well . . . through the courts when necessary . . . that noble motives are not enough, because in this country, the ends simply don't justify the means."

— DAVID KEENE
CHAIRMAN, AMERICAN CONSERVATIVE UNION

"This fascinating collection of stories puts a human face on some of the most important civil liberties issues of our time. Each of these stories reminds the reader of our duty to protect our rights and civil liberties and the rights and civil liberties of others."

— WILMA MANKILLER
FORMER PRINCIPAL CHIEF OF THE CHEROKEE NATION

"*In Defense of Our America* tosses the frequently arcane academic discussion of civil liberties to the side and presents an eloquent and moving portrait of regular Americans facing difficult choices about right and wrong within our constitutional framework. Tackling issues from terrorism and wiretapping to Katrina and religion in schools, *In Defense of Our America* shows us how everyday Americans—true patriots—fight for our nation's core values of individual freedom and human dignity."

— JOHN D. PODESTA
CEO AND PRESIDENT, CENTER FOR AMERICAN PROGRESS

"*In Defense of Our America* chronicles the lives and vastly different people whose stories and whose actions had a dramatic impact on the landscape of civil liberties in the twenty-first century. Their collective sagas form a moving narrative that is both disquieting and inspirational, and that underscores the need to respect the rule of law and ensure that basic human rights are afforded to everyone."

— MARY ROBINSON
UNITED NATIONS HIGH COMMISSIONER
FOR HUMAN RIGHTS, 1997–2002
FORMER PRESIDENT OF IRELAND, 1990–1997

"These engaging stories of ordinary people doing extraordinary things to defend our rights and liberties in these perilous times give hope that our country's promise will be fulfilled. Read this book and meet spirited patriots committed to building a country dedicated to fairness, equality and a respect for the dignity of all people."

— KATRINA VANDEN HEUVEL
EDITOR AND PUBLISHER, *THE NATION*

"The book is an engaging read, more like a novel than a collection of legal analysis. There is a dramatic edge to the interwoven narratives, and just the hint of a thriller in the way chapters are divided. Romero brings the necessity of civil liberties close to home."

—*THE AMERICAN PROSPECT*

"Brilliant. . . . [This] book clarifies the purpose of the ACLU for those who choose to distort it. It also reinforces what is now painfully obvious to many Americans, namely that those in Washington or elsewhere who abuse the Constitution may think of themselves as patriots but that title is more deservedly given to the ACLU and its champions."

—*NEW YORK LAW JOURNAL*

In

DEFENSE

of Our

AMERICA

The Fight for Civil Liberties
in the Age of Terror

ANTHONY D. ROMERO
and Dina Temple-Raston

HARPER

NEW YORK • LONDON • TORONTO • SYDNEY

HARPER

A hardcover edition of this book was published in 2007 by William Morrow, an imprint of HarperCollins Publishers.

HarperCollins books may be purchased for educational, business, or sales promotional use. For information please write: Special Markets Department, Harper-Collins Publishers, 10 East 53rd Street, New York, NY 10022.

FIRST HARPER PAPERBACK PUBLISHED 2008.

Designed by Jennifer Ann Daddio

The Library of Congress has catalogued the hardcover edition as follows:

Romero, Anthony D.
  In defense of our America : the fight for civil liberties in the age of terror / Anthony D. Romero and Dina Temple-Raston.—1st ed.
      xvi, 252 p. : ill. ; 24 cm.
  Includes bibliographical references and index.
  ISBN: 978-0-06-114256-7
  ISBN-10: 0-06-114256-5
  1. Civil rights—United States. 2. National security—United States. 3. Terrorism—United States—Prevention. 4. Intelligence service—United States. 5. Terrorism—Government policy—United States. I. Temple-Raston, Dina. II. Title.
JC599.U5 R66 2007
323.4'90973 22   2007297750

ISBN 978-0-06-114257-4 (pbk.)

FOR MY MOTHER,
*who taught me right
and wrong*

AND FOR MANUEL,
*who supported me in
righting some wrongs*

ACKNOWLEDGMENTS

WE WOULD LIKE TO THANK ALL OF THOSE WHO TOOK TIME TO help with this book, whether it was providing information, adding insight, offering advice, or patiently listening to yet another story as we tested out material before putting words on the page.

By definition, a book about ordinary people doing extraordinary things depends on the kindness of strangers. We'd particularly like to thank those people who were willing to step out from behind the scenes and allow us to pepper them with pointed and detailed questions about subjects that can make people uncomfortable, whether it be race, abortion, gay rights, or terrorism. They shared their feelings with unsparing generosity. Many took us into their houses and allowed us to rummage around in their lives. Without them, this book would never have been possible. In particular, we'd like to thank Jim Bamford, Ann Beeson, Greg Davis, Josh Dratel, Kot Hordynski, Matthew Limon, Frank Lindh, Marilyn Walker, Bert Spahr, Cecelia Fire Thunder, and the friends and neighbors they introduced us to so we could get as full a picture of the events as possible. They were always

kind enough to make time for us when we needed to add more detail
or understand the issues more precisely.

For the John Walker Lindh portions of the book we owe a great
deal to Tony West and Kerry Efigenio and George Harris. They were
available whenever we had questions and were kind enough to chase
down letters and e-mails that helped us reconstruct the events as
they happened instead of through the lens of revisionist history. Kerry,
in particular, was always gracious and helpful. Private investigators
David Fechheimer and Barry Simon helped us reconstruct John
Walker Lindh's trip through Yemen, Pakistan, and Afghanistan.

On the NSA portions of the book Ann Beeson and Josh Dratel
were very generous with their time and explained the intricacies of
the issue. Similarly, Kot Hordynski drove up from Santa Cruz to meet
us in San Francisco for dinner just so we could flood him with questions about the TALON list and its impact on him. We expect great
things from Kot in the future. He's a wonderful young man.

In South Dakota, of course Cecelia Fire Thunder was particularly
helpful. She allowed us to follow her around as she campaigned just
ahead of the abortion ban vote and permitted us to sit in on her strategy meetings, which provided invaluable insight into how the issues
of incest, rape, and abortion played on the Pine Ridge Reservation.
Also in South Dakota, our thanks go out to Kate Looby of Planned
Parenthood and the ACLU's Sondra Goldschein, who helped provide
perspective on a fiery issue.

Matthew Limon spoke with us on numerous occasions although
his parents were suspicious of our motives. He's a trusting young man
who took us at our word and tried to help us understand what had
happened to him. He is uncomfortable about being a symbol for gay
rights in this country. We think he wears the mantle well. There was
a great deal of background research necessary to do this work. We'd
like to thank the people at the Lakemary Center and Ellsworth Correctional Facility for walking us around their facilities so we could

better place Matthew and the events that unfolded around him. We also wish to thank the inmates at Ellsworth who tried to help us understand what it was like to live behind Ellsworth's bars. In particular, Herbie Harris, the ECF chaplain, has our sincerest thanks.

Help in New Orleans came from all quarters. In particular Katie Schwartzmann and Tom Jawetz of the ACLU helped us sift through hundreds of biographies to find an appropriate main character for our story the Orleans Parish Prison. The National Prison Project's groundbreaking report, "Abandoned and Abused," was invaluable. It is not only good reading, but very objective in its reporting of what unfolded in the days before and after hurricane Katrina. Pam Metzger and Katherine Mattes from the Tulane Law Center were incredibly helpful. The work they are doing in New Orleans is invaluable and we are proud just to know them.

There are always the people behind the scenes who may not realize how much they help spur a project along. Aryeh Neier was one of those positive sources of inspiration and encouragement. His reading of the early manuscript saved us from ourselves. Similarly, John Russonello, Samuel Walker, Thomas Laqueur, and Jean Strauss also provided substantive comments on the manuscript, as did Mahnaz Ispahani and Roslyn Litman.

We also owe our gratitude to the people at the ACLU who worked on these issues, provided critical information, and were often the protagonists even if behind the scenes. Among those who helped with the documents, facts, and research are Elizabeth Alexander, Ed Balaban, Graham Boyd, Ellen Chege, Terence Dougherty, James Esseks, Sondra Goldschein, Melissa Goodman, Jeremy Gunn, Jameel Jaffer, Tom Jawetz, Tamara Lange, Donna McKay, Louise Melling, Katie Schwartzmann, Steve Shapiro, Amrit Singh, Vic Walczak, Steven Watt, Emily Whitfield, Ben Wizner, and Marsha Zeesman. The ACLU executive committee and national board also deserve our thanks. Their support for a book that we believe will help focus attention on the issues of civil liberties in this country today cannot be underestimated. ACLU president Nadine Strossen is a hero for providing support and guidance throughout the book. Steve Gellers kept us out of trouble, for now. Emily Tynes provided initial encouragement to write a book on top of an already overwhelming job. Thanks a lot. Karen Simon helped us track down the photos to put the human face on these stories, and Alan Winnikoff was instrumental in helping us get the word out about the book.

Special thanks also to Bob and Alexandra for providing a clean, well-lighted place to work. We couldn't have finished this without you.

Our agents, Tina Bennett and John Thornton, as well as our publishers at HarperCollins, Jane Friedman and Rene Alegria, also deserve our thanks. Book writing is a long, drawn-out process and they helped keep us on schedule and on message.

Last, but in no way least, we would like to express our deepest gratitude to Scott Reiners. He has been a complete rock star throughout the process. He cheerfully made suggestions to improve the book and helped us bring it alive. His assistance, intellect, good humor, hard work, and support throughout this project went beyond what anyone could possibly expect from a colleague. The book would not be what it is today without his help, and for that we are both eternally grateful.

CONTENTS

INTRODUCTION

THIS BOOK IS A WORK OF NONFICTION, BUT IT READS LIKE A novel. It is a compendium of stories about people on the front lines of the battle for civil liberties: a Dover, Pennsylvania, biology teacher who refused to allow religious beliefs to be forced into her classroom; New Orleans prisoners doing "Katrina time" because of a judicial system broken long before a hurricane made landfall; a Sioux Indian concerned about rape on a South Dakota reservation.

The authors of this book chose these stories because they said something about the state of play for civil liberties at this moment in time. These pages provide snapshots of some of the most contentious issues of our time, as told in a series of vignettes that run throughout the book. We purposely did not just look at prosecutors and defendants in particular cases, but instead got down to the level of the sidewalks to find real Americans at the center of the debate on terrorism, gay rights, abortion, and religion in the classroom. The undoing of John Walker Lindh, the so-called American Taliban, for example, is told from his parents' point of view, whom we interviewed extensively. Joshua Dratel, a defense attorney who has been witness to every twist and turn of the war on terror, illuminates the fallout from the NSA warrantless wiretaps.

Some of the people described in these pages are ACLU clients, most are not. That's because this isn't a book about the ACLU. It is a book about civil liberties at a time when they appear to be under siege. As such, this book reflects the reporting and opinions of the authors, not the American Civil Liberties Union.

We are very aware that this book arrives on the scene just as many Americans—on both sides of the aisle—question whether they ought to trade civil liberties just to feel more insulated from terrorism. We hope to add to that discussion.

PROLOGUE

LONG BEFORE AMERICANS HAD INCORPORATED TERRORISM INTO their vocabulary or had started watching low-flying airplanes through suspicious, narrowed lids, terror and its effect on America's civil liberties were the twin suns around which Joshua Dratel's legal practice revolved.

In the early days of 2001, eight months before the World Trade Center attacks, the 45-year-old criminal defense attorney had a front-row seat at what would become the opening act of the "war on terror." Dratel represented Wadih el-Hage, one of four men accused of masterminding the 1998 bombings of American embassies in Kenya and Tanzania. Their trial was the United States of America's first comprehensive attempt to prosecute the growing menace of Islamic extremism in a court of law. The case, known as *United States of America v. Usama bin Laden, et al.*, laid out a terrifying narrative that, until the attacks of September 11, would go largely unnoticed by the American public. As the trial unfolded, Dratel listened with alarm as prosecutors began to sketch a portrait of a largely unknown foe determined to wage war against America. It was a global terrorism network they called al-Qaeda. And while el-Hage and three other men sat in the dock, it became clear that something much bigger was on trial, though few people realized it at the time.

Dratel was just a block away from the World Trade Center on September 11, 2001, when the prosecutors' nightmare scenario—a terrorist attack on the continental United States—came true. He heard the loud scream of a jet engine and the explosion on impact. His apartment building literally shook. He craned his neck from the window of his Battery Park City apartment to see flames licking the upper floors of the North Tower. He watched as ribbons of steel and sheets of paper rained down on the ground below. And while the rest of the world may have hoped that this was some sort of pilot error or terrible mistake, Dratel's mind immediately arrived at another place. "They bombed the World Trade Center again," he told himself, switching on the television.

In the days after the embassy bombing trial, Dratel's legal practice had changed. He became a kind of go-to guy for terror defendants. He locked horns with the government in one of its signature domestic terrorism cases against the north-Texas-based Holy Land Foundation for Relief and Development. The Bush administration accused the group of illegally raising and laundering tens of millions of dollars to Hamas, a U.S-designated terrorist organization. He was the defense attorney for David Hicks, the so-called Australian Taliban, in *United States v. David Hicks*. Hicks had been detained as an enemy combatant at Guantánamo Bay since 2001, accused of fighting for the Taliban and al-Qaeda in Afghanistan. Dratel had been prepared to defend Hicks before a U.S. military commission when his effort was cut short. The Supreme Court ruled in 2006 that the commission's tribunal process was unconstitutional. He had been one of the lead attorneys, alongside the ACLU, in suing the government over the USA Patriot Act provisions that broadened investigators' powers, allowing them to set up secret wiretaps after securing permission from a special court.

All these cases had made Dratel a resident expert on terror in the 21st century, and consequently, Dratel became, in a very real sense, the Leonard Zelig of such litigation. Just like the Woody Allen character who found himself standing next to Babe Ruth or Winston Churchill at some turning point in history, Dratel appeared at almost every key moment of America's "war on terror," blinking against the klieg lights.

So it was rather ironic that when the *New York Times* broke one of the biggest stories about civil liberties in post-9/11 America—that President Bush had sidestepped the law and hadn't bothered to secure warrants for a roster of domestic wiretaps—Dratel was one of the last to know. The December 16, 2005, front-page story remained tucked and unread in his briefcase until late that evening. Dratel had returned to his downtown Manhattan apartment, opened a bag full of take-out Chinese, and started reading through the day's headlines. He stopped in mid-chew when he read the 24-point type on the lead story: "Bush Lets U.S. Spy on Callers Without Courts."

In the months after 9/11, *Times* journalists James Risen and Eric Lichtblau reported, President Bush had signed an executive order allowing the National Security Agency to eavesdrop on international telephone calls and to monitor the international e-mail messages of people inside the United States. The program was said to track so-called dirty numbers—phone lines that might have had links, however tangential, to al-Qaeda—but there was no telling who else was inadvertently picked up in that sweep. It wasn't the suggestion of secret wiretaps that rattled Dratel. That had been done in the past after securing permission from a special court—the Foreign Intelligence Surveillance Court—created for just that purpose. It was that this time the process of getting warrants—that singular check on the power to determine whose phone calls and e-mails would remain private and whose would be monitored by government agents—had been circumvented altogether. In a very real sense, the administration decided that the gravity of terrorism put the president above the law.

Secret government spying isn't new. In fact, it goes back to the early years of the twentieth century. This kind of eavesdropping first became a major public issue during the Vietnam War when American intelligence agencies launched similar spying operations against protesters and civil rights activists. When that effort was exposed in the 1970s, Congress passed the Foreign Intelligence Surveillance Act, or FISA, to safeguard against future abuses. FISA was supposed to impose strict limits on intelligence gathering on American soil. Morton Halperin, then a staffer at the ACLU Washington legislative office, helped broker the deal that led to FISA. A former National Security Council staffer during the Nixon administration, Halperin had developed a keen personal interest in the issue of wiretapping. The FBI had tapped his own telephone after Secretary of State Henry Kissinger included his name on a list of government officials and journalists under suspicion when details of the bombing of Cambodia were leaked to the press in 1969. Halperin spent years waging a court battle against the Nixon administration over the wiretaps. A court ultimately found President Nixon to be personally liable.

The FISA deal was not without critics. Some of Halperin's ACLU colleagues saw it as a deal with the devil. Quick access to foreign wiretaps was traded for a modicum of judicial review and the promise that the wiretaps would not be used in criminal cases. Supporters of the compromise argued that the law required search warrants, approved by a secret FISA court, for wiretaps in national security cases. That would make it more difficult for the federal government to spy on critics and dissenters. Then, in December 2005, it appeared that the law no longer applied. In one fell swoop, President Bush had unilaterally bypassed Congress and the Foreign Intelligence Surveillance Court. He disregarded FISA and the Constitution in authorizing a new brand of NSA spying.

The *New York Times*'s revelations came at a time when Americans were trying to decide how much of their civil liberties they were willing to swap to avoid another terrorist attack like 9/11. Still reeling from the deadliest blow on U.S. soil, many Americans put their trust in the president, assuming that government knew better than anyone how to foil another attack. To many, civil liberties became a luxury. Certainly they could be suspended in times of peril. September 11 prompted a number of hasty changes to federal law, many of which were loaded in a shopping cart of provisions called the Uniting and Strengthening America by Providing Appropriate Tools Required to Intercept and Obstruct Terrorism Act of 2001—the USA Patriot Act. It gave the Federal Bureau of Investigation additional powers to collect personal information like library or Internet records. It watered down—and in some instances eliminated—judicial review. The Pentagon and the Department of Homeland Security asked to use public and private databases to troll for possible terrorists. The FBI and the Department of Defense were already secretly tracking and spying on peaceful antiwar protests.

While Dratel was used to thinking about how law enforcement efforts might affect his clients, this time he had reason to be personally concerned. His client list alone would have been reason enough to suspect he would have been part of a telephone sweep. He quickly ran through phone calls he had made that could have been problematic. He had been speaking to terrorism defense lawyers and potential witnesses and investigators. He called Gaza and Afghanistan. He talked to friends of David Hicks. He contacted mosques and visited jihadi Web sites. The people he called and e-mailed might well have been in touch with people who had firsthand knowledge of terrorist operations. Dratel was sure his name would pop up in any daisy chain of these numbers. "If anyone is being spied on," he remembered thinking, "it's me."

The *New York Times* article was sketchy about the details of how the spying program worked. All that was certain was that the NSA was eavesdropping on hundreds of people in the United States without judicial approval or review. The list of names waxed and waned as some people of interest were added and dead ends were dropped, the article said. What it seemed to be describing, Dratel said later, was an expansive view of the president's power when it came to issues of national security. In Dratel's opinion, that conduct was quite clearly unlawful. Permitting unchecked government eavesdropping within the "land of the free" was an enormous change in American intelligence-gathering practices. It violated the Constitution.

The fact that the program was coming out of the National Security Agency only made it more worrisome. To that point, the NSA had been in charge of spying on communications abroad. Bringing its shadowy work home raised red flags about constitutional protections against an overreaching government.

In the days after 9/11, the CIA began a series of dragnets, known as the "special collection program," targeting al-Qaeda operatives. At the same time, the FBI and the Justice Department were zeroing in on run-of-the-mill immigrants who were Muslim, Arab, and Asian. Some government officials were literally using phone book lists of Arab and Muslim names to guide their dragnets. The federal government had rounded up thousands of immigrants with no discernible connection to terrorism, detaining them on minor immigration violations. They had no access to anyone on the outside—not even a lawyer—for longer than the law allowed. A December 2003 report by the Justice Department's own inspector general cited "evidence that some officers slammed detainees against the wall, twisted their arms and hands in painful ways, stepped on their leg restraint chains, and punished them by keeping them restrained for long periods of time." Many of the detainees were ultimately deported—most of them in secret. Another inspector general's report released in June 2003 revealed how many were charged with acts of terrorism: zero.

The ACLU sought to release the names of immigrants who were detained and deported. In response, the Bush administration closed all deportation hearings. Members of the press, family members, even members of Congress couldn't sit in. The Supreme Court declined to weigh in. It let conflicting opinions in the appellate courts stand.

At the time, public opinion was on the administration's side. Immigrants—particularly Muslim and Arab immigrants—were all suspect after 9/11. Law enforcement abuses began to take root. Not since the Palmer Raids in 1919 and 1920, out of which the ACLU was born, and the internment of over 120,000 Japanese-Americans in concentration camps during World War II, had America seen such mass detention and deportations of the alleged "enemy within."

Government intelligence officials rifled through immigrants' computers, cell phones, and address books in a bid for new leads to track al-Qaeda operatives around the world. Monitoring just one phone number allowed intelligence officials to build a database of "potential terrorists" and build a web of gossamer connections. But in FBI field offices, NSA data was viewed as a distraction in the hunt for terrorist plots. Information gleaned from the NSA program often led to innocent people or dead ends. FBI agents joked that additional tips meant more "calls to Pizza Hut." Anyone calling a suspected dirty number became a potential target. Certainly anyone calling a friend they had no idea was a suspected al-Qaeda operative would likely be targeted too.

As Dratel read through the *New York Times* article, his most immediate concern was about attorney-client privilege. Though the article didn't say specifically that attorneys or physicians were in the sweep, Dratel worried that they might be. (The Department of Justice would later say that calls involving doctors or lawyers "would not be categorically excluded from interception" as long as there was a suspected link to al-Qaeda and one party was outside of the United States.) More broadly, whether or not Dratel was a target, what the article made clear was that the NSA program flew in the face of the First, Fourth, and Fifth Amendments—free speech, protection from unreasonable search and seizure, and due process. There was also the chilling effect the program could have on many Americans if they even suspected they might be on the receiving end of a wiretap. It would change the way they operate, even subconsciously.

It took two days for President Bush to confirm that the domestic intelligence collection program even existed. He defended it saying it had been instrumental in foiling terrorism in America. Under Article II of the Constitution, as commander in chief, the president had the authority to use the program, the White House told reporters. In the wake of 9/11, Congress authorized the president "to use all necessary and appropriate force against those nations, organizations, or persons he determines planned, authorized, committed, or aided the terrorist attacks that occurred on September 11, 2001, or harbored such organizations or persons, in order to prevent any future acts of international terrorism against the United States by such nations, organizations or persons." Warrantless eavesdropping, the White House argued, fell under that category.

On the Sunday talk shows, Secretary of State Condoleezza Rice claimed that the program was merely closing a seam. "Our intelligence agencies looked out; our law enforcement agencies looked in and people could—terrorists could—exploit the seam between them."

President Bush skirted the court-approved warrant process because investigators needed to be more nimble in their hunt for terrorists, Rice said. "The president is determined that he will have the ability to make certain that the seam is not there, that the communications between people, a limited number of people with al-Qaeda links here and conversations with terrorist activities outside, will be understood so that we can detect and thereby prevent terrorist attacks." But while Rice was going to great lengths to defend the NSA program and portray the warrant process as a hurdle between those whose job it is to keep us safe and secure the information necessary for them to do so, she failed to point out that FISA already gave intelligence officials the power to intercept phone calls and e-mails for up to 72 hours before getting a warrant.

The warrantless wiretaps should have been a wake-up call for Americans who believed they had nothing to fear from the war on terror as long as they were doing nothing wrong. That blind trust in government, Dratel said, was naïve. A look at American history showed that programs launched in times of emergency always became part of the larger system and they always left open the door for abuse of power.

"What worried me is that for every one thing you might discover they might be doing, there are nine you don't know about," Dratel said later. "I was sure this was the tip of the iceberg. Things that go unmonitored, like eavesdropping without a warrant, it is a prescription for abuse. And whether I was part of their listening program or not, I knew I had to do something."

Chapter 1

FINDING JOHN

THE TIMELINE OF JOHN WALKER LINDH'S journey from northern California teenager to the "American Taliban" is marked with dates in boldface. **November 1992:** John Walker Lindh sees the movie *Malcolm X* and begins to mull the possibility of converting to Islam. **Spring 1997:** John passes the California proficiency exam, allowing him to test out of the public high school system. **Fall 1997:** John starts taking history and politics classes at a local community college. **Winter 1997:** John's conversion is complete. He declares himself a Muslim. **Summer 1998:** John goes to Yemen to learn Arabic so that he can commit the Koran to memory as Muslim teacher-scholars, his aspiration, must do. **May 2001:** John e-mails his parents and tells them he is going to travel to the mountains to escape Pakistan's searing summer heat. **September 6, 2001:** John goes to the front line of a battle between Taliban forces and the Northern Alliance in Afghanistan. **December 3, 2001:** John's picture and his introduction as the "American Taliban" appear on the Internet. **January 15, 2002:** Attorney General John Ashcroft declares John a terrorist. **October 4, 2002:** John is formally sentenced to 20 years in prison.

It was just five short years, but each date marked a chronology of heartbreak for Frank Lindh and Marilyn Walker. They watched the events unfold with disbelief from the moment they realized their son was in Afghanistan until his sentencing. "The whole experience was my own personal big bang," Marilyn later said. "My life came apart and my family was under siege. Everyone keeps trying to find out what was wrong with John. Nothing was wrong with John. Everyone tried to blame us. Nothing is wrong with our family. Instead this was the most striking example of demonizing someone who doesn't see things the same way as other people I have ever seen."

Frank Lindh had just emerged from an early evening showing of Billy Bob Thornton's *The Man Who Wasn't There* when he noticed a message flashing on his cell phone. Lindh was a soft-spoken man, with a handsome face and lanky frame. He had the look of a runner, and his even temper and problem-solving demeanor were almost those of an Atticus Finch.

The voice mail was from his ex-wife, Marilyn. "Call me right away, it is about John," it said. Marilyn Walker was not a woman prone to hyperbole. Tall and thin with long flowing hair and bangs, she exuded a sense of quiet and balance. For that reason, the tightness in her voice rattled Frank. He hurried to his car and drove up the road to Marilyn's house.

Frank Lindh and Marilyn Walker had managed to construct one of those rare friendly divorces. They made decisions about their children together without rancor. They attended school plays sitting side by side. They shared the inevitable ferrying around of children as they went to soccer games or drama practice with good-natured compromise. The younger Lindhs were as likely to be found at their father's house on any given evening as they were their mother's. And after the divorce, when the Lindh parents sent letters and small notes to their children, they signed them with the slightly dated honorifics of "Mama" and "Papa."

Why a modern American would join forces with the Taliban would be the question that millions of Americans would later ask—including President Bush. The question would haunt John Walker Lindh for the rest of his life. His path to the Taliban would be a circuitous one, and it would take all of three years to complete.

JOHN WAS THE LINDHS' MIDDLE CHILD, sandwiched between Connell, his older brother, and Naomi, a younger sister who idolized him. John was a smart child, though he had always been a little introverted. He was the kind of boy who would ask for Japanese language tapes for Christmas one year and Gaelic tapes the next. He had an affinity for languages and music, and his parents, to the extent they could, tried to foster those interests. John suffered from chronic diarrhea, most likely caused by a parasite, which dramatically affected his ability to go to school. The school district, because of his many health-related absences, sent tutors to home-school him. That alone made him different. It made him solitary and by turns shy. He had beautiful hair and large brown eyes when he was little, and when people commented on it, Marilyn could see John's writhing discomfort. "He hated attention," she said.

When he was little, Men at Work, an Australian pop group, was constantly playing on the radio. Their hit was a song called "Be Good." His father used to sing the song to John. The song had one voiceover that said: *"So, tell me what kind of boy are you, John?"* When his father used to sing it to him, John was embarrassed but in that secretly de-lighted way children are when their parents dote on them.

The song was the furthest thing from Frank Lindh's mind when he walked into his ex-wife's house. Marilyn had a poster of Pakistan up on the wall in her entryway. She had always kept close tabs on John when he went overseas. She marked the four or five cities on the map where John had been with push pins. It seemed like as good a way as any to keep track of him.

For a man who would later go to fight for the misogynistic Tali-ban, John thrived in a family of strong women. In addition to hav-ing strong bonds with his mother and his paternal grandmother, Kate, John had developed a particularly close relationship with his sister, Naomi, eight years his junior. He was the protective older brother outside on the streets, and a nurturing buddy at home. After school, John would whip up some macaroni and cheese for the two to share. Frank and Marilyn were used to coming home to find their two youngest kids talking furiously with their mouths full of cheesy pasta.

When Marilyn left Frank the voice mail, the Lindhs hadn't heard from their son in seven months. He e-mailed them in the spring say-ing that he would be leaving Bannu, Pakistan, where he was studying the Koran, to take refuge in the mountains.

From his parents' distance, the move made sense. John's stomach was acting up again and he had trouble bearing the sweltering Paki-stani summers. The climb to a higher altitude, his message said, would provide some relief. But when the Lindhs had heard nothing from John by midsummer, Marilyn began to worry. She started plan-ning a trip to Pakistan to find him. His father visited local mosques in the San Francisco Bay Area searching for some clue as to where he had gone and how he might find him. Then Marilyn left that ominous voice mail on Frank's cell phone.

Marilyn led Frank back to her computer and pointed to the screen.

There was an e-mail from a cousin of Frank's with a single line: "Do you think this could be John?" Frank leaned in. There was a fuzzy photograph on the MSNBC Web site of a young man with a beard and long matted hair. His face was smeared with dirt. Frank Lindh stopped breathing. The picture looked eerily like his twin brother twenty years earlier. It took a moment for Frank to realize that he was harking back to the wrong generation. He and Marilyn had finally found John.

The Lindh parents had come to expect extraordinary things from John. Born in Washington, D.C., in 1981, the Lindhs' middle child has two famous namesakes: Chief Justice John Marshall and John Lennon, who had recently been shot outside the Dakota apartment building in New York City by Mark Chapman. John's mother, a photographer, stayed home with John and his older brother while Frank Lindh was finishing up law school at Georgetown University. A short time later, Frank started working at the Federal Energy Regulatory Commission. John was 8 when his father landed a job at LeBoeuf, Lamb, Leiby & MacRae. When John was 10, the firm transferred his father to its San Francisco office.

In hindsight, his parents say that John never really liked California. He missed the Washington suburb, Silver Spring, Maryland, where he had grown up. And for whatever reason, it was with the move to California that John's lifelong bout with intestinal diseases began. John's chronic diarrhea had a debilitating effect on an adolescent growing into a young man's body. He became reclusive, shying away from potentially embarrassing situations with other kids his age. It was heartbreaking for his parents, who watched the emerging young man struggle. Finding one's way and acquiring confidence as a teenage boy was hard enough without the discomfort and embarrassment of an unpredictable stomach ailment. The loneliness that followed would teach John other skills. His father would later say that John developed an ability to remain active in his mind and to find peace in being alone. "He would use those same skills later in jail," he said wistfully.

If there was a turning point, one event from which the others appeared to flow, it was John Walker Lindh's decision to go see Denzel Washington in Spike Lee's *Malcolm X*. He was moved by the movie's climax when Malcolm X makes a holy pilgrimage to Mecca just after he split with the Nation of Islam. (He was assassinated in Harlem a short time later.) The film's scene at the Haj prompted Lindh, at the age of 12, to begin exploring Islam. He started studying religion with his school tutor. She tended to assign papers according to his interests, so Arabic history and the roots of Islam became common choices. Against that backdrop, it is not so surprising that John Walker Lindh made the weighty decision to convert at the age of 16. He went to the Mill Valley mosque in late 1997 and he took *shahada*, his confession of faith.

When someone becomes a Muslim, he utters the first principle of Islamic teaching: "There is no god but God and Muhammad is the messenger of God." John Walker Lindh took the name Suleyman, or Solomon. His parents didn't find out until sometime later when a friend from the mosque called for Suleyman at home. His parents say now that John was always calm, and centered, and still. His choice of religion may have surprised them—he had been reared in the Catholic Church—but they saw nothing wrong with it. "It didn't seem to be a bad thing," his father said later.

Later, outsiders would say Frank and Marilyn should have had their son on a shorter leash. They saw them as being permissive "northern California" parents. One thing was sure, however. They loved their boy.

AS WITH ALL RELIGIONS, Islam is made up of a series of beliefs and practices. At its root, Islam entails "submission" to the will of God. A Muslim, in the strictest sense, is "one who submits" to the will of

God. All Muslims believe that God revealed his will in scripture, including the Jewish Torah and the gospels in the Christian Bible. Muslims also believe that all these scriptures teach that God created all human beings as equals and that the duty of believers is to treat one another as such. That's why for Muslims there is an unending effort to remedy injustice. If people are suffering, it is the duty of Muslims to try to reduce that suffering. While no one person can fix the world, each Muslim is expected to contribute to a just society. That could mean anything from being a good student to striving to be a good parent. Muslims are expected to make career choices, for example, based on where they think they can make the greatest contribution. This struggle, for a Muslim, is called *jihad*.

Military jihad, the one most people associate with the 9/11 attacks, is very different. Military jihad is carefully regulated by Islam. Some Muslims believe that jihad can be initiated only by a duly constituted government. They believe that since the Ottoman Empire, there has been no authority in the Muslim world qualified to call for jihad. Others believe that the current Islamic governments are profanely secular, therefore leaving room for the true believers to take action outside of government. The jihad debate rages with enormous intensity among Muslim scholars.

Contrary to what many Americans may think, military struggle is not considered the highest form of jihad. The "greater jihad" is the struggle to control one's selfishness and pride. And that was what John Walker Lindh was trying to do when he joined a local San Francisco Bay Area branch of a global missionary Islamic group, Tablighi Jama 'at—which means "a group that propagates the faith." Its network stretches the world over—through Europe, Asia, and the Middle East. Its members visit mosques and college campuses in small groups and preach a return to purist Islamic values.

After joining the San Francisco branch of Tablighi Jama 'at, John asked his parents to let him attend the Yemeni Language Center in

Yemen so he could learn Arabic. It would be the only way, he told his parents, that he could become a teacher-scholar in the tradition of Islam. While today Americans see Yemen as largely synonymous with terrorism, when John Walker Lindh went there to study in 1998, the country was fairly obscure. The bombing of the USS *Cole* in October of 2000 brought Yemen to wider public attention, but by and large, Yemen was better known by average Americans as the site of a goodly number of foreign kidnappings. The abductions weren't always meant as anti-Western statements, however; and Americans living in Yemen at the time were quick to say that most of the tourists held hostage were eventually released unharmed. Many even claimed that they were well treated. The purpose of the kidnappings was to exact some sort of concession from the Yemen government, and in general, the strategy worked. The kidnappers often got what they wanted.

"People are under the impression that we just let John go; just threw up our hands and said, 'Yemen, sure, dear, anything you want,'" Marilyn said, growing visibly angry. "We did a lot of research before he left. He did a lot of research. And the best place in the world to learn classical Arabic is Yemen. It still is. And that's why he wanted to go there." Experts don't disagree that Yemen is the undisputed center of Arabic learning.

Lindh left for Yemen in July 1998, came home for ten months, and then returned to continue his studies. John's time in America in 1999 and 2000 was unremarkable. There wasn't agitation or anti-Americanism when he returned, his mother said. He was just as she had remembered him, a gentle, quiet young man. He worked part-time in a women's clothing warehouse to earn pocket money and then flew back to Yemen, where he attended the Yemen Language Center in Sana'a. But in John's estimation that language center was full of foreign coeds who had traveled from home just so they could party. He quickly looked for another school where, he said, the other students took their studies more seriously. He transferred to

Al-Imam Islamic University of Sana'a for a total Arabic-immersion program.

By the following fall, in 2000, Lindh's Arabic was good enough to allow him to take the next step: to begin the memorization of the thirty chapters of the Koran. For that, he decided, he needed to go to a madrassa, or religious school, in Pakistan. He traveled around Pakistan for a couple of months and then attended a conference of the Tablighi Jama 'at in Lahore before his Koran classes began.

Every fall, the Tablighi Jama 'at conferences draw over 1 million believers to the city of Raiwind, near Lahore. The words *Tablighi Jama 'at* literally mean "proselytizing group." The group is considered law abiding. They are described as an apolitical grassroots missionary operation seeking to shape individual lives, and promote introspection and spiritual development. Some scholars compare them to Alcoholics Anonymous. Given the group's focus on spiritual development and growth, it's not hard to see how a spiritual boy from Northern California might be drawn in.

John Walker Lindh took his place among the other students in Pakistan. Lindh chanted and rocked and memorized chapters of the Koran. In late-night conversations, they told John that if he really wanted to be a good Muslim he should go fight in Kashmir. By standing alongside Muslim brothers fighting for an Islamic homeland, John was told, he would achieve religious peace. For whatever reason, the idea appealed to the young Lindh and he made plans to do exactly that. His parents learned all of this later. In the summer of 2001, all they knew was that their son was escaping the heat by going up to the mountains for a couple of months. He told them not to worry.

"In Bannu, it's starting to heat up," John wrote in an e-mail to his parents. "And Indian heat is not like Californian heat. I haven't decided 100% where I'll go, but this should be worked out in the next two weeks. I'll try to keep in touch, but in the mountains I may not have e-mail access so I could end up sending you a letter or calling you before I go, then keep in contact by way of postal mail until the end of the summer." To his parents, this sounded like a reasonable plan.

JUST WEEKS BEFORE LINDH WAS TRAVELING to higher ground, in April 2001, the U.S. government awarded $43 million in grants to the Taliban government for opium eradication. The *New York Times* called it "a first cautious step toward reducing the isolation of the Taliban" by the Bush administration.

The Taliban developed as a political force in Afghanistan in the mid-1990s, after the anti-Soviet, multinational Afghan mujahideen campaign defeated invading forces in 1989. The withdrawal of the Soviet forces after ten years of occupation left a power vacuum in Afghanistan. Infighting between various factions claimed many thousands of lives. In the midst of all this, the Pakistani government created the Islamic Movement of Taliban (which literally means "students"). It was an army of Afghans from the Islamic schools and refugee camps of Pakistan. The Pakistani government saw supporting the Taliban as an opportunity to install a friendly neighbor to the west to offset the hostilities it faced with India to the east. With Pakistan's blessing and backing, the Taliban ended factional infighting and brought 90 percent of Afghan territory under its umbrella. The Northern Alliance held the remaining fraction.

The women of Afghanistan, in particular, endured years of extreme violence and discrimination under Taliban rule. The Taliban restricted virtually every aspect of their lives—including their movement, behavior, and dress. Women could not show their faces in public. They were required to wear the chadari, or burqa, and to be accompanied by a male relative at all times. Women who disobeyed the law—particularly the dress code—were publicly beaten by the religious police, who wielded metal-studded batons.

Illiteracy among women in Afghanistan under Taliban rule was a staggering 90 percent. Access to health care was abysmal, resulting in the deaths of nearly 45 women per day due to pregnancy-related issues. In July 2000, the Taliban banned all Afghan women from working in aid agencies except for those in the health care sector. These and other restrictions on women's employment led to an increase in women begging on the streets and participating in prostitution. The Taliban also targeted civilian ethnic minorities and frequently used the rape and abduction of minority women as a weapon of war.

AFTER SEVERAL YEARS of studying Arabic in Yemen and goading from his classmates, John had come to the conclusion that just studying and memorizing the Koran wasn't enough. He wanted to take his belief and his commitment further. "I believed it was the part of every good Muslim to train" for military jihad, he said. He hoped he might be able to find a way to help create a "pure Islamic state" and thought he could do that by joining Harakat-ul-Mujahideen (HUM), a Pakistani organization that trained Muslims to fight against Indian forces in the disputed border regions of Kashmir.

Those who doubt John Walker Lindh's naïveté point to this decision as proof that he had decided he would take up arms for Islam. In going to Kashmir, Lindh was stepping into one of the bloodiest disputes between two nuclear powers on the world stage. And HUM, in particular, was an organization with questionable, even violent, factions within it. Lindh told investigators later that he had no idea that HUM might have been a terrorist organization. People who talked to Lindh after he was captured, including FBI investigators, said that he had a rather romantic view of Islam. And that innocent view might have led him to the HUM camp.

Contrary to John's expectations, the camp was not full of Islamic scholars and well-intentioned Muslims. Instead, it was a fat farm of

sorts for doughy Saudi teenagers. The three-week basic-training portion of the class was like elementary school phys ed. There were lots
of calisthenics and running. There was no live ammunition. This
camp wasn't quite as advertised. It was not preparing young men for
an Islamic struggle. Instead it was all about getting Kashmir annexed
back to Pakistan. Lindh saw Kashmir as an independent Islamic state,
a possible Muslim homeland, not an arm of secular Pakistan. Pakistan shouldn't be in charge of Kashmir any more than India should
have been, he concluded. After three weeks, he dropped out of the
HUM program and decided instead to follow the route that many of
his Muslim brothers had: he would help save Afghanistan.

It was June when Lindh crossed the Khyber Pass and reported to
the Taliban recruitment office in Kabul. He asked to go to the front
line, the place where he could lay his life on the line for the Taliban
forces—and Islam. Instead, they assigned him to Al Ansar, a non-
Afghan, Arabic-speaking unit. They said that without Pashto or Urdu
language skills he would have to be assigned to what they deemed a
"foreign force." His training at HUM would not be enough to qualify
him for a role in the Afghan army. He checked into the Al Ansar training camp in Kandahar in late June.

The declaration of jihad has been a difficult issue in the Muslim
community. There has never been a consensus on whether military
jihad is a genuine religious obligation. Local Saudi chapters of the
Muslim Brotherhood, for example, said that their members just
needed to do relief work in Afghanistan and Pakistan. There was no
need to be fighting on the front line. Concerned Saudi fathers went
to the training camps to drag their sons back home. Many of the
people in these camps were holiday fighters—students looking for an
exciting way to spend their breaks from school.

While all this was taking place, Osama bin Laden had a vision of
creating an Arab force—a sort of rapid-reaction force—that would fight

for Muslim causes. Violence and terror were part of its playbook. As part of that project, bin Laden set aside money for Arabic-speaking recruits who came to the training camps in Afghanistan and Pakistan. John Walker Lindh ended up in that part of the Al-Farouq camp that was financed by bin Laden. Lindh wasn't directly training with al-Qaeda; rather, he was training to be part of the Afghan army—a distinction that would later be lost on U.S. authorities. But the money came from bin Laden all the same, something that would return to haunt him.

There were two training tracks one could take at Al-Farouq. The al-Qaeda training aimed at fighting civilians or the military training, focused on toppling the Northern Alliance. FBI officials say that Lindh participated in the military training, aimed at waging a traditional war against the Northern Alliance forces. He enrolled in what he thought was an infantry training camp with three weeks of weapon familiarization. Each recruit was permitted to fire ten rounds of a pistol and a shoulder weapon, as well as one rocket-propelled grenade. They spent a week practicing map reading and using the sun and the moon for navigation. They also got a week of battlefield training using camouflage and defensive positions and moving under fire.

Lindh was there when Osama bin Laden arrived. He gave evening lectures on the local situation, political issues, and old Afghan and Soviet battles. He thanked the recruits for taking part in the jihad. Lindh later told investigators that he wasn't impressed by bin Laden. In fact, he fell asleep during one of his speeches. Lindh eventually volunteered for duty as a foot soldier in the Afghan army. The assignment took him to Takhar, in northeastern Afghanistan.

Lindh would say later that he thought the war between the Taliban and the Northern Alliance was merely a continuation of the war between the mujahideen and the Soviets. The mujahideen of that era had been supported by the U.S. government. Since the Soviet pullout, the American government's stance had changed. By 2001, the

U.S. was backing the Northern Alliance, something Lindh said he didn't know. "I went to Afghanistan with the intention of fighting terrorism and oppression, not to support it," he said.

Experts supported Lindh's claim that his allegiance was to the Taliban, not al-Qaeda. Rohan Gunaratna made a career out of interviewing terrorists and writing about what leads them to terrorism. He wrote *Inside Al Qaeda*—the definitive book on the organization—and served as an expert witness both for and against the U.S. government. Few people know al-Qaeda better than Gunaratna. He spoke to John Walker Lindh for eight hours and was sure he wasn't a terrorist. "There is a difference between the Taliban and al-Qaeda and the government has conflated that difference in this case," he said. "At Al-Farooq there was military training for soldiers in the Taliban and separate training for al-Qaeda. He trained as a solider and wore a Taliban uniform. He didn't receive any civilian warfare training. He didn't have the skills or the expertise to become a terrorist or to conduct terrorist operations. He was an ideologue. He was naïve and went headlong into the arms of the Taliban. That doesn't make him a terrorist," he said.

Al-Qaeda, particularly at that time before 9/11, was a secret organization, Gunaratna explained. Lindh couldn't foresee that the conflict with the Northern Alliance would later be connected to 9/11. According to Gunaratna, "Lindh was asked by an al-Qaeda leader, Abu Mohammad al-Masri, if he wanted to go to the United States or Israel for a martyrdom mission. He said no. He said he came to Afghanistan to serve on the front line against the Northern Alliance. That wasn't easy, to say no, in a place like Al-Farooq, but he did. That says something."

John Walker Lindh arrived on the Taliban's front line on September 6, 2001. He was with 75 other recruits in one of the last deployments of soldiers to be flown to the Takhar region. The brutality of the Northern Alliance, by this time, was renowned. Castration followed by execution was just one of the many atrocities Northern Alliance prisoners were likely to face. General Abdul Rashid Dostum, the founder and leader of the National Islamic Movement of Afghanistan (a faction of the Northern Alliance comprising mainly ethnic Uzbeks), had punished soldiers and prisoners by tying them to the treads of tanks. When Dostum was driving out of Kabul in 1997, his forces reportedly slaughtered about 50,000 people and raped young girls and mutilated their breasts. When John Walker Lindh landed in Takhar, he was handed a rifle and two grenades—the standard issue for new recruits. He was a foreigner, his commander told him, so he would be doing guard duty.

John possessed another unique skill that the Taliban exploited. He knew how to make instant noodles. Those afternoons of macaroni and cheese with his sister were paying off. Before Lindh, bags of egg noodles would arrive at the camp and be pushed around by the Taliban fighters with quizzical expressions. Lindh knew how to cook the food and said as much. For a brief time, before the fighting eclipsed such trivial things, John Walker Lindh was the Taliban's king of macaroni.

KOT HORDYNSKI WAS HOME for his 2005 Christmas break when a disturbing e-mail came over the transom: apparently the Department of Defense found him (and a handful of his friends) to be a "credible threat" against the nation.

Hordynski, a tall, loose-limbed 21-year-old who still gets carded when he wants to buy a beer, blinked in disbelief. One of the founding members of Students Against War (SAW) on the University of California at Santa Cruz campus, Hordynski seemed more on the way to embodying the American dream—his parents had emigrated to the United States from Poland when he was in grade school—than battling against it.

His résumé, such as it was for a junior in college, was full of earnestness. His objective was to obtain a job "in a challenging and meaningful area" and to that point his work experience, including translation projects from Polish to English, training students to raise money over the phone for the California Peace Action in Berkeley, and working at the Inter-Library Loan office at UCSC, reflected that. He was, the résumé said without a great deal of description, a "library assistant III," which presumably was better than a library assistant I or II. In nearly every way, Kot Hordynski seemed like a typical college kid. But a story on the MSNBC Web site over Christmas break suggested that he was a leader of something insidious.

Hordynski clicked on the link and started reading about a covert Pentagon program that had been tracking a series of antiwar and counterrecruitment meetings at a handful of the nation's colleges. The document cited in the news story was a rather exhaustive list of student political movements on campus, including what looked like threat assessments of some 1,500 "suspicious" incidents. Ten colleges were highlighted in the document. Among the incidents listed: an April 5, 2005, UC Santa Cruz Students Against War protest in which Hordynski and his friends had set up a booth near a military recruiter to provide information to students who the military had been trying to sign. For every argument that the recruiter made to get young men and women to enlist, SAW provided a counterargument. It was more like a benign version of CNN's *Crossfire* than a protest. For their efforts, the internal Pentagon documents labeled the members of SAW a "credible threat."

"If we, as students, are being labeled a credible threat," Hordynski remembered thinking, "then no one is safe."

Chapter 2

TWO WRATHS
FROM GOD

THERE IS A CREEPY STILLNESS IN THE Lower Ninth Ward of New Orleans. Even more than a year after hurricane Katrina, nearly every house is deserted. Many are frozen in midcollapse, contents open to sky, with doors ripped from hinges and windows punched out. The houses look like their mouths are agape, as if they are still surprised by such wholesale devastation. Katrina left perfect disorder in a place that didn't have much to start with. The Lower Nines (as it was known locally)—which sits at the bottom of New Orleans's famous Ninth Ward— is two square miles of concentrated Bayou poverty. Even before Katrina, the area was considered the most dangerous neighborhood in the most dangerous city in the nation. The number of murders in New Orleans peaked in 1994 with 421 dead—a higher murder rate than in any other U.S. city. In 2004, 265 people were murdered. Many of those murders happened in the Lower Nines. The area's proximity to the city's industrial canal and its violent reputation earned it another nickname: CTC, "Cross the Canal," or, more often, "Cut Throat City." The neighborhood street signs belie the meanness of the place. They carry gentle, religious names like "Piety" and "St. Ann." Shotgun houses, long and thin on tiny lots, are crammed cheek-by-jowl.

Fourteen thousand people lived in the Lower Ninth Ward before August 2005—less than 3 percent of the city's population. Then, on the morning of August 29, an enormous wave washed over the houses in the Lower Nines with such force that it pulled nearly a full square mile of the homes off their foundations. When the waters receded, not a dwelling in the Lower Nines was untouched. Those that didn't collapse or get wrenched from their postage-stamp-sized yards were flooded to the rooflines. The Lower Ninth Ward, by the fate of geography, was all but snuffed out.

Some might say that those who stayed could, with some ingenuity, have found a way to leave. To be sure, there were many residents, through sheer inertia, who figured they would wait out the storm, banking on the hyperbole of weather reporters—knowing that the doom casters had been wrong before. "Billion-Dollar Betsy"—the hurricane that had wreaked havoc 40 years earlier—was a distant memory for some. And the country had long forgotten about the great 1927 Mississippi flood, when rescuers saved white women and children who were left homeless. Blacks were left behind, and in some cases held at bay—at gunpoint.

In 2005, the decision to stay put in New Orleans proved ill-fated, but for most, at least, it was a decision made after a moment of reflection. For some 7,000 prisoners—many of whom called the Lower Nines home—at the Orleans Parish Prison, the decision to wait out the storm was made by someone else: a freshly minted sheriff named Marlin Gusman. "The prisoners will stay where they belong," he told the Department of Corrections when they offered to help with an evacuation. He called a meeting of his deputies on the Saturday before the storm and told them they were welcome to bring their families to the jail for safety. He assured them there were generators and water and flashlights.

A deputy at that meeting said that one of the cooks warned there wasn't nearly enough food to sustain the inmates and workers' families for more than a day or two. There was a shortage of batteries for the flashlights, piped up another. Gusman assured everyone that everything would be just fine. Gusman seemed to have forgotten that OPP was not built to shelter prisoners, but merely to contain them. And this became OPP's undoing.

GIVEN ALL THE SUFFERING that occurred in the wake of Katrina, it was easy to shrug off what happened to the prisoners as part and parcel of unanticipated tragedy. There were casualties everywhere. Clearly, prisoners were bound to be among them. The sheer size of OPP—almost half as big as the entire Lower Ninth Ward—meant that people were bound to get hurt.

New Orleans's incarceration rate reflected its violent reputation. But it was hard not to notice that the jailhouse population was racially skewed. While only 66 percent of Orleans Parish was black, African-Americans made up nearly 90 percent of its prison population. Outsiders assumed the inmates they saw on television who ended up on a highway overpass to escape the rising water were murderers and rapists. In fact, more than half of the people sitting on the asphalt were men and women arrested on municipal charges—public drunkenness, or unpaid fines—and most of them were pretrial detainees. They hadn't yet had their day in court.

Greg Davis was in jail when Katrina made landfall. A handsome, sturdy 51-year-old who gave off the air of an old-timer who had seen it all, there was something immediately likable about Davis. It could have been his manner. He was easy with himself. He bore no grudges against anyone and had found an equilibrium: he asked little of life and expected little in return. Davis liked to wear a big silver cross around his neck and trim, fitted black jeans. Despite his poverty—he worked odd jobs when he could find them—he was fastidious about his appearance. He kept his house clean. His yard was spotless.

One afternoon shortly before Katrina, he went to the store to get cigarettes. Police arrested him on his way out. He was suspected of having taken part in a burglary. To that point he'd been a man arrested on an array of relatively minor charges: trespass or drunkenness or drug paraphernalia. But because he was suspected of taking part in a theft, Davis found himself in jail just weeks before Katrina, sitting in OPP waiting to be charged. As he awaited arraignment on the burglary charge, he missed a court date for a separate incident at which he was supposed to pay about $440 in fines. He didn't have a public defender assigned to his case, so no lawyer was there to explain that Davis was already in jail and that's why he couldn't show up. The judge issued a warrant for the incarcerated man's arrest. Davis's burglary charge was dismissed, but right after he was released, he was picked up on a warrant for his outstanding fines.

Greg Davis's story wasn't unusual. The inmates on the overpass were not a collection of the meanest of the mean. Instead they were mostly a motley crew of indigent African-Americans, many of whom wouldn't have been in jail at all had they lived just about anywhere but New Orleans. The penal system in New Orleans was broken— and had been for some time. It just took a category 5 storm to get the rest of the country to sit up and take notice. At least for a while.

———

ORLEANS PARISH PRISON WAS an archipelago of more than a dozen buff-colored structures in an area of New Orleans called Mid-City. The complex is within walking distance of the Broad Street overpass and rises above Interstate 10 amid a blighted neighborhood of shotgun houses and rusted, abandoned industrial buildings. The Ernest N. Morial Convention Center sits about two and a half miles away, near the river. The Louisiana Superdome is just about halfway between the two.

Orleans Parish Prison began as just a single jailhouse. In 1929, the city built it to hold 400 to 450 people. In the fifty years that followed, the population had merely doubled. Then, in 1974, a man named Charles Foti was elected sheriff. Over the next three decades, under Foti's guidance, OPP's capacity would jump 1,000 percent. When Foti left in 2003, the prison's population had grown from 800 to 8,500 prisoners. While New Orleans before Katrina was the thirty-fifth most populous city in America, OPP was the ninth largest local jail in the country. It was a city within a city, and as things tended to happen in New Orleans, it became a power unto itself.

New Orleans had long had the dubious distinction of the highest incarceration rate in the country: double the national rate. Foti's skyrocketing prison population is even more striking when one knows that in the same period that the number of prisoners increased, the actual population of Orleans Parish had fallen almost 20 percent, from some 600,000 in 1970 to 485,000 at the time of the last census in 2000. The number of Foti's stewards rose not because of a miraculous crackdown on local crime. Instead, the population ballooned because in the mid-1970s, OPP began to take in prisoners on behalf of Louisiana's Department of Corrections, raking in substantial state per diems in the process.

Orleans Parish offered to take on the state's overflow after a federal court ruled in 1975 that Louisiana's prisons were so overcrowded as to be unconstitutional. Louisiana's DOC, the judges said, violated the Eighth Amendment rights of the prisoners housed there; the amendment prohibits the infliction of cruel and unusual punishment. The court found that the state was showing "deliberate indifference" to conditions that posed a substantial risk of serious harm to prisoners. Orleans Parish Prison officials said they would be happy to help the department remedy the situation. Thirty years later OPP would find itself accused of doing the very same thing.

On the face of it, the court decision was a financial boon for Sheriff Foti and Orleans Parish Prison. To accommodate the DOC population, he began to build annexes and dormitory structures. There was a House of Detention, a ten-story tower with a psychiatric ward; a Community Correctional Center for administration; five dormitory structures known as Templeman I–V; a work release center; and the Conchetta's women's facility, which was a converted motel. Together they were, literally and figuratively, the "big house." The new mini city of incarceration, as it was envisioned, would be paid for by stepping up the type of prisoners that would come to OPP. Foti, a former police department attorney, aggressively pursued contracts to house federal inmates, which brought in about twice as much money— $42.50 a day—as the state and city prisoners did. He offered to take the overflow of prisoners from neighboring parishes.

At the same time, the government's "war on drugs" and move toward mandatory minimum sentences in the 1980s and 1990s helped boost the OPP bottom line. New Orleans, a city known for letting the good times roll, instituted a zero-tolerance policing policy, like the one made famous by Rudy Giuliani in New York City. The idea was to attack quality-of-life problems with the goal of reducing bigger crimes, though attorneys on both sides of the courtroom agree that New Orleans may have taken this to an extreme. Foti was known for encouraging his police to make more arrests when prison beds were empty. As time passed, the prison made Foti as powerful as the mayor, if not more so. By 2003, he was overseeing a $70 million budget, 1,200 employees, and a jail full of prisoners who could work for free. With those kinds of resources, Foti became a kingmaker and political force. His employees were largely nonunion, so there were no labor leaders to cry foul when guards or deputies were sent out into neighborhoods to canvas for candidates in their spare time. There was a jail full of prisoners who could be dispatched to clear garbage or repaint unsightly graffiti at opportune times during the election cycle. At Thanksgiving, the sheriff presided over an enormous public feast for the elderly, usually held at the Hyatt hotel. All the meals were courtesy of the prison. Clearly, rehabilitation was not the job of those who ran OPP. They had become warehousers of human beings, and without putting too fine a point on it, they were storing a large number of people who had lived in the Ninth Ward.

Marlin Gusman took the job as New Orleans's chief jailer in 2003. He was the first black sheriff the parish had ever had, and it would fall to him to keep the empire safe when Katrina made landfall two years later. Today the prison is announced by oversized bright green letters on the outside wall of the administration building. Marlin Gusman's name is spelled out in letters so large one could be forgiven for thinking it was named after a former civic leader, as a memorial gesture, instead of the current sheriff.

DEPUTY BERNARD REED WORKED with troubled inmates in the psychiatric ward of OPP's House of Detention. A deputy at OPP since 1998, he arrived for his shift the Sunday before the storm feeling anxious. His wife had asked him to quit. This storm, she was convinced, would be different. She asked Reed to wait out the storm in Georgia with the rest of their family. But Reed felt he had a responsibility to the jail, and to the other deputies, to show up. "I went in to work because it's like a family there, and one less person on staff can make a big difference, especially since I'm big, strong, and experienced," he said. Reed was six feet seven, and at the time weighed about 500 pounds.

The trouble started before Katrina ever made landfall. On Friday, August 26, three days before the hurricane struck, the prisoners' phones died. That meant that no one could call to find out where their family members were going to be—whether loved ones would try to wait it out or evacuate. The problem made an already anxious prison population even more so.

Tiers A and B in a unit known as Templeman III were where new prisoners were held after their arrest and booking. The receiving tiers, as they were known, were still doing a brisk business as the storm closed in. While those who could evacuate were climbing into their cars and heading east on Interstate 10, OPP was still admitting new prisoners. One man was arrested just five days before the storm because he had failed to pay $100 in old fines. Over 100 of the men who were held in the receiving tiers during hurricane Katrina had been arrested and booked on minor charges on August 27 and 28. The prison went into lockdown a day later, on Monday. Greg Davis was put in a cell built for two with seven other prisoners.

For guards, lockdowns provide a sense of relief. When inmates are all in their cells, what is stressful for officers fades away. The gates are closed. The PA system is quiet. Typically, lockdowns happen after unusual incidents—be it gang-related violence, attacks on guards, a problem with the count that implies an inmate is missing, or the discovery of some contraband. Calling for a lockdown isn't done casually because, while it is a relief to jailers, it is stressful to inmates.

Before the storm hit, Greg Davis's chief concern was his mother. He didn't know if she was going to try to wait out the storm or evacuate with a neighbor. When the phones in the jail went dead three days before the storm, prisoners in his section of OPP were crazy with worry. When the power went out on Sunday night, Greg Davis said it was so dark he couldn't see his own hand in front of his own face.

Then water started streaming into OPP. Greg Davis said, "Water was just pouring in . . . through the windows, through the walls, and through the vents and stuff. . . . We really found ourselves locked in, and nobody watching us and nobody to let us out. And we started panicking."

"Once the power went out, deputies started quitting left and right," Deputy Reed, who was on the 10th floor of the House of Detention, said afterward. "We really didn't have any problems with the inmates except that they were upset because they didn't know what was going on with their families."

As Reed saw it, the guards were woefully unprepared for the storm and managed to enflame an already volatile situation. The prisoners had a right to know about their families, he said. "Even though they are in jail, they are human beings." It would be easy to blame the guards for what went wrong in the days leading up to and after the hurricane, but it was hardly their fault. Before the storm, they didn't have any training or emergency drills to help them handle the situation. Reed said Sheriff Gusman's policies were to blame. Gusman was always trying to trim costs. When he started work as a deputy in 1998 there were always enough supplies on hand. His floor never ran out of toilet paper. Under Gusman "you had to jump through hoops just to get what you wanted for your floor," he said. "All I know is that the supplies were so low during the storm that we ran out of food." Reed said he ended up not eating for three days.

ON FEBRUARY 26, 2000, Matthew Limon was with a friend in one of the dormitory rooms at Lakemary School. In and of itself, that was a problem. Anyone attending Lakemary, a special needs institution in Miami County, Kansas, would tell you that going into someone else's dorm room was not allowed. Rooms were oddly sacred there: they offered a zone of privacy that other residents were not supposed to invade. If Lakemary had a golden rule, the room prohibition was it. The typical Lakemary student recited the school's regulations the way a third-grader might recite his times tables or spell words by rote. ("You cannot go into someone's room without being invited." "You are not allowed to go beyond the trees." "There is no touching of another student.") So Matthew and his friend knew better than to be on their own. But on this particular evening, in those untapped hours after supper but before bed, Matthew, just turned 18, and his friend, just shy of 15, had found themselves without supervision. And as teen-agers often do, they took the opportunity to engage in some sexual experimentation. The age of consent in Kansas is 16, but the two boys almost certainly had other things on their minds.

Matthew and his friend were in Matthew's dorm room. The younger of the two, identified only as M.A.R., consented to oral sex, but then asked Matthew to stop. Matthew did so right away. What happened next changed the course of Matthew Limon's life: a Lake-mary counselor walked in on the two of them. The police were called. Officers in squad cars arrived on campus. And Matthew Limon in-stantly made the transition from high school student to sex offender.

MATTHEW LIMON, A DOE-EYED BOY with an easy smile, is big-boned in that way football players can be. There is a largeness to him that belies his soft-spoken demeanor. Matthew could easily fit into the crowd of young gay men who saunter up and down Eighth Avenue between 14th and 23rd Streets in Manhattan's Chelsea neighbor-hood. Unlike the Chelsea boys, many of whom also herald from small towns, Matthew Limon was struggling with being gay in a place where that just wasn't done.

Matthew was born on February 9, 1982, in Satanta, a small agri-cultural town of 1,200 nestled in the hills of southwestern Kansas. Now 25, he lived in the tiny city of Larned, and worked the night shifts at a local Wendy's. If Matthew was Larned's Chelsea boy, Wendy's was its East Village—the epicenter of a small-town counter-culture. During a visit there, a young black man in Chuck Taylor high-tops came in with a piercing on his lip and a ring through his eyebrow. He stayed a while, made Starbucks-like small talk, and then left. The young girl behind the counter also had an eyebrow pierced.

Matthew's father, Mike Limon, was both Christian and a cowboy, and by all accounts lived his life in that order. His church and his religious beliefs guided just about everything he did. He was a descendant of one of the town's oldest Mexican families, whose forebears came to Satanta to work for the Santa Fe Railroad. Matthew's father was a "full-blooded Mexican" as Matthew described him, and spoke a proud Spanish. One of Mike Limon's first disappointments in his boy was when Matthew never took to the language, shedding the mother tongue as the younger generations often do. The Limon clan was led by two brothers, known simply by their initials: A.P. and E.P. They were men who achieved standing in a community simply by being rock solid. They were dependable people who worked hard and kept to themselves. The next generation was born in America and began with Gilbert Limon, Mike's father, who, as expected, continued to carry the family's good name. The Limons, right down to Mike and Matthew, were considered the kind of people one wanted to have as neighbors. Helpful, but not intrusive. Quiet, but not unfriendly.

Mike Limon was the embodiment of the rural Kansas life. He had his first horse at the age of 12 and nursed a lifelong passion for horses and livestock and cattle. As he matured, he gravitated toward his strengths and became a cowboy. He could lasso cows, sing, and play guitar with the best of them. Anyone who knew him said that what defined Mike Limon was not his work, but his faith. God was his savior and there was barely a moment in the day when Mike Limon didn't remember that and act accordingly. When he married his wife, a white woman named Debby, it was clear he was determined to rear a family that wouldn't just mouth the word of God but would live it.

To that end, the Limons practiced a life of self-sacrifice. They were the first to volunteer for church activities, the first to help with funerals or Sunday school classes, the first to coach the choir. And as life unfolded before them, be it triumph or setback, they embraced it all as part of a larger plan from above—the wisdom of which would reveal itself as long as their faith remained unbowed. They reared two children, Kendra and then Matthew, to think that way as well.

AT FIRST, YOUNG MATTHEW's slow response time to the world around him led his parents to believe he had a hearing problem. They consulted doctors, and it appeared that in that regard, their boy was fine. They enrolled Matthew in a Christian kindergarten and it was there that it became clear that he had a learning disability, although for years its severity eluded the experts. His problem was masked, people said later, by his affinity for music. While God might have denied Matthew in one way, he gifted him in another. Matthew never took a piano lesson but was able to mimic songs on the keyboard by ear. His parents gave him church hymns to learn and soon Matthew was writing his own songs, some about God, others about love. Many were about redemption. Matthew would say later that music was the one thing he thought he did well. It was the one thing he had in common with his cowboy father. Mike would play the guitar while Matthew accompanied him on piano. The father-son duo would even play in church—"old gospel songs," as Matthew remembered it. Music provided a refuge of sorts: while playing music Matthew didn't feel different or special or slow. He felt free.

When there wasn't music, and when Matthew was forced to read and write and do arithmetic, life was harder. He started attending special education classes in local Christian schools. When that wasn't enough, his parents tried a center for the developmentally disabled, in Liberal, Kansas—35 miles from Satanta. Debby or Mike would carve out the time in an already busy day to drop Matthew off at the center in the morning and pick him up every afternoon. That might have been enough to get him through school, residents said, had it not been for a tragic accident that set the young Limon reeling. A close friend was killed in a car crash. Her name was Allison. She was only 14. Confronted for the first time with life-and-death issues, the loss of a friend, and an outside world that didn't strike him as particularly friendly, Matthew quickly descended into such a deep depression that his parents didn't know how to respond. They were afraid he wouldn't finish school. They prayed for guidance. Eventually, Mike and Debby Limon came to the conclusion that their son would be better off in a group home with others who shared his difficulties.

Doctors said that Matthew's intelligence fell somewhere between "borderline intellectual functioning" and "mild mental retardation." In Matthew's own words: "I'm a little slow with things but I have no problems and get on." If one wasn't trying to teach him spelling or math, one might not have noticed the problem. Matthew was talkative and when he chose the wrong word it was usually a bigger word than the one he needed. It was something that poorly educated individuals often did to make themselves sound more sophisticated. Unless they knew about Matthew's learning disability, people tended to dismiss the stumbles, pauses, and bad word choices as one of the shortcomings of growing up in rural Kansas or perhaps a sign of an innocent lack of interest in those details, but nothing more.

LAKEMARY BILLS ITSELF AS a school for "exceptional children." Its campus has the feel of a small community college. There are neatly manicured lawns, winding sidewalks, and pine trees. The dormitories and regular classrooms are one-story stone-and-concrete affairs, separated by flower beds and low hedges. While Lakemary talked about "exceptional children," what they meant were special needs kids—children with mental retardation, behavior disorders, and other developmental disabilities—which the Kansas public school system was not sufficiently equipped to handle. While Lakemary was both private and nonprofit, two-thirds of its six dozen residents were in the custody of Kansas Social and Rehabilitation Services—kids whose parents had come to the end of their ropes, who had decided that they were not able to care for their children themselves. Sometimes it was a violent outbreak at school that convinced them to send their children away. Other times, as in the case of Matthew, it was minor brushes with the law. The Lakemary kids were not murderers or gang members. Instead their problems were of a more innocent variety—impulse control, suppressing the urge to strike out when frustrated. Lakemary's safe and controlled environment was meant to blunt the sharp edges of day-to-day life. The state picked up Lakemary's $121.50 a day fee for most of the residents. Parents applied for aid and much of the bill, almost as a matter of course, was absorbed by state programs for troubled kids. Matthew was one of the school's few private clients.

Anyone bringing their child to Lakemary would be hard pressed not to feel that their children might be happier there than in the outside world, where people didn't understand them. There was something unendingly cheerful about Lakemary. Construction-paper drawings dotted the walls. Colorful tiles, designed by the students themselves, lined the hallways. There was a sensory room full of colorful lights and soft fabrics, a treat doled out to children when they had performed particularly well. The place had that elementary school disarray that children and parents alike find oddly comforting. For Matthew Limon, however, the experience quickly seemed demeaning. With an IQ of 84, Matthew was a borderline case. His "special needs" were barely severe enough for placement at Lakemary. But after his friend's fatal car accident, Matthew had problems keeping his hands to himself at school, so a kind of segregation from the world seemed necessary.

Neighbors said Mike Limon was torn about the decision but came to believe that sending Matthew away was the best way to unscramble his sexual confusion, to guide him to a different choice than a homosexual one. God certainly did not mean for Matthew to be gay, his parents told their son. God didn't approve of this kind of life. But as much as they prayed, it seemed to have no effect. Matthew had been gay as long as he could remember. "I like it," he says plainly. His parents learned of Matthew's orientation in 1999. A few years earlier, there had been another minor incident—a 14-year-old Matthew experimenting with two boys his own age—that had rattled his fundamentalist Christian parents. ("They didn't appreciate my gay lifestyle," Matthew said. "They thought that maybe I would grow out of it and were disappointed when I didn't.") As they saw it, the only thing left to do was to drive their son into the Kansas hills, hours from Satanta, to Paola. Matthew arrived at Lakemary School in July 1999 and he said later that as he watched them drive away, he was convinced his parents had given up on him.

ACCORDING TO HIS COUNSELORS, Matthew had settled in quite comfortably at Lakemary, and he seemed happy enough with his schooling there. Given Matthew's history of not keeping his hands to himself, the Lakemary counselors felt they had no choice but to call in the police when he and M.A.R. were caught alone in the dorm room. Later, some of the same school officials expressed regret at involving the police. But then again, Matthew was an adult—albeit a very young one—and the boy who was with him was not quite 15. Kansas's statutory rape law prohibited "criminal sodomy," including oral sex with teenagers younger than 16. Furthermore, Kansas's law protecting teenagers who have consensual sex with younger teens specifically excluded consensual sex among boys. If Matthew had had sex with a girl, and the state had decided to prosecute him at all, the longest sentence meted out would have been 15 months. But because M.A.R. was a boy, Matthew didn't have the benefit of the romantically named "Romeo and Juliet" statute. Instead, he was facing a sentence that approximated that of a murder rap.

There are only a handful of states with Romeo and Juliet laws. The statutes attempt to accept the reality that as much as parents don't want their teenagers to have sex, they often do anyway. There are times, Kansas lawmakers conceded in 1999, when a boy over 18 might have sex with a girl who was, legally, too young to say yes. That boy, they decided, didn't deserve to be treated as a rapist or sex offender. While young love was often stupid, it was rarely equivalent to rape. The Kansas legislature passed the law to make sure that young love—or teenage lust—didn't accidentally become a serious felony. According to the Kansas Court of Appeals, the law was meant to differentiate sex between a full-fledged adult and a young teen from sex between teens of different ages.

The 1999 decision to create the law clearly didn't come easily to Kansas lawmakers, who had already been moving toward the right. In order to win passage, legislators wrote a number of clarifications into the statute. They recognized that there may be developmental differences in the teen years: a 17- or 18-year-old boy or girl was much more aware of the consequences of sex than, say, a 14-year-old. So the law stipulated that the ages of the sexual partners had to be less than four years apart. The law was not meant to legalize or condone teenage sex, lawmakers stressed on its passage. Instead it was designed to greatly reduce the penalties involved in punishing it.

In the eyes of the state, however, boys who had sex with boys didn't deserve such protection. As lawmakers saw it, gay sex was much more insidious. Boys who got blow jobs from other boys were so impressionable that they might "turn gay," they thought. They ignored any research that indicated sexual orientation was innate. In Kansas, sexually active gay teenagers were predators to be charged under a sodomy law that was written in 1855, when Kansas was still a territory. It was revised more than a hundred years later, in 1983, to specifically exclude heterosexual sex.

There was one lawmaker in particular who was steadfastly opposed to the 1999 Romeo and Juliet statute: a young state legislator from Shawnee, Kansas, named Phill Kline. In his view, the legislation was tantamount to giving teenagers a free pass to have sex at a time when they weren't emotionally equipped to handle it. He voted against Senate Bill 149. Kline would later come to play a key role in Matthew Limon's case.

Had they been asked at the time, Matthew's parents might well have sided with Kline. They were clearly horrified by the turn of events at the Lakemary Center and there was a part of them that thought the seriousness of an arrest and trial would help deter their son from this aberrant lifestyle he had chosen. "They thought that maybe prison would cure me of this gayness," Matthew said. "I wanted to have that happen, I really did. But I think deep down inside I knew that no matter how hard they prayed I wasn't going to wake up one morning and be different."

The police arrived on the Lakemary campus and interviewed Matthew in one of the school's conference rooms. He didn't have a lawyer present. He was read his rights, but the Miranda protection of having "the right to remain silent" quickly evaporated in Matthew's case. Matthew tried to lie to the officer, who, he said, "saw through it." M.A.R. confirmed he was a willing participant and that Matthew stopped when he told him to, but that didn't matter. Matthew Limon had entered the criminal justice system.

Chapter 3

OUTSIDE FORCES

To hear a good number of people in Dover tell it, Bertha Spahr and the science department of Dover High School had decided to wage war against God. This wasn't an overly dramatic characterization, they insisted. Spahr—a chemistry teacher and the head of the high school's science department—and the young faculty that worked with her were threatening to undermine a basic tenet of Christian belief: that God had a hand in creating the world. For evangelical Christians in this rural Pennsylvania town, Spahr and her colleagues' decision to teach Darwin's *Origin of Species* without giving equal time to God smacked of nothing less than atheism. And their differences over that issue—whether there was a place for God in the high school science curriculum—ignited the most serious legal challenge to the teaching of evolution in the public schools in decades. It was a modern-day Scopes trial in which religious liberty and the separation of church and state were at stake.

It says volumes about Bertha Spahr that almost everyone knows her affectionately as "Bert." A small-boned, compact woman with a practical haircut and penchant for comfortable shoes, Spahr has a presence that makes clear that she brooks no nonsense, and quite possibly never has. She doesn't gesture wildly or speak loudly. Instead she sits with her hands calmly clasped before her, making all her points in the measured way a parent might patiently explain to a child how to cross the street. She has those qualities that good students associate with their favorite teachers. When Spahr started teaching science 41 years ago at Dover High School there were no women teaching chemistry in the school district. A nun was teaching science at York Catholic High School. Spahr was fond of saying that at those early countywide science teacher meetings it was "all men, one nun, and me."

The students naturally assumed that the diminutive Spahr, who looks to weigh as much as a small collie, would be a pushover. From the outset she clearly was not. "I had to show them who was in charge right at the beginning," she recalled. She did that with what came to be known as Spahrisms—good-natured threats that kept the students in line. Spahr, who is Sicilian, would tell students who had not done their work, "Will it be necessary for the little Sicilian to jump up and down on your tabletop?" Students who didn't follow lab directions typically heard, "Don't judge me by my size because I will take you out at the knees." One enterprising student dutifully collected the Spahrisms over the course of a year and presented them, bound, to his favorite teacher. Spahr reckons there are 30 or 40 in the book, though she said she is constantly modifying them to keep up with the times.

Spahr, whom students teasingly call "Big Bird" because of the obvious irony in her size and her penchant to wear bright yellow, clearly loves teaching science. A stuffed Big Bird sits on the top shelf of her science lab. A stuffed panda with an ironic smirk sits one shelf over. Spahr's enthusiasm is infectious. Her colleagues credit her with single-handedly turning would-be English majors into science geeks just by attending her class. "Bert is a force," one of the teachers at Dover said. A force that for 41 years had taken generations of Dover's youth through frog dissections and DNA strands and, more important, Darwin's *Origin of Species*. She taught whole generations of Dover students. And then she taught her former students' kids years later. For four decades Spahr and the members of the Dover High School science faculty treaded carefully around two issues: evolution and God. "We've always been very aware of the community we serve," Spahr said evenly. "So we tried not to upset the apple cart. When students asked us about God's role, we danced around the issue. We felt it was something their parents or their church should address. We didn't talk about where things came from but how things adapted to their environment."

Dover is a sleepy town of small family farms and retirees in rural Pennsylvania. The landscape is what you would expect: rolling hills punctuated by those abbreviated small-town strip malls that typically contain a supermarket, a dollar store, and a nail salon. Drivers headed to Dover from Harrisburg on Route 83 South pass a billboard that reads, "In God We Trust. United We Stand." Dover is a highly religious town—90 percent of its residents call themselves Christian. About a third of them say they are evangelical and most of the rest are Lutheran. Dover streets are dotted with churches, nearly two dozen of them in all, with names like Dover Assembly of God, Harmony Grove Community Church, Saint David's Evangelical Congregational Church, and Calvary Lutheran. There is a single Methodist church, a handful of new denominational churches, and two United Church of Christ congregations. With that number of houses of worship, it almost goes without saying that God was always relevant in Dover, though people tended to avoid talking about the details of their faith. It seemed best for all concerned if no one paid much attention to who was affiliated with which church. Privately, however, townsfolk outside the evangelical circles did have a nickname for those who were more activist about their beliefs: they called them "fundies," short for "fundamentalists."

Religious affiliations aside, Dover was the kind of place where neighborliness transcended such divisive issues. If there was a fire, everyone pitched in to help. Parents packed the halls for school assemblies whether they had children onstage or not. Agricultural fairs—with prize cows and healthy pigs—brought out residents of every stripe. The fire department was still an all-volunteer force. The city ambulance was driven by a teacher. Dover is a workingman's town, filled to bursting with generation farmers and factory workers who, until recently, had punched the clock every morning at either New York Wire or Consolidated Freight. When those businesses shut their doors in 2004, the workers retired but didn't move. Staying wasn't easy. Some 6,000 jobs left Dover in a span of four years, and looking back on it, residents said it did cast a pall over just about everything in the community.

It could have been the unanticipated job losses that made the people of Dover look outward for relief. Or perhaps it was just the general feeling that God, at this point in Dover's history, was needed more than before. But whatever it was, there was a definite feeling among the evangelicals at Harmony Grove Community Church that the time had come to step up their efforts to save the people of Dover. With a dearth of outlets to choose from, the school board—where fundamentalists outnumbered the modernists—seemed as good a place as any to start.

———

THE DOVER AREA SCHOOL DISTRICT encompasses the borough of Dover, Dover Township, and a neighboring lower-income area called Washington Township. The high school, a flat nondescript brick building, serves a little over 1,000 teenagers. Some 92 percent of them are white. The saying goes in Dover that the minority population swells when the exchange students come in.

Bill Buckingham had lived in Dover for 28 years. He sent his children to Dover's schools and would tell anyone who would listen that he grew up at a time when students prayed and read the Bible during religion class in the public schools. As he rose through the ranks of the Dover Area School Board, he came to wonder where that sort of spiritual discipline had gone. If he were to blame anyone it would be the liberals, he decided. Those liberals in "black robes"—the nation's legal elite—had stripped Christians of their fundamental rights. He was determined to do something to bring it back. A former police officer and prison guard whose pronounced limp was the most poignant reminder of an inmate's surprise attack, Buckingham had a bifurcated view of the world. There were those whom God had saved and those waiting for God to save them. Buckingham associated with the first group and was always on the lookout for someone who might fit into the second.

For Buckingham, teaching Darwin's *Origin of Species*—that man basically descended from apes—was a prime example of one of those Christian issues that had been overtaken by activist courts. It seemed patently wrong to talk about Darwin's theories without also telling students that Darwin's theory was by no means ironclad. There was lots of wiggle room in Darwin's study, as Buckingham saw it, and it was a Christian's duty to let the students know.

Bert Spahr said later that she saw the first signs of the assault on evolution in August of 2002. That's when she discovered that a janitor at the high school had taken it upon himself to dispose of a project a graduating senior had given to the science department several years earlier. It was a four-foot-by-six-foot mural of his interpretation of the ascent of man. The artwork was good, but it was nothing terribly original or controversial. It was merely a series of painted apelike figures, knuckles dragging, that, by stages, became what we think of as man: an upright figure with a brow somewhat less protruded and knuckles no longer skimming the dirt. Spahr took the mural in the spirit in which it was intended and thought nothing more of it, until the head of the school's janitorial services, knowing his granddaughter would be in the biology room the next fall, decided the best thing to do with the artwork was burn it. Not throw it away, but burn it. "It was a little extreme," Spahr said later. "You don't burn something unless you are making a statement."

Spahr complained to the superintendent of schools. She was told to mind her own business. For Spahr it was a shot across the bow. She knew immediately that the argument over Darwin had only just begun. She braced for the next offensive.

The salvo arrived six months later when the Dover Area School Board began discussing how it could weigh in on a debate about the Pledge of Allegiance. In the summer of 2003, a California man sued the Sacramento County School District over the Pledge of Allegiance. Michael Newdow, an atheist, objected to the words "one nation under God." He said the teacher-led recitation of the pledge violated his nine-year-old daughter's religious liberty. Even though the pledge was a voluntary act, Newdow's suit contended it was unconstitutional for students to even be forced to hear the words. A teacher leading the students through the pledge, he argued, was tantamount to government-sanctioned religion in the classroom. That summer, the U.S. Court of Appeals for the Ninth Circuit banned the pledge for some 10 million schoolchildren in the nine Western states under its jurisdiction. The ban was put on hold until the Supreme Court weighed in.

For Bill Buckingham, an attempt to distance God from the Pledge of Allegiance was just more proof of America's wrongheadedness. "Two thousand years ago someone died for us," Buckingham said he told the board, which had found itself with a goodly number of creationist fundamentalists as members. "Shouldn't someone stick up for him?"

He wanted to write a letter to the Supreme Court, or file a friend-of-the-court brief, saying that the people of Dover thought "under God" in the Pledge of Allegiance wasn't unconstitutional at all. In fact, stripping it out smacked of anti-Americanism. "I thought we'd have a slam dunk to support the pledge. I was surprised it was ever controversial," Buckingham said later.

In fact, the words "under God" were not in the original Pledge of Allegiance written by Francis Bellamy in 1892. The pledge has changed numerous times over the years. The original began, "I pledge allegiance to my flag" without any reference to the United States of America or "the Republic for which it stands." The American Legion and the Daughters of the American Revolution stirred up fears that the pledge's vagueness might confuse immigrant children. So, despite Bellamy's objection, it was revised in the 1920s. The recitation was also originally accompanied by an arm held aloft, instead of over the heart. That requirement was changed in the 1930s. It was uncomfortably similar to the Nazi *"Sieg Heil."* Political leaders, seeking to rally the American public against the rise of atheistic communism, added the phrase "under God" in 1954.

The 2003 Dover Area School Board was made up of nine citizens: six born-again Christians, a Quaker, an Episcopalian, and a Lutheran. Some members of the board wondered why Dover would want to enter the fray on the issue at all. "This is not our job," Casey Brown, the Episcopalian member, told Buckingham. "This is not our business. Leave it alone."

Eventually, Buckingham was obliged to do exactly that. He couldn't get the board to agree on the wording for a letter and by the time he had started to sway members, the Supreme Court had already made its decision. It was a no-win situation either way the court ruled. If it found that the words "under God" had no religious meaning, it would alienate a large portion of religious America, who obviously felt otherwise. If it ruled that the words "under God" communicated a religious purpose, it would be hard to square that meaning with established precedent on religious liberty and the importance of keeping government out of private religious affairs. The justices sidestepped the controversy on procedural grounds. The Pledge of Allegiance, and "one nation under God," remained in place. Even so, Doverites said later the entire episode sowed the seeds of religious conflict in town. Six school board members who saw God as their savior had been dissuaded from speaking out against what they saw as an onslaught against their Lord.

IN THE FALL OF 2003, science teachers at Dover High School noticed that the assistant superintendent of schools, Mike Baksa, had become a frequent guest in the teachers' lounge at lunchtime. They saw him there, chatting up the science teachers as they ate their lunches and corrected last-minute papers. Bert Spahr recalled that through all the small talk, Baksa seemed to be interested in just one thing: how the faculty was handling the issue of evolution. It soon became clear that Baksa was looking at how he might do the bidding of some conservative members of the school board. They were eager to have creationism enjoy equal billing with evolution in the high school's biology class. He kept asking Spahr if the teachers in her department were teaching man comes from a monkey. For Spahr, a teacher in Dover for 41 years, this was anathema. As far as she was concerned, "balancing" evolution with creationism was a nonstarter. Darwin's *Origin of Species* was science. Creationism, assuredly, was not.

But Baksa, a born-again Christian, began making the rounds sell-ing a whole new idea—something called "intelligent design." It wasn't biblical literalism, its supporters began to tell people in Dover's churches and school meetings. This wasn't about the earth being created in six days or about fossils unearthed when the waters receded from the flood. Intelligent design actually embraced evolution, to a point. Its supporters admitted that there had been evolutionary fine-tuning of life on earth. Where they differed from traditional creationism was in folding it into what science has discovered unequivocally. Intelligent design focused on gaps in the record. The underlying supposition was that there were organisms on earth that were so complex they could not possibly have developed by evolutionary "accident." Some greater force must have intervened to coax the process along. As they saw it, that greater force—call it God, call it the "designer"—deserved a fair hearing in Dover's biology classrooms.

The concept that underlies intelligent design is not new. It began with an 18th-century theologian named William Paley, who used a watchmaker analogy to explain intelligent design to the masses. He saw the universe as a giant watch. Living creatures were the gears in the timepiece. A watchmaker assembles the whole product, winds it, and it begins to tick. As Paley saw it, living organisms were infinitely more complicated than watches, so if a watch had a creator, then life must have one too. Paley thought the intelligent designer was the Christian God. Modern intelligent design proponents were careful not to name names.

Bill Buckingham recalled that the first mention he had ever heard of intelligent design came from Baksa. He thought nothing of it until his curriculum committee on the school board was asked to approve a new textbook for the coming school year.

Textbooks in public schools are generally updated and replaced on a continuing and rotating basis. In the summer of 2004, the curriculum committee of the Dover Area School Board was supposed to approve a new biology textbook, one that would replace a seven-year-old text that teachers complained was badly out of date. In 2004, Bill Buckingham was the head of the curriculum committee. When the purchase of the new biology textbook was delayed by a year and then again, Dover's science teachers got worried.

At first it seemed almost assured that the board would support buying *Biology*, a two-pound tome by Kenneth Miller and Joseph Levine, published by textbook stalwart Prentice Hall. It was an updated version of what the students were already studying, and teachers agreed it offered a straightforward, easy-to-follow biology education. But as summer wore on and the deadline loomed for approval of the book, there was an unexpected twist. Buckingham objected to the proposed text because it was "laced" with Darwinism. "It is inexcusable to teach from a book that says man descended from apes and monkeys," he said at a public board meeting that June. "We want a book that gives balance to education."

Days later, the phone rang in the Harrisburg, Pennsylvania, office of the ACLU. A newspaper reporter from York, Pennsylvania, asked a staff attorney a basic question: was teaching intelligent design in the public schools constitutional?

AT THE OUTSET OF the 21st century, Dover was not the only American town struggling with how to handle subjects with religious overtones. School boards and state legislatures around the country struggled with conflicts similar to the one that had pitted Clarence Darrow against William Jennings Bryan in the Scopes "monkey trial." Intelligent design/creationism battles raged in Mississippi, Louisiana, Montana, Georgia, Ohio, and Kansas. Even "liberal" California had become a front line of the intelligent design war.

The original Scopes case involved a Tennessee teacher, John Scopes, who was found guilty of teaching evolution in his science class, which was against Tennessee law at the time. Scopes's trial, over the years, has become more mired in lore than fact. Scopes has been presented as naïve, a teacher merely trying to pass knowledge on to his pupils. But neither the Scopes monkey trial nor Dover's modern rendition of it came about by happenstance. The romantic version begins with a chance meeting between Scopes and three men at the Rexall drugstore in downtown Dayton. An argument started over evolution and Scopes, a 24-year-old shy, religious, strawberry-blond man, agreed to be arrested to test Tennessee's prohibition against teaching Darwinism. The real story is somewhat more complicated.

In the spring of 1925, ACLU secretary Lucille Milner had been clipping newspapers and happened upon an interesting item: Tennessee had just passed a law forbidding the teaching of evolution. She brought the article to ACLU founder and executive director Roger Baldwin, who immediately put an ad in local Tennessee papers offering the ACLU's assistance to anyone willing to challenge the statute. The ACLU rarely provided counsel at the trial level at the time, but Baldwin had been concerned about a trend toward hogtying teachers as a wave of Protestant fundamentalism began sweeping the country. A few days after the advertisement went into the papers, the phone rang at ACLU headquarters. It was a local Dayton engineer named George Rappleyea. He thought challenging the law might provide some publicity for Dayton. Locals had already sent a telegraph to William Jennings Bryan, a widely known fundamentalist, asking him to take on the case. Clarence Darrow, a notorious self-proclaimed atheist, offered to represent Scopes. Rappelyea thought the case would put Dayton on the map.

The case created a media frenzy. Baldwin and other officials at the ACLU saw the case as embodying the first cause the organization had defended with which the national press and its audience could identify. The trial lasted eight days, but the jury took just nine minutes to find Scopes guilty. He was fined $100. Bryan died just a week after the trial, long before the Tennessee Supreme Court would over-turn the verdict on a technicality. Tennessee law required that fines of more than $50 be set by juries, not judges. Judge John Raulston himself had imposed Scopes's fine. The case transformed the ACLU. The *St. Louis Post-Dispatch* hailed the ACLU as "the only organiza-tion of its kind in the United States, if not the world." It was the first endorsement the ACLU had ever received from a major American newspaper.

In a way, Dover offered Scopes in reverse. Instead of drawing a bead on a law that prohibited teaching Darwin's theory of evolution, Dover's school board was taking aim at the Constitution and its pro-hibition on the use of government power to promote religion. The Scopes trial—beyond leaving us with Spencer Tracy's depiction in *Inherit the Wind* and Clarence Darrow and William Jennings Bryan providing legal performances that surpassed even the greatest of ex-pectations—never addressed the fundamental issue of whether evo-lution was plain, basic science. That field of battle had been left untouched.

Tennessee and Georgia had endorsed teaching of creationism as late as 1996. Alabama had a disclaimer, inserted into biology text-books, that said evolution was a "controversial theory." In the 1980s, the Supreme Court confronted a Louisiana law that required the teaching of "creation science" in any public school that taught the theory of evolution. The central question was whether a 1981 state law, backed by fundamentalist Christians in the state, was adopted for a religious purpose in violation of the First Amendment ban on establishment of religion. The case, *Edwards v. Aguillard*, set the stan-dard by striking down Louisiana's "balanced treatment" law. It said that teachers were required to teach creation science for the same amount of class time that they spent on evolution. The Supreme Court voted seven to two, ruling the law was unconstitutional. Justice William Brennan Jr. said that the First Amendment's requirement of separation of church and state meant that teaching must not be "tailored to the principles or prohibitions of any religious sect or dogma."

ACLU lawyer Steven Shapiro called it the "legal end of the creationism movement." Shapiro was clearly overly optimistic at the time. He would later spend decades shaping the ACLU's legal docket on religious freedom.

The ruling in *Aguillard* didn't end the debate. The justices did not ban teaching an alternative to evolution in the public schools—they provided some room that could be seen as allowing some form of creationism. And it was that gray area that members of the Dover Area School Board, and some outside forces, would come to exploit.

IN HINDSIGHT, NO ONE should have been surprised when South Dakota emerged as a battleground in the war over abortion rights in this country. The state is religious, conservative, and largely Republican. It is a place where headlines in the local paper read: "61% of South Dakotans Support the Death Penalty" and "Families with Children are the City's Growth Engine." So it is little wonder that on the issue of when life begins, South Dakotans have been sanguine: the last resident doctor who performed abortions in South Dakota retired ten years ago, deciding that offering the procedure was not worth the stigma of being branded a baby killer. The local Planned Parenthood chapter has been flying doctors in from Minnesota once a week ever since. It isn't just a dearth of doctors that has made a woman's right to choose so difficult. South Dakota's legislature has erected other obstacles, to make the state one of the most restrictive places in the country for an abortion. State law requires a 24-hour waiting period, mandatory counseling to discourage the procedure, and parental notification if the patient is a minor. It is one of three states in the Union that has only one abortion provider; Mississippi and North

Dakota are the other two. And while the nation was focusing on civil liberties and the "war on terror," right-to-life advocates were establishing a new beachhead in South Dakota.

When Planned Parenthood built its clinic in Sioux Falls six years ago, architects factored in the hostility the clinic was likely to face. There are no windows in the front of the building. It was easier to prevent abortion protesters from looking in. The parking lot and entrance are in the back, on private property, to guard against picketers. If that weren't enough, the glass in the waiting room is bulletproof and the inner doors are deadbolted. Visitors have to show identification to be buzzed in. Until recently the protesters who came to the clinic were of just the pesky variety. One in particular would wait outside the clinic on the sidewalk and videotape anyone driving in or out. What happens to the videotapes no one knows, but the cameraman is there to menace just the same.

Kate Looby, the South Dakota state director of Planned Parenthood, is a tall, lanky brunette who looks more city catwalk than South Dakota country. On a morning in November 2006 she is wearing jeans, a pink fleece vest, and pink slip-on ostrich boots. A fifth-generation South Dakotan, she speaks with the soft, swallowed accent one associates with that part of the country. She is a mother of four and has been involved with reproductive rights for about as long as she can remember. She was South Dakota's NARAL state director at the age of 25 and was the administrator at an Omaha, Nebraska, independent clinic in the early 1990s—a time when America's abortion battles were at their most violent. It was the era of Operation Rescue, clinic bombings, and murdered doctors.

"I am not one to back off a fight, but that time was a lot for anyone to handle," she said from her office in Sioux Falls. "We'd have people follow us home from work, we had break-ins in the clinic once a week. They would call our house. It was a very difficult time."

Looby was pregnant with her first child in the 1990s, but even that was not sacrosanct. Workers at the clinic had planned a baby shower for her for one Saturday morning when her home phone rang at six in the morning. "Kate, we just wanted to let you know that we can't make your baby shower today," a voice on the line whispered.

"This was all about intimidation," she said. "They wanted me to know that they could get to me, that they were on the inside. They even publicized my due date. Eventually I left. Bringing a new baby into that kind of environment was more than I could handle."

Looby and her new family later moved back to South Dakota, where she continued to work as a reproductive choice advocate. After an unsuccessful bid for secretary of state in 2002, Looby signed on with Planned Parenthood, where, until late 2006, the battle over a woman's right to choose was on a low simmer. The abortion landscape in South Dakota was shifting. For anyone watching the debate, it was clear that lawmakers in Pierre intended to move toward an outright ban of abortions in the state.

In 2004, the state legislature passed one only to have the governor send it back, without his signature, for what he called "technical reasons." Another effort was staged in 2005. It died in committee. It was only a matter of time, Looby said, before lawmakers managed to tinker at the edges of the law enough to get a ban passed.

WHEN THE 2004 BILL PASSED the state legislature, eager and pissed-off ACLU lawyers started drafting legal papers. Clearly, the South Dakota legislation was crafted as an attack on *Roe v. Wade*. Up until South Dakota, conventional wisdom among abortion rights lawyers was that *Roe* wasn't about to be overturned. It was established law; the Supreme Court didn't have a penchant for flipflops. Even the conservative justices had stated their respect for the court's prece-

dent. Most abortion rights advocates thought *Roe* was basically secure even if it was being chipped away bit by bit: a woman's right to
choose diminished by a waiting period here, a parental notification
law there, a counseling requirement here.

But under the public's radar screen was a new deference to the
states' decisions. As a new federalism was ushered in, choice advocates continued to play the *Roe* card at the federal level—claiming
that the Supreme Court was one vote away from a reversal. In a
perverse way, such warnings only served to increase public apathy on
abortion issues. Until South Dakota.

As the legislative process slowly came to a boil in 2005 and 2006,
an alternative strategy was considered, even if more costly and potentially more dangerous. Over the last decade, the choice movement
had been criticized for relying too heavily on the courts and doing too
little to change people's minds. So-called activist judges were "legis-
lating" in areas where the body politic wasn't convinced. The criticism resonated among many proponents of abortion rights who saw a
need to supplement their legal strategy with an on-the-ground effort.

THE SEISMIC SHIFT FINALLY came in March 2006 when the South
Dakota governor, Mike Rounds, signed a bill known as HB 1215. It
was written, quite literally, to fly in the face of *Roe v. Wade*, the landmark 1973 case in which the Supreme Court declared that abortion
was a constitutionally protected right and, by extension, had to be
legal in every state. HB 1215 wasn't just written for South Dakotans.
Instead, it presented the antiabortion position in its purest form:
under HB 1215 there could be no abortions unless a mother was in
danger of dying. There would be no exceptions for rape or incest.
Doctors who performed abortions in violation of the law would be
charged with a felony punishable by up to five years in prison. The

mother could not be charged. And with that, HB 1215 became the vessel in which the anti-*Roe* forces put all their hopes.

"In the history of the world, the true test of a civilization is how well people treat the most vulnerable and most helpless in their society," said Governor Rounds, a Republican, as he signed the bill into law. "Supporters of this bill believe that abortion is wrong because unborn children are the most vulnerable and most helpless persons in our society. I agree with them. We must help each mother to see the value of the gift that is a child, and nurture the mother for her own sake and for the sake of her child."

For the pro-choice movement, South Dakota provided an opportunity to use a ballot initiative to defend rights. The plan was to go on offense and rally the public. South Dakota was as good a state as any to pitch this battle. The small population would make the costs of advertising and get-out-the-vote strategies more manageable. Using the electoral process to win in a "red" state would send a message to the Jerry Falwells and the antichoice forces that they could be beat on their home turf. Legal papers were shelved, but never too far away, as this was a leap of faith for many working on abortion rights. Focus groups were commissioned. Public relations experts were retained. Ads were prepared. Organizers were hired. Advocacy dollars were raised. Almost all of it came from outside South Dakota.

Inside South Dakota, about 300 miles from Sioux Falls, near the state's border with Wyoming, sits South Dakota's Indian country. At one time the state was home to the Cheyenne, Arikara, and the Sioux. Today, the Lakota and Dakota, two of the seven tribes that make up the Great Sioux Nation, live in the western part of the state. The Oglala Sioux, a Lakota tribe, live on the Pine Ridge Reservation amid thousands of acres of uninterrupted grassland. The trip to Pine Ridge takes one through giant dun-colored sandcastles, fossil beds, buttes, and pinnacles of Badlands National Park and into another world of another time—part *Dances with Wolves*, part *Legends of the Fall*. Long ribbons of two-lane roads cut through hills that are mostly empty. Nothing but wind seems to be moving there.

Amid the quiet beauty there are visual reminders of just how difficult life has become for the American Indian. The reservation is a place of extreme poverty. Rusted cars perch atop cinder blocks. Trailer homes look tired and almost flaccid. The unemployment rate in Pine Ridge is 85 percent. Life expectancy is 46 for men and 55 for women. At a time when one in six American women has been the victim of rape or attempted rape, the rate of rape and sexual assault among American Indians is three and a half times higher than that. Domestic violence on the reservation is rife.

News of the state's abortion ban arrived at the Pine Ridge Reservation in the form of an e-mail. Cecelia Fire Thunder, the first female president of the Oglala Sioux and a former rape crisis worker, skimmed the message quickly; she had her assistant print it out, and put it aside for a time when she could read it without interruption. The news actually surprised her. Because the reservation was sovereign, the machinations of state laws did not have direct legal effect on the residents of Pine Ridge. They had to follow tribal law and federal statutes. So while Fire Thunder had heard about the abortion ban discussion in the Pierre legislature, she hadn't followed it. There had been abortion ban bills before. Governors had never signed them. She assumed this time would be no different. But if abortions were outlawed in the rest of the state, even Native American women would lose access to services.

"Frankly, I was taken aback," Fire Thunder recalled later. "The way I saw it, Mike Rounds just signed a law as a Catholic instead of as a governor."

The law's no-exceptions clause for rape or incest hit Fire Thunder particularly hard. Rape and sexual assault were crimes that tended to go unpunished on the reservation. Rape and sexual assault were considered the purview of outside law enforcement; they couldn't be prosecuted in a tribal court. When accusations of rape surfaced, the federal authorities or criminal investigators from outside the reservation came in. The response had been lackluster, at best, for more than 15 years, Fire Thunder said. As a result, rape had become almost accepted, something that was swept under the rug because it was a crime without consequences. Women on the reservation had come to think of rape prosecution as a dim possibility, like a light on a flat field, miles off.

"I was furious once I realized what the law did," Fire Thunder said. "A group of white men who know nothing about women of my culture had made a decision that children could be created in an act of violence and women had no options. I don't think God wanted the future of the human race to be created in violence. I couldn't let this stand."

Fire Thunder picked up the phone and started talking to some of the women elders of the tribe. They began to map out how best to respond.

Chapter 4

THE SEARCH FOR CREDIBLE THREATS

PRESIDENT TRUMAN CREATED THE NSA in 1952 so that a single agency could concentrate on breaking Russian codes and eavesdropping on the Soviet government's most secret communications. For a long time the National Security Agency was so under wraps the joke was that NSA actually stood for "no such agency." From the start, it was always envisioned as an organization that would lurk in the shadows.

The NSA's roots can be traced back to a small, highly secret group known as the MI-8 or the "Black Chamber," the country's first peacetime code-breaking organization. The Black Chamber originally operated out of a small brownstone in New York City and was headed by Herbert O. Yardley, a former code breaker with the American Expeditionary Forces in France during World War I. Disguised as a company that made commercial codes for businesses, it was responsible, among other things, for deciphering messages to and from delegates during the war's disarmament talks. The Black Chamber dispatches gave the American delegates the inside track on the discussions.

Secretary of State Henry Stimson shuttered the operation in 1929 when he found out that the chamber's cryptanalysts were spying on friends and foes alike, saying—as the legend goes—"Gentlemen do not read each other's mail." Unemployed and in need of cash, Yardley published *The American Black Chamber,* exposing the secrets and extent of U.S. code-breaking work in the 1920s. (Not surprisingly, two years after its publication, a law was passed that made the unauthorized disclosure of cryptologic secrets a crime.)

For a short time, the government got out of the code-breaking business, until the army secretly resurrected the operation in 1930. They called the group the Signal Intelligence Section. Eventually that operation merged with code breakers in the other service branches to become the Army Security Agency. It didn't become the NSA as we know it until Truman decided to beef up American intelligence operations after the country was caught by surprise when the North Koreans crossed the 38th Parallel and captured Seoul.

On October 24, 1952, just months before he would leave office, Truman scrapped the AFSA and in its place created the National Security Agency. It was to be so secret, he and his advisers decided that afternoon, it would be hidden from Congress, the public, and the rest of the world.

ANN BEESON WAS CELEBRATING New Year's Eve 2003 in style. She was in Vermont with her husband, Robert, and their two-and-a-half-year-old son, Oscar. Visiting a friend's house, they went ice-skating on a frozen pond and sledding with their little boy. In Beeson's words, they were "detoxing" after another busy year. She was unaware that at that same moment, her own country was kidnapping her future client Khaled El-Masri. But 2003 had been a great year for Beeson. She had been given a promotion and she had just argued the first federal case challenging the constitutionality of the USA Patriot Act.

Beeson's case challenged Section 215, the so-called "library records" provision, which gave the FBI expanded powers in accessing library, business, and financial records. The Patriot Act also diluted the standard of judicial review because it greatly expanded the government's ability to seize documents without any court oversight through something called National Security Letters (NSLs). And under both the "library records" and NSL provisions of the Act, people who received such orders were gagged from publicly disclosing the government's seizure of the information. Beeson argued that the Act violated the First, Fourth, and Fifth Amendments. It was the first case of its kind.

Before September 11, Beeson was one of the top experts on free speech and the Internet. Freedom of expression had become a cause célèbre for Beeson. Before joining the ACLU in 1995, she worked at Human Rights Watch, where she documented threats to free expression in Albania and pushed for the application of the Universal Declaration of Human Rights to the Internet. A graduate of Emory University School of Law, she became a lawyer only after abandoning a Ph.D. track in socio-anthropology at the University of Texas. She had been working with the indigent in Texas and came to the conclusion she could do more good by lawyering for the poor rather than studying them.

Beeson had a very personal connection to 9/11. She was on a Newark tarmac that Tuesday morning. Had she noticed the plane taking off ahead of her own Washington flight, she might have caught a glimpse of one of the airplanes that would be hijacked that morning. United flight 93, which eventually crashed into the fields of Pennsylvania, was the last flight out of Newark that day. Beeson's plane was scheduled next for departure. By 2003, Beeson had become one of the country's leading litigators on national security and civil liberties.

FAST-FORWARD TO THE MORNING of December 16, 2005. The day was already shaping up to be a busy one. Beeson began scanning her e-mail. One had come in overnight from an ACLU staffer in Washington. It was a link to a *New York Times* article. The subject line read: "This is huge." The story, of course, was James Risen and Eric Lichtblau's revelation of a warrantless NSA spying program. Beeson was on the phone within minutes, lining up lawyers to respond. There were conference calls to schedule, talking points to work out, Freedom of Information Act requests to file, legal research to start, clients to identify, and press conferences to hold. Beeson hit the ground running.

This wasn't how Beeson had expected to spend the week before Christmas. The holiday should have had all the earmarks of a quiet vacation. Only the week before, Beeson and her staff were wrestling with a major case. Khaled El-Masri was a German citizen of Lebanese birth, a father of six. When Beeson was on vacation in Vermont, El-Masri was on his way to a holiday in Macedonia on December 31, 2003, when he was abducted by Macedonian officials and turned over to a team of CIA agents. He was transferred to a hotel room where he would spend the next 23 days in captivity, curtains drawn. The U.S. government suspected him of terrorism. He was questioned about activities he knew nothing about and people he had never met.

On January 23, 2004, El-Masri's nightmare only got worse. Several men entered the room. They handcuffed him, blindfolded him, led him to a vehicle, and drove him to another building. There, he was severely beaten and his clothes were sliced off his body. Men in black ski masks placed him in a diaper and a track suit, chained him at his wrists and ankles, placed earmuffs over his ears and eye pads over his eyes, blindfolded and hooded him. He was led to an airplane (leased by U.S. government agents) and forced to its floor, facedown.

He was injected with drugs and flown to what he would later find out was a secret base in Afghanistan. He spent months in the notorious "Salt Pit"—a secret U.S.-run prison just north of Kabul—locked in a small, dirty, cold concrete cell. He was interrogated and tortured.

As it turned out, it was a case of mistaken identity. But the CIA continued to hold El-Masri incommunicado in Afghanistan long after it realized its mistake. Five months after his abduction, he was finally led out of his cell, blindfolded, handcuffed, chained to the seat of a plane, flown to Albania, and—without explanation—abandoned on a hillside at night. He was never charged with anything. Beeson and her team at the ACLU had filed a federal lawsuit against CIA director George Tenet, the unidentified CIA agents, and the corporations that owned the aircraft used to transport El-Masri.

The El-Masri case came more than a year after the pictures of torture at Abu Ghraib prison in Iraq came to light. But this was different. This was a case of a German citizen whisked off the streets in Macedonia and "rendered" to a military base to be tortured by his American jailers.

The El-Masri case would end up souring Secretary of State Condoleezza Rice's first visit with the new chancellor of Germany, Angela Merkel. The ACLU filed suit on the day Rice arrived in Berlin. The two leaders had difficulty shaking questions about why an innocent German citizen was kidnapped and tortured by the American government. The U.S. government would later move to dismiss the ACLU lawsuit. It said that either confirming or denying El-Masri's detention would expose "state secrets." Ben Wizner, Beeson's colleague who argued the case in federal court, would answer that there was little about the El-Masri case that was secret. Both the European Union and the German Parliament had conducted inquiries. President Bush had confirmed the existence of a network of secret prisons. The practice of "extraordinary rendition"—abducting foreign nationals for detention and interrogation overseas—had been documented by press reports. What the world was waiting to see, Wizner argued, was whether the American government would make amends to an innocent man. What was on trial was nothing less than the principles of fairness and due process—whether a man who had been tortured by the U.S. government would have his day in court.

Ultimately, El Masri wouldn't get his day in court. Justice Department lawyers would claim that allowing the case to proceed would jeopardize national security. The U.S. District Court for the Eastern District of Virginia sided with the government and dismissed El Masri's case. In March 2007, the U.S. Court of Appeals for the Fourth Circuit followed suit and upheld the dismissal. And then in October 2007, the U.S. Supreme Court refused to review El Masri's case. The *New York Times* editorial page labeled the decision a "supreme disgrace." An innocent man who was tortured by the U.S. government would not have any recourse in an American court of law.

After filing the initial *El Masri v. Tenet*, "we thought we would have a week to take a breath," Beeson said later. "Then the NSA wiretapping story broke."

Since the attacks on the World Trade Center and the Pentagon, Beeson and her colleagues had been concentrating on opposing provisions in the Patriot Act that trampled on civil liberties. In particular she was concerned about the expansion of the administration's wiretap powers under the Foreign Intelligence Surveillance Act. The *New York Times* story suggested her worries were misplaced. The broadening of FISA warrants wasn't the biggest problem. The administration was doing an end run around the FISA court altogether. What little oversight there had been was now moot. "We were suddenly in a position of defending FISA. The debate had suddenly shifted," Beeson said.

ACLU attorneys called James Bamford—one of the country's leading experts on the NSA. His book *The Puzzle Palace* was the definitive work on the NSA's surveillance of political dissidents and civil rights leaders in the 1950s and 1960s. Bamford had unearthed the shadowy practices and clear dangers of a government agency turned on the American public. Thanks to his work, Congress reined in the NSA. Bamford uncovered decades of illegal spying on Americans that was unbeknownst even to several presidents. When in 1969 Richard Nixon asked the NSA to undertake such surveillance, NSA deputy director Dr. Louis Tordella called it a "heaven sent opportunity." Nixon revoked the order a week later under pressure from J. Edgar Hoover, but the spying continued. Bamford's book made Bamford persona non grata at the NSA. Then in 1999, NSA director Michael Hayden invited him to the agency to show how much it had changed. Bamford was impressed. The agency had made significant changes.

For Bamford, the revelations in the *New York Times* regarding the NSA's eavesdropping were devastating. He felt personally betrayed. When Beeson called, he was only too happy to help.

FISA warrants required the government to demonstrate that the target of the surveillance was a "foreign power or an agent of a foreign power." There were some exceptions in cases of emergency, such as tapping a foreign power fifteen days before going to war. What was clear was that the government could count on the FISA court being sympathetic to its warrant requests. Since 1978, about 19,000 FISA warrants have been granted. Only five of them were denied. The NSA program simply went around the FISA judges.

It took a week for Beeson and her team of lawyers to put together the FOIA requests to get an idea of just how broad the NSA wiretapping had been. Just days before Christmas, ACLU staffers gathered at the New York headquarters to come up with a group of plaintiffs to challenge the NSA program in court. They needed organizations or individuals who would have legal standing to challenge the program and attract attention to the case. Terrorism defense attorney Josh Dratel, not surprisingly, came up as the perfect candidate.

DRATEL WAS IN HIS WALL STREET OFFICE when the phone rang. Ann Beeson was on the line. Dratel is more down-to-earth than many lawyers. A Brooklyn boy who made good by going to Columbia University and Harvard Law School, there was something about the way Dratel carried himself that made him immediately likable. No one could mistake him for one of the slick corporate lawyers who worked down in the financial district. There appeared to be more Brooklyn in the man than Harvard. He wore dull gray suits and cream-colored shirts that weren't pressed quite right. When the headset broke on his telephone, he switched to the handset. When that broke too, he took to taking all his calls on a speakerphone.

Dratel's office is small and announced by piles upon piles of paper. There are four-foot stacks of documents on his desk. Other case files sit around the room, frozen in what looks like midcollapse, almost waist high. There are Xeroxes and the requisite plaques from associations and law schools, but what strikes one most about Dratel's law office is the unpretentiousness of it all. It looks like the office of someone who needs a secretary but can't be bothered to hire one.

Beeson called that December morning to discuss who at the National Association of Criminal Defense Lawyers would be best positioned to sue the government over the NSA program. Dratel was cochair of the nonprofit, Washington-based group. The question was: who could best allege that they were likely to have been targeted? Dratel and Beeson both knew the answer. Dratel called and e-mailed people in the Middle East, South Asia, and Africa as a matter of course, just as journalists, scholars, and other groups had done.

"Ann and I both found it ironic that a week earlier we had been talking about the problems with the broadening of the FISA court's authority and now we were going to have to talk about its virtues, to treat it as a constitutional floor," said Dratel. "It was a weird turn of events."

With Dratel on board, Beeson and her colleagues discussed other potential plaintiffs. Muslim and Arab organizations would be likely targets. They could articulate a well-founded fear of government spying. Other likely targets: journalists and scholars with connections to the wars in Iraq and Afghanistan. ACLU lawyers contacted authorities on those countries and signed up the leading expert on the Taliban, Barnett Rubin of New York University and Iraq expert Larry Diamond of the Hoover Institution. Bamford himself became a plaintiff as well. *ACLU v. NSA* was beginning to take shape.

The government had already conceded all of the facts in the case. So Beeson filed a motion for a summary judgment, hoping to stop the program in its tracks. The ACLU's 60-page complaint named the NSA and its director, Lieutenant General Keith Alexander, as defendants. "The prohibition against government eavesdropping on American citizens is well-established and crystal clear," Beeson said in announcing the lawsuit. "President Bush's claim that he is not bound by the law is simply astounding. Our democratic system depends on the rule of law, and not even the president can issue illegal orders that violate constitutional principles."

The White House spokesman at the time, Scott McClellan, called the lawsuit "frivolous." It does "nothing to help enhance civil liberties or protect the American people," he said.

WHITE HOUSE OFFICIALS LAUNCHED a public defense of the National Security Agency domestic wiretap program just days after the *New York Times* story broke. Attorney General Alberto Gonzales led the charge. Gonzales was not new to controversy. He was White House counsel when President Bush secretly approved the NSA spying program. He authored a 2002 memo that called the Geneva Conventions "quaint" and "obsolete." His appointment to attorney general against that backdrop was worrisome. The ACLU was concerned, and clearly the reservations turned out to be well founded.

Joshua Dratel was visiting his in-laws in Kentucky when Gonzales began defending the NSA program as a necessary "tool" in the fight against terrorism. "The vigor of their defense told me that there was something more there," said Dratel. "I was worried their hiding behind national security would work. But as they stepped up the defense of the program I became convinced this was only the beginning. There was something they didn't want us to find out or to know."

To the White House, the necessity of the warrantless eavesdropping program was clear. The nation was waging a new kind of war against a dangerous enemy and needed to be able to use all of the tools at its disposal to fight them. "If you're talking with al-Qaeda, we want to know what you're saying," Bush and Gonzales said.

The FISA court that had been used to approve the secret wiretaps in the past had been very effective in dealing with terrorists, Gonzales told reporters at the time. "Many, many presidents have exercised their inherent authority under the Constitution to engage in electronic surveillance of the enemy, particularly during a time of war. That's been long recognized by the courts and long recognized by practice," he said on PBS's *Newshour.*

"Now, some would argue that in 1978 that changed when FISA was passed, that that was intended to cabin the president's authority," he continued. "Our response to that is that we have to look at the authorization to use military force, which was passed in the days following the attacks of 9/11, and we believe that the Congress intended for the president to engage in all of those activities that are fundamentally incidental to waging war, including electronic surveillance, and therefore we don't get to the question as to whether or not FISA is constitutional or unconstitutional."

Civil liberties weren't in peril, he continued, because the program was so limited. The only calls they were tracking were ones in which one party of the communication was a member of al-Qaeda or a group linked to al-Qaeda. "Electronic surveillance is something that is very, very, I think, sensitive," Gonzales said in its defense. "It can be very political. Of course, we understood that this would be something that some people would disagree with. I think it would have been irresponsible for anyone acting as president to not take action to further protect the country once he's told that we have the technology to do something and once the attorney general says yes you have the legal authority to do so. Our enemy is very patient and very diabolical. And they watch very carefully what we do. And so we very much worry that as there is more continued discussion about the operations, not the legal justification but the operations, that we may compromise the effectiveness of this program."

Dratel watched all of this from the living room of his in-laws' house in Kentucky and couldn't help but smile to himself. If the White House had just left this alone and not been so defensive, he thought, the story might have died. Their vigorous defense only got the press that much more interested. The story had legs.

THREATS TO DEFENSE DEPARTMENT PERSONNEL or military installations were supposed to be picked up in an early warning system the DOD calls TALON, the Threat and Local Observation Notice. The idea was for it to capture raw information about "anomalies, observations that are suspicious . . . and immediate indicators of potential threats" to the Defense Department, according to the military.

Among the types of information worth recording, according to a TALON report guide, are threats or incidents that "may indicate a potential for a threat . . . whether the threat posed is deliberately targeted or collateral." Another trigger for reporting would be individuals who appear to be monitoring U.S. facilities. Suspicious photographs, maps, or drawings of installations and strangers using binoculars were all in the crosshairs of this program. The mandate was ambiguous enough that it gave the Defense Department wide latitude in how it was applied. The problem was one person's threat was another person's innocent, nonviolent protest. Or at least that is what Kot Hordynski thought.

The TALON system is part of the Defense Department's growing effort to gather intelligence within the United States, which officials saw as important to detecting and preventing terrorist attacks. The TALON reports—how many are generated is classified, a Pentagon spokesman said—are collected and analyzed by Counterintelligence Field Activity or CIFA, an agency at the forefront of the Pentagon's counterterrorism program. Very few people know how big CIFA is or the size of its budget. That information is also classified. It is also unclear how many TALON reports are filed each year. But just one of the military services involved in the program, the air force, generated 1,200 during the 14 months that ended in September 2003, according to a newsletter released by the inspector general's office.

Military officials say TALON came out of an earlier operation called Eagle Eyes, an air force Office of Special Investigations anti-terrorist program that basically had air force members and people all over the country keeping tabs on anything that looked "suspicious." It was, in a real sense, a neighborhood watch program for military bases. After the September 11 attacks, it morphed into a reporting system that, according to a background paper on TALON, was supposed to "assemble, process, and analyze suspicious activity reports to identify possible terrorist pre-attack activities."

Kot Hordynski, his friends at UCSC, and at least nine other college campus antiwar protests apparently qualified for TALON inclusion. When their names appeared on a 400-page TALON list it reminded some people of the 1960s, when the Pentagon collected information about anti–Vietnam War groups and peace activists. That effort led to congressional hearings in the 1970s and eventually to limits on the types of information the Defense Department could gather and retain about U.S. citizens.

The ACLU had paid scant attention to TALON until NBC News broke the story in December 2005. Before then, there was much greater concern about political surveillance and infiltration of peaceful groups by the FBI, and the use of the Joint Terrorism Task Forces (JTTFs), which brought together state and local law enforcement agencies with the FBI and other federal agencies.

FOIA requests found the FBI and JTTFs monitored or infiltrated a "Vegan Community Project" event at the University of Indiana, a 200-person peace march in Ohio, and a planned protest of Cindy Crawford's decision to become a llama fur spokesperson. The FBI compiled over 1,100 pages of documents on the ACLU's activities after September 11, 2001. They redacted all the documents about the ACLU before turning them over. Environmental groups like Greenpeace and antiwar groups like United for Peace and Justice were also targeted. A JTTF file included the names and license plate numbers of dozens of nonviolent activists—critics of the timber industry who protested at a lumber convention in Colorado. The file read "counterterrorism." The FBI also subpoenaed membership information and minutes of an antiwar group at Drake University.

It turned out that FBI and JTTF spying was only the tip of the surveillance iceberg. The NSA and TALON programs went a step further.

IT IS DIFFICULT NOT to like Kot Hordynski. A good-looking, clean-shaven boy with dark hair and an easy smile, he tended to wear Oxford cloth shirts and V-neck sweaters. He looked like the kind of guy any girl would be happy to take home to meet her parents. He had a soft voice and a sharp intellect, and while he had the gift of gab, he was modest about his ability to sway a crowd. He usually let other people speak first.

He immigrated to America from Poland when he was in grade school. His mother and father were both intellectuals and had left Poland in the heady days of the early Solidarity movement when dockworkers led by Lech Walesa—who would eventually become president of Poland—founded the Soviet bloc's first independent trade union. While Hordynski didn't remember much about his life in Poland, his parents talked often about the days of martial law. They told him how dangerous it had been to speak out. Maybe that was part of Hordynski's motivation to take full advantage of the rights he was afforded in America. So when America went to war with Iraq he decided to protest, to make his voice heard. That, he said later, was what he had always thought was the American way.

Hordynski went from soft-spoken college student to "credible threat" on April 5, 2005, when he and more than 200 students with Students Against War flooded the Stevenson Event Center during an annual spring job fair. As students lined up in jacket and tie to meet with recruiters from Broadcom and American Express, Hordynski and fellow SAW members swarmed the room to protest against marine corps officers also recruiting students at the fair. They waved signs and chanted the typical, rhyming fare that characterizes campus protests. "Racist, sexist, antigay, hey, recruiters, go away," went one.

Campus police, caught unprepared by the protest, blocked the doors, keeping more than 100 students waiting outside for the melee to clear. UCSC officers appeared in riot gear and protective helmets. There was yelling and pushing and shoving, but the protest for the most part was peaceful. Eventually, the SAW students got the military representatives to leave the building. Members of SAW then provided their own counterrecruitment information: a list of alternatives to military careers.

UCSC administrators said the military recruiters were on campus thanks to the Solomon Amendment, a law that denies federal funding to universities that bar military recruiters from campus. (The ACLU had previously argued that the Solomon Amendment violated the free speech rights of universities and school administrators. The Supreme Court upheld the law in 2006.) Hordynski and other members of

SAW thought UCSC should follow Harvard Law School's lead and ban military recruiters.

What they didn't realize was that their protest at the job fair had attracted the attention of the Defense Department. Hordynski and SAW were seen as nefarious individuals who needed to be tracked and cataloged against some sort of evil they might get into later. "In a way it was really cool finding out that we were on this TALON list," Hordynski later said. "At first, I was kind of proud in the sense that student activists are supposed to have a message, to make the government take notice. Putting us on the TALON list meant we were having an impact and that was a huge ego thing. But the more we thought about it, the scarier it got. We saw ourselves as exercising our right to free speech and we got labeled as terrorist threats."

That said, their first response was typical college-age levity. They had T-shirts made for members of SAW that read, "Credible Threat."

Then they called the local ACLU.

Chapter 5

TAKING THE GLOVES OFF

BILL BUCKINGHAM SAT BEFORE HIS COM-
puter and typed the words "intelligent design"
into a search engine. Hundreds of hits lit up
the screen and above them all was one name:
the Discovery Institute. Buckingham double-
clicked on the Web site link and began
reading.

Founded in 1991 as an arm of the Hudson Institute (the conservative think tank established by Herman Kahn), the Discovery
Institute was named after the ship that explored Puget Sound in 1792. Its leader was
Bruce Chapman, a Rockefeller Republican
turned Reagan conservative who had, among
other things, served on the Seattle City
Council and run an unsuccessful campaign
for governor of Washington. Eventually his

politics took a sharp right turn and he ended up as director of the Census Bureau during the Reagan administration.

The Seattle-based organization's intelligent design crusade started with an article in the *Wall Street Journal* by a professor at a Christian college in Spokane, Washington, that focused on a biologist who was chastised for discussing intelligent design in the science classroom. The professor, Dr. Stephen C. Meyer, was friendly with conservatives Howard and Roberta Ahmanson, wealthy religious philanthropists, and together they hatched the idea of creating the Discovery Institute's Center for Science and Culture. Dr. Meyer is its director. Other backers include stalwarts in the conservative movement like Philip Anschutz and Richard Mellon Scaife. The Ahmansons were by far the biggest supporters of the Discovery Institute, having provided some 35 percent of the $9.3 million the science center raised from its inception. Mr. Ahmanson sits on the Discovery Institute's board.

As a general rule, the institute supports the work of a number of conservative thinkers. It provided almost $4 million in fellowships to some 50 researchers so they could write books on intelligent design. After the reelection of President George W. Bush in 2004, Discovery was involved with no fewer than 78 evolution battles in 31 states. It took advantage of the No Child Left Behind education law to help states rewrite curriculum standards. Ohio, New Mexico, and Minnesota signed on to the institute's "teach the controversy" approach— where there was Darwin, they said, there ought to be an alternative idea presented too. (Pennsylvania's own Senator Rick Santorum, a Republican, had tried to include a passage from the institute's talking points in the No Child Left Behind legislation. Santorum's amendment didn't make it into the law, but a modified version did appear in the bill's conference report. It read, in part: "Where topics are taught that may generate controversy (such as biological evolution), the curriculum should help students to understand the full range of scientific views that exist, why such topics may generate controversy, and how scientific discoveries can profoundly affect society." Proponents of intelligent design, including Dr. Meyer, have used the statement to argue that federal education policy calls for teaching ID in science classrooms.)

What was clear to Buckingham as he perused the Web site was that he and the Discovery Institute were of like mind. The very next morning, Buckingham had the phone to his ear, waiting to be connected to Seth Cooper, one of the institute's attorneys. He thought Cooper might be able to help with the evolution controversy in Dover. The conversation would be a life-changing one for Buckingham. As he began to tell Cooper about the unfolding debate, he had a calming sense that he was on the phone with someone who understood him. Cooper explained that the institute worked with nearly 50 fellows who produced research and articles on the wisdom of intelligent design. The team included some of the biggest names in the ID movement, Cooper continued, reading from the roster of its scholars, including Michael Behe, a professor of molecular biology at Lehigh University, and William Dembski, formerly of Baylor University. These Discovery Institute fellows all held advanced degrees from some of the best universities in the country and, by virtue of that, had changed the complexion of the argument. The disagreement over Darwin was no longer a religious debate. Suddenly, scientists were arguing with scientists over evolution, Cooper said. They weren't discussing creationism; a court had already said that it had no place in the public schools. Instead, intelligent design offered an alternative theory to evolution that the courts had not rejected—a theory with "scientific" underpinnings.

Cooper helpfully suggested a solution to Buckingham's textbook dilemma as well. The institute had backed a book called *Of Pandas and People: The Central Question of Biological Origins,* which addressed Buckingham's concerns about Darwinism, and they would be happy to provide some copies for the Dover students. *Pandas* is a thin volume—just 170 pages long—which was first published in 1989 and went into its fifth printing in 2004. The authors, Percival Davis and Dean Kenyon, were college professors who suggested that Darwinism's gaps demanded an explanation for what scientists could not understand. (Davis's writing credit was dropped from the book after it surfaced that he had cowritten a book called *Case for Creation,* which was published by Chicago's Moody Bible Institute.) Talking about his work on *Pandas,* Davis was quoted in a 1994 *Wall Street Journal* story as saying, "Of course my motives were religious. There's no question about it."

The quote would come back to haunt supporters of intelligent design. They were trying to make the case that their work had its foundation in science, not religion. In a user's guide to the book, the authors and editors of the volume say they have written it on two levels: a lighter, easy-to-understand treatment with more depth in what they called "excursion chapters." "It is easy to sacrifice accuracy when trying to make a scientific subject easy to follow," the authors write. "And this is a subject where accuracy is important."

The book begins with a quote from Carl Sagan, "one of the foremost popularizers [*sic*] of science in our time." The introduction helpfully explains that *Of Pandas and People* is not intended to be a balanced treatment by itself. "We have given a favorable case for intelligent design and raised reasonable doubt about natural descent," it reads. "By now you are aware that you have a mind of your own. Here is a good opportunity to use it."

What later became crystal clear was that the Discovery Institute had a very specific agenda in mind. In 1999, an internal document from the organization, known as the Wedge Document, suddenly appeared on the Internet. It described not only the Discovery Institute's goals but how the group was prepared to accomplish them. The document said that the idea that human beings are created in the image of God was "one of the bedrock principles on which Western civilization was built." People like Darwin, Marx, and Freud had "infected virtually every area of our culture" and their ideas needed to be "overthrown."

BERT SPAHR IMMEDIATELY SAW "intelligent design" for what it was—a bid to cast a patina of doubt over the scientific theory of biological evolution. She was clear: "We were not going to bastardize science." She would ask herself, "This business of keeping our children ignorant serves what purpose?" Darwin's studies on the Galapagos Islands showed how animals adapted and changed to survive. Finch beaks changed shape. Brains modified. A potent cocktail of random mutation and natural selection had tinkered at the edges of species and ultimately improved them. Those advances were passed along to the next generation and over billions of years organisms evolved to become better suited for their surroundings. In 1870, about ten years after the publication of Darwin's *Origin of Species,* most of the world's biologists had signed on to the idea of evolution. Fifty years later, natural selection was embraced as well. This was science, pure and simple—theories based on observable evidence that made for testable predictions.

Supporters of intelligent design said the gaps in scientific knowledge had given rise to alternate theories. They pointed to molecular biologists in the 1950s deciphering incredibly complex cells—organisms that were far more intricate than anyone had previously imagined. And, ID advocates said, those organisms were too complex to have been an accident of nature as Darwin had written. This was not a testable prediction, simply an argument as to why evolution wasn't the answer.

This might well have remained a debate between scientists and creationists were it not for Michael Behe. Behe is a small, bespectacled man who looks like the classic absentminded professor. His beard is a little scruffy. His hair is a bit out of place. In other words, he looks as though he would fit in quite well at any university biology department were it not for one thing: he is one of the fathers of intelligent design.

The classic argument from intelligent design, which has been around for hundreds of years, is that biological systems are so complex that a "designer" must have set all this in motion. In Western culture, this went back to a book called *Natural Theology* that was written by the Reverend William Paley and published in 1802. Paley's book is considered the best pre-Darwin classical formulation of the idea of intelligent design. Behe provided his own twist by bringing all these design theories forward using the new language of biochemistry. For Behe, life's complexity lay in what he called "irreducible complexity," and his favorite example of this is something called a bacterial flagellum.

High school biology taught us that bacteria are very, very simple cells. They are everywhere in nature. Some bacteria have little whiplike structures called flagella. Under a microscope, they look like little outboard motors that whip the bacteria around at breakneck speed. Scientists have not yet explained how flagella came about. And, for a long time, they seemed satisfied with the idea that sooner or later they would, indeed, work out how flagella came to be. For Behe, this was not a scientific mystery so much as a divine one. It isn't that scientists have not come up with a solution to flagella; in Behe's worldview, scientists never will, because a designer created it. Darwin's evolutionary theory breaks down, Behe says, just by looking at everything around us. Living cells contain complex biochemical systems and machines and are composed of many parts. But if you start to take away any of those parts, to see if there might be a simpler machine below, you realize that the machine breaks down. Organisms like bacteria are irreducibly complex and could not possibly have come about by slight, successive modifications as evolution might have produced them. As he saw it, there were organisms that didn't function until the last part was snapped into place. If that was the case, the theory of evolution unraveled. "The complexity of the system dooms all Darwinian explanation to frustration," he wrote.

That conclusion was at the heart of the arguments in *Pandas*. If evolution could not provide a complete explanation for life's mysteries, then there was an alternative: it was the work of a benevolent designer.

And although creationism had not fared well in the courts, science educators felt the chilling effects of the dust kicked up by the legal challenges. Jen Miller, a young biology instructor from Dover High School who had more than a passing resemblance to Ally Sheedy, was one of those teachers.

Given the fact that fundamentalists in Dover were so vocal, Miller found herself dancing around the issue of evolution in her classroom. One of her favorite lessons had involved taking a large roll of cash register tape and running it down the school corridor so students could build a time line. The idea was for everyone to help write in dates for the origins of the earth and various species. By its very design, the lesson explicitly supported the standard scientific theory about the age of the earth: four and a half billion years. Creationists put the earth's age at about six to ten thousand years, believing the geological column of the planet was formed in a single worldwide flood. That made Miller's lesson plan, at best, problematic. Eventually, not wanting to rock the boat, Miller dropped the exercise from her regular classroom instruction. To be sure, the arguments were heating up. Other school board members started passing on to the teachers a roster of materials, including a video called *Icons of Evolution*, which criticized Darwin's theory.

"I feel embarrassed to admit it, but I was intimidated," she said later. "These intelligent design people scared me."

FRANK LINDH HAD RIDDEN what was known as "the stockbroker bus" from his home in Marin County to San Francisco in the wee hours of September 11, 2001. He was rushing to his Market Street office in time to patch into a 9 A.M. eastern time conference call. He was in the middle of a sentence when the first airplane flew into the North Tower of the World Trade Center. It was announced on the call in a very matter-of-fact way—a plane had crashed into Manhattan's tallest building. "We thought the same thing everyone did when it first happened, some Piper or Cessna had gone off course and had an accident; we kept talking on the call until the second plane crashed," said Lindh. "It is odd, but I remember thinking at the time, 'How did they get all those people out of the airplane before they flew into the towers?' It was inconceivable that they would just kill 300 passengers just like that—and then they did."

Marilyn Walker was home when the telephone rang the morning of September 11. A friend was on the other line. "Turn on the television," the friend said. She did, just in time to see the second plane crash into the South Tower.

John Walker Lindh was on the Afghan battlefield when he heard about the attacks. He told investigators later that he wasn't sure how he found out, though he suspected it was through the BBC or Taliban radio. Conspiracy theories have a way of gaining incredible traction in remote areas. Some reports said Osama bin Laden was behind the attacks. Others said Mossad, the Israeli intelligence agency, was behind it in an effort to make Arabs look bad. Lindh wasn't sure what to believe. There had been rumors at the Al-Farouq camp that bin Laden had dispatched some 50 members for a martyrdom mission. Everyone assumed it would be a Saudi or American attack but no one knew when or how the mission would be carried out. Lindh heard later that all the al-Qaeda camps were closed on September 11. It is hard to fathom how Lindh must have felt when the news of the attacks filtered through the Taliban front line. He was worried they would kill him for being an American.

Frank Lindh and Marilyn Walker, thinking that their son was still in the mountains of Pakistan to escape the summer heat, also had reason to be concerned. They worried that when the U.S. military started bombing the tribal areas between Pakistan and Afghanistan, John might be killed.

That weekend, Frank Lindh took some photographs of John to local mosques and asked if anyone had heard of or seen John. He drove to the Tenderloin District of San Francisco and began asking Muslims milling around a small mosque there if they knew John. "In a way it was very sweet," he said later. "People knew him because he was this white kid who had converted. I can't tell you how many people said, 'Hey, I know this guy.' There was a real tenderness to it. They kept trying to tell me that if he was with Tablighi Jama 'at I didn't need to worry. They were really trying to make me feel better. I hadn't expected that."

In fact, Frank Lindh and Marilyn Walker did have good reason to worry about their son. He had volunteered to go to the Taliban front line in Takhar facing Dostum's Northern Alliance. By early November 2001, the Northern Alliance had breached the Afghan army's front line and Lindh's commanding officer ordered a retreat. The unit began a painful two-day march to Kunduz, trudging fifty miles through dusty desert landscape. Nighttime temperatures dropped below freezing. The ragtag group, some in plaid shirts, others with soft slipper boots on their feet, had to keep marching just to stay warm. The retreat had been such a hasty one, the Taliban troops had no water or food. Lindh, for his part, could barely walk. He had been battling his old intestinal problems for weeks and he was dehydrated, exhausted, and dirty.

At the same time, a nagging fear began to filter through the ranks of the retreating forces. They worried about what lay ahead. They were marching right into the arms of Dostum's troops, and stories of his wrath rattled the young men as they headed for Kunduz. Hundreds of Taliban soldiers had surrendered to Dostum in Kunduz ahead of Lindh's unit. Dostum had summarily executed them. The best the retreating Taliban could hope for was some sort of negotiated safe passage that would end better than the one that had preceded them.

Days later, toward the end of November, John Walker Lindh found himself on the back of a truck with 400 Taliban foot soldiers bound for Herat, one of the three largest cities in Afghanistan. A treaty, commanders said, had been reached with the Northern Alliance. The troops would be given safe passage to Herat in exchange for turning over their weapons. Lindh's health was declining and he knew it. He began mapping out his escape. When the truck arrived in Herat he would make his way back to Pakistan and try to return home to the United States.

Lindh's best-laid plans were dashed when the convoy began to head for Qala-i-Jhangi, an old fortress outside Mazar-e-Sharif. The men were headed right into the arms of Dostum. Clearly the safe passage agreement had been broken. Lindh's heart sank as he and 300 Taliban sat helpless on the truck beds speeding toward their fate.

LINDH STEPPED DOWN FROM the truck when the convoy pulled up in front of a rubble-littered fort. He was almost immediately greeted by a loud explosion. One of the Afghan army soldiers, sure that the group had been double-crossed, had detonated a grenade. Dostum's guards began hustling the Taliban soldiers into a dark, cramped basement under the fort—a military building known as the Pink Building. The Taliban forces were now captive. To retaliate for the earlier attack, Dostum's soldiers dropped a grenade down an air shaft. Lindh was nearly killed. He spent the night crouched in a corner of the basement near a toilet. His jihad, he was sure, was about to come to an untimely end. As Lindh cowered in the basement of the Pink Building, his parents were reading the stories of what would become the massacre at Qala-i-Jhangi fortress. They had no idea their son was witnessing it firsthand.

On Sunday, November 25, there were foreign cameramen at the fortress. Video footage of that morning showed a calm scene. Prisoners, with their arms tied behind their backs, were kneeling in a horse pasture next to the fortress. The tapes show Dostum's men passing along the lines of Taliban prisoners. They kicked some of them. They beat others with sticks. Two Americans in civilian clothes moved among the prisoners as well, pointing things out to Dostum's guards. One of them, a man named Dave Tyson, donned a long Afghan shirt, a gun, and a video camera. The second, a former marine named Johnny Michael Spann—who went by the name Mike—was wearing a black shirt and jeans. Lindh thought they were mercenaries, working with the Northern Alliance, and he instinctively crouched lower as they neared. They moved over by Lindh, took him away from the other prisoners, and started questioning him. The video picked up the interrogation.

"Irish? Ireland?" Spann asked him.

Lindh sat mute.

"Who brought you here? You believe in what you are doing that much, you're willing to be killed here?"

Lindh kept his head down.

Then Tyson turned to Spann and said, "The problem is, he's got to decide if he wants to live or die, and die here. . . . We can only get the Red Cross to help so many guys."

Lindh probably should have realized that the mere mention of the Red Cross might have signaled these two weren't mercenaries. He was criticized (and nearly charged) for lying to the two men about his nationality. If he had to do it again, maybe he would not have. But at the time, with the stories of Dostum's brutality still ringing in his head, Lindh didn't pick up on cues that a savvier observer might have seen. Neither Spann nor Tyson had made it at all clear that they were working for the U.S. government, but their interrogations of prisoners should have made Lindh think twice. Instead, he assumed the best thing to do was stay quiet. So he did. John was returned to the main body of prisoners, while others were still being led out of the basement and forced to kneel in the horse pasture. Lindh was seated in the dusty compound of Qala-i-Jhangi with his arms tied behind his back just above the elbow and his head bowed.

What happened next is still muddled. Some say it started with a thrown rock. A Taliban soldier knocked out a Northern Alliance soldier and grabbed his gun. Other Taliban recruits snatched nearby arms and all hell broke loose. Still tied up, the Taliban started charging Northern Alliance soldiers, crying, "Allah-u Akbar" ("God is great"). Gunfire mowed down the front line. Those who escaped that attack found an arsenal in the Pink Building and began fighting Dostum's troops at close range.

According to British journalist Luke Harding, "It was then . . . that Spann 'did a Rambo.' As the remaining guards ran away, Spann flung himself to the ground and began raking the courtyard and its prisoners with automatic fire. Five or six prisoners jumped on him, and he disappeared beneath a heap of bodies." (Spann's body was later recovered by U.S. Special Forces. He was the first American to die in combat in Afghanistan.) John tried to run but he was shot in the thigh. He lay motionless for the next 12 hours, pretending to be dead, thinking that was his only chance at staying alive.

American helicopters and special forces soon followed. Massive 2,000-pound bombs rocked the area. When one bomb missed its target and accidentally hit Dostum's soldiers, the air strikes ended. Journalists who visited the compound afterward were shattered by what they saw. How an American CIA agent was caught in the crossfire is still unresolved. The official version was that a Taliban soldier rushed Spann and blew himself and Spann up. Another person said he had seen Spann's body and he had been beaten and shot through the chest. One Northern Alliance source said that Spann's body had been found with a booby-trapped body on top. Spann was removed by tying a rope or cable around his foot and attaching the other end to an armored vehicle to pull the CIA agent out from under.

However the scene unfolded, there was no debate about the carnage that was left. There were 150 Taliban twisted and blown apart on the compound. One body, crushed by a tank, was no thicker than a piece of cardboard. Northern Alliance soldiers were stealing shoes from the corpses and using daggers to remove gold fillings from the mouths of the dead. The Taliban soldiers who survived the onslaught had slipped back down into the Pink Building's basement, awaiting the next wave of violence. Against all odds, John Walker Lindh was among them.

Deep in the complex of underground tunnels, the Taliban hunkered down for safety. A short time later, an American bombardment began. Thundering overhead, dozens of bombs fell on the fort. Lindh said later that he couldn't understand why the Americans were helping the Northern Alliance. It never occurred to him, he said, that the Afghan civil war had a terrorism component or that the Taliban were seen as accessories to the World Trade Center attacks. When the

American bombing didn't drive the Taliban fighters out of the Pink Building, the Northern Alliance decided on a more direct approach. They tried to freeze them out. They diverted a water channel directly into the basement. The basement filled with four feet of water, Lindh said later. Those who were injured and lying down drowned. Lindh kept himself propped up on a stick. Two days later, on December 1, the last Taliban fighters surrendered. Only 86 of the original 300 survived. John Walker Lindh was one of them. He came to the top of the staircase with his hands in the air and said, "I'm an American."

Colin Soloway of *Newsweek* broke the story of the "American Taliban" that day. He interviewed Lindh for about 40 minutes outside the Pink Building. He told another journalist there that Lindh was "a kid" who had gotten himself "into the wrong place at the wrong time." Hours later, Marilyn Walker was showing Frank Lindh a photograph of their son on the Internet.

"I knew immediately that there would be a problem," Frank said later. "Seeing his picture cut both ways. It solved the mystery of where John was, but I knew he was in for trouble. The media was immediately talking about him serving life in prison."

On December 4, Frank Lindh arrived at his local Red Cross chapter in San Rafael. He sat alone at a desk in a small office and composed a note to John, who he assumed was a prisoner of war. The parameters of the note were circumscribed by the form letters of the Red Cross:

Dear John,

> *I hope you recognize my handwriting. Mama and I love you very much and are trying to find out where you are being held. I have retained a lawyer to help you. Please ask the U.S. authorities to allow*

*me, Mama, and the lawyer to come visit with you as soon as possible. I
hope you're feeling OK.*

Love,
Papa

P.S. Connell and Naomi both send their love!

(The Lindhs learned later that this letter would never reach John,
nor would any of the other letters sent from the Red Cross that
month. John would later read copies of the letters through a glass
window in an interrogation room—held up against the glass by his
father.)

It would turn out that John Walker Lindh wasn't the only American apprehended on the battlefield fighting for the Taliban. The second was Yaser Hamdi. Hamdi was born in Baton Rouge, Louisiana,
and held dual U.S. and Saudi citizenship. His Saudi parents moved
back to the kingdom when he was still a little boy. But as luck would
have it, Hamdi's fate would end up very different from that of the guy
from Northern California.

IN 1999, THE KANSAS legislature passed what was known as the
Romeo and Juliet law to differentiate sex between a young adult and
a young teen from sex between teens of different ages. The idea was
that if two childhood sweethearts had sex, the one who happened to
be 18 shouldn't be treated as a sex offender. The legislature very deliberately decided not to make the statute apply to gay teenagers. Instead, teens of the same gender who had sex were subject to the
state's criminal sodomy laws, which prohibited sex with a child less
than 16 years of age. Under the Romeo and Juliet law, first and sec-

ond offenses received probation. A third offense carried a maximum sentence of 15 months in prison. The criminal sodomy laws involved hard time. The first offense carried a sentence of 55 to 61 months. The second offense merited 89 to 100 months. And the third offense provided for as much as 228 months in prison. Criminal sodomy was seen as a sexually violent crime under Kansas law. As a result, violators had to register as sex offenders. Most states had some kind of Romeo and Juliet law and tended to be neutral on the issue of the sexual orientation of the teens involved. Only Kansas and Texas had laws that treated gay teens differently than straight ones. And this, of course, was Matthew Limon's bad luck. Because he was gay in Kansas, the courts saw him as a predator, not a teenager.

Matthew Limon's first lawyer, a public defender named David Estes, immediately filed a motion to dismiss the charges, arguing that Limon was being discriminated against. Excluding him from the lesser penalties of teenage love spelled out in the Romeo and Juliet laws denied Matthew equal protection under the law, he said. The court denied the motion and set the case for trial. The rights guaranteed by the 14th Amendment—namely, equal protection under the law—did not appear to apply to Matthew Limon. Matthew's next court-appointed attorney, Anthony Lupo, advised Matthew to waive his right to a jury trial. Because Matthew had already admitted to having sex with M.A.R., a jury was certain to find him guilty. Instead, Lupo said, the strategy should be to appeal his sentence. Matthew followed his advice and had a three-day bench trial. The facts weren't in dispute, so Matthew had little choice but to beg for the mercy of the court. And that's precisely what he did when he appeared in Miami County Court for sentencing on August 10, 2000.

Judge Richard Smith asked him if he wanted to make a statement. Matthew nodded. "I prayed to God many times and asked him to change my life, asked him—I've asked him to change my ways," he began. "First I gave up all hope that I couldn't change, and I'm willing to change. I want to change." He talked about how God had given him his music, the thing that brought him closer to his family, and said he wanted to get his relationship with God straightened out. "Please, please, Your Honor, give me some treatment," he said. "I asked a few people about prison and most of the people said I wouldn't survive or wouldn't make it . . . they said I was too soft and I was weak. Some other people said if I just mind my own business and just kept my mouth shut that I'd probably be okay. I know I deserve some major punishment, but I'm also asking for just one more chance to change my life."

Judge Smith didn't provide it. In August 2000, he sentenced Matthew Limon to 17 years and 2 months in a correctional facility, followed by 5 years of court supervision after his release. Matthew later said about the verdict, "Oh my God. A bomb dropped. I felt so bad." He was also to be classified as a sex offender, a categorization that would stay with him the rest of his life. His name, address, and photograph would be publicly available—kept on file at police departments or included in searchable, online sex offender registries.

Phill Kline, the former state legislator who had just become Kansas's new attorney general, learned of the sentence with some satisfaction. This type of offense, he said, merited the toughest of punishments.

ELLSWORTH CORRECTIONAL FACILITY SITS at the intersection of Highways 56 and 40 in northwestern Kansas, about two hours north of Wichita. The landscape around it is beautiful: emerald green hills dissected by two-lane blacktop roads that disappear into the distance. The facility is announced by a giant silver water tower and a series of fences and low-slung brick buildings visible from the street. If it weren't for the razor wire and the series of identification checks needed to get inside, one might be forgiven for thinking this wasn't a prison at all.

For Matthew Limon, the irony of Ellsworth was that it looked very much like the Lakemary Center: all manicured lawns, winding concrete paths, and low shrubs. Built in 1988, it looked more like a community college than a medium-security prison housing murderers, experts in forgery, and drunk drivers. "We see the inmates here as having made bad decisions and that's what brought them here," one prison official said. "We don't think of them as murderers. We see them as people who made mistakes and are trying to set things right."

With that philosophy in mind, they sought to create an environment conducive to allowing men to set their lives straight. Prison officials arranged an array of public service activities for the prisoners, something to keep them busy while they awaited the day of their release. Some inmates refurbished bicycles to be donated to needy children at Christmas. Others participated in Wheels for the World, a program in which prisoners repaired previously owned wheelchairs. In four years, 35 Ellsworth inmates managed to restore some 2,774 wheelchairs that were sent to people around the world who needed them. For animal lovers, there were dogs. Ellsworth had established a partnership with Canine Assistance Rehabilitation Education and Services (CARES), an organization that trained dogs to help handicapped individuals. Inmate handlers lived with puppies for 12 to 18 months, right in their cells. And the dogs, mostly labs and boxers and retrievers, appeared to love the arrangement. An animal might leave Ellsworth to eventually become a medic-alert dog for an owner in Manhattan, trained to notify paramedics if its master took a fall. Wherever the dogs ended up, for the time they were at Ellsworth they provided an atmosphere that made some inmates, even for a short time, almost forget they were in prison.

But Matthew didn't like fixing things or working with dogs. His strength was music. He almost immediately signed up for the spiritual center's choir. For protection, Matthew made friends with his cellmate. His cellmate was "my best friend. Like my brother."

"I was pretty lucky that for the first two years I had a cellmate who was my best friend. He got me into working out and we lifted weights together. He watched out for me and told me who to avoid and how to get along in prison. There have been a couple of people like that, ones who have watched out for me. Between that and music, I figured I could get through all this."

While life at Ellsworth wasn't ideal, Matthew did manage to make the best of it. His mother and father donated the family piano to the prison in the hopes that it might make Matthew's time behind bars pass more quickly. Three months later, prison officials auctioned off the piano—citing the fact that it didn't work very well and that Matthew had taken an interest in another instrument. The auction garnered $50 for Ellsworth. Limon later said about the auction: "That hurt me. That piano had so many memories. I said I'll even buy it back." But the family piano was gone.

There was so much musical talent at Ellsworth—keyboard and bass players like Matthew, singers and drummers and guitarists—chaplain Herbie Harris decided to bring professionals in to help the men record a CD. The idea was to create a compilation of songs the inmates wrote themselves—religious tunes with names like "Look to Him," "Jesus Loves His Nobodies," and "Like Jesus Did for Me."

Matthew had been at Ellsworth for two years before the CD recording opportunity presented itself, and for a time, it was all-consuming in that healthy way that allows one to forget that time is passing. In all, it took nearly 10 months to produce. Friends of Chaplain Harris brought in recording equipment and donated their time. Another volunteer did the mixing. Matthew played bass and piano on two of the 14 songs on the album. About the same time that the

CD—*Freedom Within*—hit the prison store, Matthew learned that his appeal had been denied. Matthew was dumbfounded and thought to himself, "To serve ALL that time . . ."

By then, Matthew's parents had moved to the small town of Larned, some 63 miles from Ellsworth, to be closer to their son. They visited him twice a week; though Chaplain Harris remembers that the visits were often contentious. They wanted Matthew to stop this nonsense about being gay. "My parents will never accept me for who I am," Matthew would say. "But I am happy with who I am."

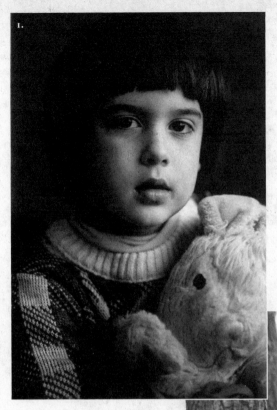

1. John Walker Lindh was a smart child, though a little introverted. He was the kind of boy who would ask for Japanese language tapes for Christmas one year and Gaelic tapes the next. He always had an affinity for languages and music. (*Courtesy of the Lindh family*)

2. Lindh's beautiful hair and eyes attracted compliments from adults when he was a little boy. Marilyn Lindh recalled her son's writhing discomfort when it happened. "He hated attention." (*Courtesy of the Lindh family*)

3 AND 4. John was the Lindhs' middle child, sandwiched between older brother Connell and Naomi, a younger sister who idolized him. Connell sits far left in this photo, beside Naomi, John Walker Lindh, and his father Frank Lindh. Lindh's mother, Marilyn, is seated behind John. Below, a teenage John mugs with his father for the camera. (*Courtesy of the Lindh family*)

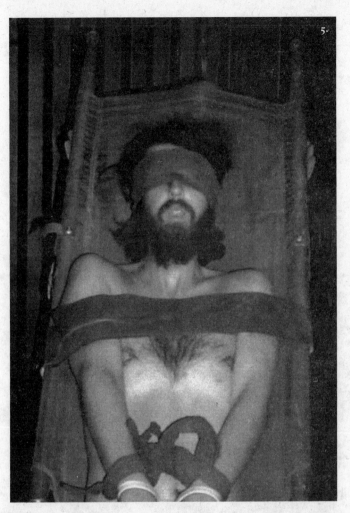

5. When photographs of John Walker Lindh, naked and duct taped to a stretcher by the American military, surfaced the public thought nothing of it. In retrospect, the photographs should have alarmed lawmakers in Washington about the treatment of prisoners captured in the "war on terror." *(U.S. Military Photo)*

6. Colin Soloway of *Newsweek* broke the story of the "American Taliban" just weeks after the September 11th attacks. He interviewed John Walker Lindh for about 40 minutes when he emerged exhausted and dirty from a Taliban compound. He told another journalist at the time that Lindh was "a kid" who had gotten himself "in the wrong place at the wrong time." This photo is from a television image on December 1, 2001. (*AP Photo/APTN*)

7. U.S. Attorney General John Ashcroft holds up the 12-page criminal complaint filed against John Walker Lindh during a press conference at the Justice Department in Washington, D.C. Ashcroft said Lindh was charged with conspiracy to kill U.S. nationals and with "providing material support and resources to designated foreign terrorist organizations." *(Tim Sloan/AFP/ Getty Images)*

8. Marilyn, Frank, and Naomi Lindh console each other outside the Albert V. Bryan Federal Courthouse in Alexandria, Virginia in July 2002 after John Walker Lindh pled guilty to helping the Taliban in violation of U.S. law. *(Paul J. Richards/ AFP/Getty Images)*

8.

9 AND 10. Kot Hordynski, right and below, was a member of the nonviolent anti-war group Students Against War (SAW) at the University of California, Santa Cruz. The Pentagon included SAW in a terrorism watch database and deemed Hordynski and his friends a "credible threat." The ACLU filed a lawsuit on the students' behalf to open up the Pentagon's database. *(Right: Courtesy of the ACLU) (Below: AP Photo/Eric Risberg)*

9.

10.

11. Police watch over prisoners from Orleans Parish Prison (OPP) caught by the flood waters of Katrina. Prison officials had made the decision to wait out the storm, but when the prison flooded they were obliged to transfer prisoners, by boat, to a highway overpass where some of the inmates were forced to wait for days. (*AP Photo/David J. Phillip*)

12. On the Broad Street overpass, prisoners were ordered to sit in rows back to back and weren't allowed to move. Shuttling thousands of prisoners out of OPP to the streets outside became one of the largest prisoner evacuations in U.S. history. (*Photo by Mario Tama/Getty Images*)

13. "The prisoners will stay where they belong," New Orleans Sheriff Marlin Gusman, far left, told the Department of Corrections when it offered to evacuate his charges. (*AP Photo/Bill Haber*)

14. Greg Davis was caught at Orleans Parish Prison during the flood and ended up doing what prisoners called "Katrina Time." While he was in prison for a charge that was eventually dropped, he was lost in the morass and confusion of the New Orleans correctional system for seven months before a volunteer attorney from Tulane found him and got him released. (*Photo courtesy Steve May of* The Independent Weekly)

15. Bertha Spahr started teaching science at Dover High School 41 years ago, when there were no women teaching chemistry in the school district. She was fond of saying that at those early county-wide science teacher meetings it was "all men, one nun, and me." *(Anthony D. Romero)*

16. The ACLU's Witold Walczak led the courtroom battle over the Dover school board's decision to include "intelligent design" in its biology curriculum. *(AP Photo/ Bradley C. Bower)*

17. Lehigh University professor Michael Behe, wearing hat, is a leading advocate of "intelligent design." He was the lead witness in a federal trial deciding whether intelligent design could be mentioned in public school science classes as a possible alternative to the theory of evolution. (*AP Photo/Bradley C. Bower*)

18. Former Dover school board member Bill Buckingham, right, was keen to have creationism taught alongside evolution in high-school biology classes. He felt that it was wrong to talk about Darwin's theories without also telling students that they were by no means ironclad. (*AP Photo/York Daily Record/ Sunday News, Jason Plotkin*)

OF PANDAS
AND PEOPLE
The Central Question of Biological Origins

Second Edition

19. *Of Pandas and People* is the biology textbook preferred by advocates of Intelligent Design. Teachers in the Dover public schools were concerned because they found the book to be factually inaccurate and poorly written.

20 AND 21. Cecelia Fire Thunder was the president of the Oglala Sioux tribe on the Pine Ridge Reservation in South Dakota. She created a stir on the reservation when she told reporters that she would put a Planned Parenthood clinic on her tribe's land if South Dakota voters upheld a law banning abortions. (*Left: Courtesy of the ACLU*) (*Below: Photo by David Melmer. Reprinted with permission of* Indian Country Today)

22. Kate Looby, South Dakota director of Planned Parenthood, right, helped organize volunteers to canvass voters to battle the state's anti-abortion law. It sought to ban all abortions, even in cases of incest or rape. (*AP Photo/Nati Harnik*)

23. Matthew R. Limon, shown here in his Department of Corrections photograph, was sentenced to more than 17 years in prison for having sex when he was 18 with a 14-year-old boy in 2000. Under Kansas' "Romeo and Juliet" law, Limon would have been sentenced at most to one year and three months in prison had his partner been an underage girl. (*AP Photo/Kansas Department of Corrections*)

24. Matthew Limon wipes his face while waiting for a hearing in Miami County District Court, in Paola, Kansas. Limon was in court less than a week after the Kansas Supreme Court ruled that the state can't punish underage sex more harshly if it involves homosexual acts. (*AP Photo/Orlin Wagner*)

23.

24.

25. ACLU attorney Ann Beeson, left, and author James Bamford, right, had opposed the National Security Agency spying program that trampled on civil liberties. *(AP Photo/Al Behrman)*

26. Josh Dratel had become, in a very real sense, the Leonard Zelig of terrorism litigation. Just like the Woody Allen character who found himself standing next to Babe Ruth or Winston Churchill at some turning point in history, Dratel appeared at key moments of America's "war on terror," blinking against the klieg lights. *(AP Photo/Mark Wilson, Pool)*

Chapter 6

ETHICAL LAPSES

NEW ORLEANS HAS SOME OF THE MOST draconian antiprisoner laws of any American city. Before ever seeing a judge or a lawyer, people can be detained for up to 45 days for a misdemeanor and 60 days for a felony. This is standard procedure. It doesn't matter whether the charges are well founded.

From a distance, reasons for arrest can seem almost whimsical: reading tarot cards without a permit; "aggravated bike riding" (both hands were not on the handlebars). More often than not the arrested came from the ranks of the city's homeless and poor. In New Orleans, the people who fit those criteria tended to be black. The numbers tell the story: one in seven African-American men in Louisiana ends up in the prison system. Only one in 35 ends up in college.

The way the city defended the indigent made an already bad situation that much worse. Public defenders were part-time employees of the city. There was no public defenders' office, per se—no handful of lawyers watching out for the rights of the indigent. If you couldn't afford an attorney in New Orleans, the one appointed to you by a court of law was, at best, preoccupied. Lawyers defended the poor while juggling private practices. Two-thirds of the money to pay for the public defenders came from traffic and parking fines. Attorneys got $17 for every one of their clients who pled guilty. They got nothing if their clients fought the charges. The system gave lawyers little incentive to be advocates for their clients. The way this system was structured, the indigent were not afforded a simple 6th Amendment protection: the right to effective counsel.

Lawsuits had been filed in other states challenging the inadequacy of indigent defense systems. In Montana, a class-action ACLU lawsuit prompted the passage of legislation in 2005 that created a statewide public defender system for the state's poor. But the system in New Orleans was still broken. Lawyers for the indigent in New Orleans tended to tell their clients that they could get released if they just pled guilty in exchange for time served. On the surface that seemed like good advice. What their clients often didn't understand was that doing so meant they would have to pay court costs and probation fees of $40 a month for up to five years. Many of the people who were in OPP when Katrina made landfall were there because they couldn't come up with the money to pay their fines and fees.

New Orleans's public defenders were assigned to specific courtrooms and were essentially attached to specific judges. As a result, the lawyers came to see themselves as an extension of the court. "There is a culture of inadequate representation here," said Katherine Mattes, codirector of the Tulane Law Center, which provides legal assistance to the indigent in New Orleans. "Because there is no training and there are no case load limits, basically the public defenders are taking on double the number of cases the American Bar Association recommends. People actually got lost in the system for months after Katrina. They just disappeared. We're still finding people today who have been in jail for a year just awaiting trial. The part-time public defenders had maybe 250 clients and no paperwork and no way of tracking these people. It was a mess."

In March 2004, the National Association of Criminal Defense Lawyers and the National Legal Aid and Defender Association released a report that found that Louisiana failed to meet "9 of 10 national indigent defense standards." The upshot, the report concluded: "If you are poor in Louisiana, you have no real access to justice."

There was a lengthy list of accusations leveled against OPP's guards and its administration as well. In 2004, two guards were indicted for beating a prisoner to death after he was picked up on charges of public drunkenness. The same year, OPP was ranked among the top five prisons in the country for facing substantiated reports of sexual violence. Almost a third of the prison's $17.3 million insurance fund was set aside to pay claim liabilities in 2002.

To be fair, the problems didn't start with the current sheriff, Marlin Gusman. The former sheriff, Charles Foti, was the chief defendant in *Hamilton v. Morial*, a lawsuit the ACLU filed in 1969 on behalf of some 3,000 inmates at OPP, challenging the conditions of their confinement. To many Americans, the idea of "prisoners' rights" is oxymoronic—in other words, you get what you deserve when you are in prison.

The ACLU's first round of prison-condition cases took on the most egregious violations: overcrowding, inadequate health care, rampant violence among prisoners, and guard-on-prisoner assault. While progress has been made, many of the same issues are often at play some thirty years later. In 2003, for example, a Mississippi court found that the treatment of prisoners on that state's death row was cruel and unusual punishment. For a Mississippi court to rule in favor of such an unpopular group of plaintiffs meant that conditions had to be really bad. Inmates were denied access to showers for days at a time, held in cells with no air-conditioning and where the heat index would frequently reach 100 degrees in summertime. There were mosquito infestations, and sewage would back up into the cells because of malfunctioning toilets. The court found "no excuse" for the situation "no matter how heinous the crime committed," and placed the prison under consent decree, which obligates the prison to improve conditions.

Orleans Parish Prison is also under a consent decree and is involved in one of the longest-running cases of prisoner litigation in the country. *Hamilton* forced OPP to make substantial changes in its medical program and psychiatric facilities. There remained, however, other problems, including the investigation of inmate deaths. The sheriff's own staff, as opposed to the police, conducted them. They had little incentive to actually conduct those inquiries and even less incentive to find themselves culpable. Prisoners also received poor medical treatment. The court ordered it to make improvements. What was clear to anyone looking at New Orleans's penal system was that it was riddled with problems before Katrina. It completely collapsed in its aftermath.

"When the storm hit, the whole building was swaying side to side," Deputy Reed told the ACLU's National Prison Project. "I was scared. The floors and the stairs got real slippery and there was water coming in from places you didn't know water could come in from. The first day of the storm was all right—you were looking out at the rain and the water. It had to be about two or three feet at the time. But it was rising and rising even after the rain stopped. That was such a weird thing to see."

On Monday, August 29, the floodwaters began to pour into the lower levels of the OPP complex. Deputies gave prisoners on the bottom floors brooms and mops for the Sisyphean task of sweeping the water out of their cells. In Templeman II, water started seeping into the dorm through floor drains. Women in Templeman IV were climbing onto the second and third level of the bunks to stay out of the water.

In Templeman III, one deputy said the water rose from just an inch to three feet deep in a matter of minutes. When it rose to chest height, prison officials decided to start moving prisoners to higher ground. By that time, cell doors had shortcircuited under the deluge. Deputies had to use crowbars to get some prisoners out. There were screams for help and panic as inmates became convinced that they would drown in their cells.

Reed was one of the few deputies who stayed on duty during the entire ordeal. As the water rose, officers started to go missing. Some threw their badges on the ground, turned their shirts inside out, and just left. At one point, there was only one deputy per floor supervising over 120 inmates. They didn't have working radios or any way to call for help, so they stayed put in a sort of defensive crouch. Prisoners started fighting among themselves, shouting for help, and jimmying open the gate locks. Eventually, one of the associate wardens started locking the doors behind the deputies when they reported for duty. Reed said he was trapped on his floor for an entire 12-hour shift.

At first, the prisoners lit fires just to provide some light in the darkened prison. Later, the flames seemed like a good way to let rescue helicopters know that they were still inside, waiting for help. Deputies instructed prisoners to break windows so they could escape the smoke and get fresh air. In one building inmates ripped metal tables and dayroom benches from where they were bolted to the floor and used them as battering rams to punch holes in the prison's cinder block walls. Others started tying bedsheets together to lower themselves out of the broken windows into the swirling water below. Some got caught on the razor wire around the perimeter fence. One deputy said later it was like watching the movie *Attica*.

"No one from our building escaped," Reed said later. "But you could see people getting shot by snipers on the roof around the jail. It was almost like a third world country. It was unreal. It looked like people were getting picked off. You see somebody fall into the water and that was enough for me to see right there." Reed didn't look to see what happened to the inmates once they splashed into the muddy waters below. He never found out whether the prisoners were being shot with live rounds or rubber bullets. Sheriff Gusman claimed that every OPP prisoner was accounted for and no one died.

Pearl Cornelia Bland was jumped by a bunch of other female prisoners in Conchetta Women's Facility on the far side of the OPP compound the first day of the storm. By her account, she had just told some of the women in her cell to be quiet so she could hear a deputy's instruction. Whatever set the women off, Bland came out the loser. Eight women were beating her up as she cried for help. The deputy on the floor closed the door and refused to break up the assault. "Let them fuck that whore up," the deputy reportedly said. Another woman in the cell finally pulled the prisoners off her. There is a photograph of Bland taken days later. Her left eye was swollen shut and her jaw looked inflamed. Bland said that when she complained to the guards, one laughed and said if she didn't shut up he would let the women take another shot at her.

Bland was another inmate who shouldn't have even been in OPP when the storm hit. She had been arrested for possessing drug paraphernalia. At an August 11 arraignment, Bland pled guilty. A judge ordered that she be released the next day and placed in a drug rehabilitation program. Bland was indigent, so the judge waived all the fees and fines leveled against her. Instead of releasing her on August

12, OPP held Bland because she owed fines and fees from a prior conviction.

Under normal circumstances, Bland might have then gone to court to have outstanding fines and fees waived because of her inability to pay. Her August 23 hearing to do just that, nearly a week before the storm, was postponed to September 20. (Bland contacted the ACLU for help after the storm had passed. She ended up spending 10 months in jail because of $398 in unpaid fines.)

After the water subsided, a local reporter spotted a plaintive sign taped next to a broken cell window. "We need help," it read.

THE TALON DATABASE EXPOSED by NBC News listed more than fifty antiwar meetings and protests, some of which took place miles from any military installations. In addition to the protest at the University of California at Santa Cruz, the database included an antiwar protest in Los Angeles at Hollywood and Vine in March 2005. Other listed protests—from Boston to Florida—had annotations like "threat" or "exercising constitutional rights." Another 200 entries in the database had no connection whatsoever to the Department of Defense, but they appeared on the list all the same. NBC's report also showed that the Defense Department was stepping up its domestic monitoring of individuals. One briefing document, stamped "secret," said: "We have noted increased communication and encouragement between protest groups using the Internet, but no significant connection" between the incidents and no recurring "vehicle descriptions." That meant they were actually collecting information about the individuals at the protests.

The Pentagon's domestic intelligence and security operations were traditionally limited to things directly related to the military—counterespionage, sabotage, and investigation of personnel. The Pentagon had been burned before for tracking innocent civilians who only happened to disagree with the government. In 1970, a former Army intelligence officer named Christopher Pyle revealed, in an article in *Washington Monthly*, that during the Vietnam War, the Department of Defense had compiled dossiers on individuals and political organizations involved in antiwar and civil rights protests. And the people in the crosshairs were not just Black Panthers and the Weathermen. The NAACP and the ACLU were under surveillance as well.

Fear of government spying had led to one of the darkest moments in the ACLU's history. ACLU leaders provided government officials with inside information on ACLU activities and membership lists during the 1950s. This didn't come to light until the 1970s under the leadership of Aryeh Neier, who courageously led the organization during some of its most turbulent times—including the defense of neo-Nazis' First Amendment right to march through Skokie, Illinois. In 1940, the ACLU expelled Elizabeth Gurley Flynn from its national board because she was a member of the Communist Party. ACLU leadership—Irving Ferman, Herbert Monte Levy, and Morris Ernst— gave information on the ACLU to the FBI. They wanted to protect the organization from J. Edgar Hoover and from congressional investigation committees like HUAC. The organization's own ethical lapses later eclipsed its successes. ACLU efforts against the anti-Communist provisions of the Smith Act and advocacy to ensure Communist candidates' access to the ballot in the 1940s were largely overlooked because of this checkered history.

The Department of Defense began its domestic intelligence program in 1967, when the Army was trying to help local authorities quell violence in the nation's inner cities. When the antiwar movement went into overdrive, the Army reasoned that the FBI, Justice Department, and local law enforcement authorities were incapable of collecting intelligence. So the Army started spying on protesters.

They went to marches; they watched high school activists; and they gathered data on what they saw as the impending threat. Information came in on thousands of Americans, without congressional approval, and it might well have never come to light were it not for Christopher Pyle.

The ACLU sued the government, charging that the Army's activities inhibited civilians from exercising their constitutional rights of free speech and petition. Americans would be afraid to speak out, debate, and take stands on the issues that really mattered if they feared government surveillance. Eventually the Army withdrew and promised not to investigate civilians without the Secretary of the Army's approval. A lengthy congressional investigation followed. The military had conducted probes on at least 100,000 American citizens. Pyle convinced more than 100 military agents who had been ordered to spy on U.S. citizens—many of them antiwar protesters and civil rights advocates—to testify. In the wake of the investigations, such military spying inside the U.S. was discredited.

The TALON program suggested the problem wasn't gone. In the program's first year alone, the Department of Defense received more than 5,000 reports, and those details were fed into data-mining programs within CIFA. From March 2004 to the spring of 2006, CIFA awarded at least $33 million in contracts to corporate giants like Lockheed Martin, Unisys Corporation, Computer Sciences Corporation, and Northrop Grumman to develop databases that could comb through classified and unclassified government data, commercial information, and Internet chatter to help sniff out terrorists. Hordynski was shocked to find out that his e-mails fell under their purview.

Another data-mining program—the Defense Advanced Research Projects Agency's Total Information Awareness program—was stopped dead in its tracks because of civil liberties concerns. The ACLU initiated an unusual array of groups—including the American Conservative Union, Americans for Tax Reform, the Eagle Forum, and the Free Congress Foundation—to oppose it, and Congress killed the program in 2003. It was spearheaded by Admiral John Poindexter, who had been indicted because of his role in the Iran-Contra scandal. Rather than "connect the dots," Poindexter's and other data-mining programs collected more dots. More names. More information. Such efforts squandered limited law enforcement dollars by casting too broad a net, experts said.

Acting Deputy Undersecretary of Defense Roger W. Rogalski admitted in a letter obtained by NBC News that peaceful demonstrators had been wrongly added to the TALON database, including Kot Hordynski, the UC Santa Cruz student. "The recent review of the TALON Reporting System . . . identified a small number of reports that did not meet the TALON reporting criteria," the letter said. "Those reports dealt with domestic anti-military protests or demonstrations potentially impacting DoD facilities or personnel. . . . While the information was of value to military commanders, it should not have been retained in the Cornerstone database." Rogalski said there were people in the TALON database who shouldn't have been there. "They did not pertain to potential foreign terrorist activity and thus should never have been entered into the Cornerstone database. These reports have since been removed from the Cornerstone database and refresher training on intelligence oversight and database management is being given," the letter said.

The ACLU of Northern California didn't think the mea culpa letter went far enough. It pressed the Pentagon for further information on its monitoring of student protests in Berkeley and Santa Cruz. The ACLU filed Freedom of Information Act (FOIA) requests seeking documents from the Defense Department on the TALON program. The requests came just as the Senate Judiciary Committee was to begin probing the National Security Agency's warrantless wiretaps of domestic-based phone calls. Hordynski was shocked to be in the middle of the maelstrom. "We thought we were just exercising our constitutional rights of free speech and assembly," he told reporters at the time.

December 11, 2001

Dear John,

We all send our love to you, and hope you are well. This is now our second message to you—I hope you've received the first. We did get your message dated December 3—my birthday. You have our unconditional love and complete support. We are begging to get to see you. Trust in God!

Love,
Papa

P.S. We've hired a lawyer who also wants to see you!

Before Frank Lindh had sent the second of three Red Cross letters to his son, Defense Secretary Donald Rumsfeld told the military to "take the gloves off" when interrogating John Walker Lindh. Requests for a lawyer went unheeded even though letters had been sent to the government on December 3 that said that a lawyer had been retained for John. With a bullet still in his thigh, Lindh was flown to Camp Rhino, an American Marine base about 70 miles south of Kandahar. He was stripped naked and bound to a stretcher with duct tape wrapped around his chest, arms, and ankles. It was winter in Afghanistan and Lindh was left in a steel container outside, unclothed, to shiver in the cold for two days. He was then taken into a building at Camp Rhino and placed before an FBI agent who demanded he sign an advice-of-rights form that basically waived his right to counsel. Lindh said later that when he reached the part of the waiver that concerned his right to retain a lawyer, the agent stopped and said, "Of course, there are no lawyers here."

Lindh signed the waiver. He didn't know that his parents had already hired a lawyer who was willing to fly to Afghanistan, so he didn't feel he had much choice. (Frank Lindh called the national ACLU for help with his son's case. But the family had already retained one of the finest criminal defense lawyers, James Brosnahan. The ACLU had little expertise to add at the time.)

It wasn't just Lindh's parents who would be shocked to learn that their own government had tortured their son. People within the Justice Department were concerned as well. Government documents obtained through a FOIA request indicated that some Justice Department officials, including FBI agents, were concerned about torture.

The ACLU wrangled loose 100,000 pages of U.S. government documents shedding light on the extent of the torture and abuse of detainees in Afghanistan, Iraq, Guantánamo, and elsewhere. Senior Bush administration officials would later argue that Abu Ghraib was an isolated incident involving a few rogue soldiers—a few "bad apples." Thousands of pages of internal government documents begged to differ.

The FOIA request—filed months before the images of torture at Abu Ghraib came to light in April 2004—would show that there had been a debate within the government over whether such actions were justified and whether they ever extracted reliable intelligence. Several FBI agents warned that the use of abusive interrogation methods would come back to haunt the government. Even officials at the FBI headquarters instructed field agents not to participate in interrogations that used abusive techniques. Warnings from the top brass of the FBI were sent out from the executive offices of the J. Edgar Hoover Building, just down the hall from where one could view the oil painting of J. Edgar with his pinkie ring reflected in the tabletop. These warnings would come long after the U.S. military had already tortured a homegrown American, John Walker Lindh.

In internal e-mails, a lawyer in the Justice Department's ethics office specifically warned against the tactics the FBI used at Camp Rhino. Attorney Jesselyn Radack of the Department of Justice Professional Responsibility Advisory Office concluded that questioning Lindh without a lawyer present was not only unethical but unlawful. "I consulted with a Senior Legal Advisor here at PRAO and we don't think you can have the FBI agent question Walker," Radack wrote in a December 7, 2001, e-mail message. "It would be a pre-indictment, custodial overt interview, which is not authorized by law." That was before she learned that the FBI had already gone ahead and done it. On December 10, Radack wrote, "You just advised that the Deputy Legal Advisor of the FBI stated that an agent went and interviewed Walker over the weekend, not knowing that Walker was a represented person. Please keep me in the loop as you learn more details. The interview may have to be sealed or only used for national security purposes; however, I don't have enough information yet to make that recommendation." It was possible that, despite signing the waiver, anything Lindh said would be inadmissible in court.

Just after Christmas, Frank sent another Red Cross letter:

December 27, 2001:

Dear John,

> *This is now my third letter, so I hope you received the other two. Mama, Connell, Naomi and I all love you very much, and hope to*

see you soon. Your lawyer, Jim Brosnahan, also wants to visit you with us. You will like him. We hope you are well. God bless you!

Love,
Papa

John Walker Lindh was abused and photographed years before the shocking photos from Abu Ghraib would come to light. After he was stripped naked and blindfolded, Lindh was told by one soldier that he was "going to hang," and that they would sell the photographs after he was dead.

In a photo never released publicly, U.S. soldiers had scrawled "shithead" on his blindfold and posed next to him. Some of those photographs, along with a videotape of Lindh, were destroyed by a commanding officer.

The ACLU received hundreds of pages of government documents investigating the treatment of John Walker Lindh and the "shithead" photograph in particular. Described as "barracks humor," a "momentary lapse," and a "mild embarrassment" in various documents, the photo apparently did raise questions within the military about whether Lindh had been abused. The soldiers who had taken the photo said in sworn statements that they wrote "shithead" and posed with him, "because I felt based on his situation that he was a shithead." Another sworn statement said that "the sentiment conveyed by the inscription is certainly sh[a]red by the vast majority of Americans." Years later the photograph of army Pfc. Lynndie England—holding a leash attached to an Iraqi prisoner who was lying on the floor—brought new focus on the treatment of detainees in U.S. military custody.

One partially redacted government document went to great lengths to show that Lindh wasn't abused. The "generosity toward M. Lindh was humbling," it said. The commander of the U.S. Army

Special Forces Command (Airborne) at Fort Bragg, North Carolina, was told that soldiers "gave up their own food and supplies to him for consumption and warmth, confiscated an electric heater (FOB Supply Room) and even another man's cot (SSG [redacted]) for Mr. Lindh to use while [redacted] continued to sleep on a concrete floor, in a separate unheated room. Mr. Lindh was given soap, a toothbrush, toothpaste and towel for his personal hygiene and was permitted to practice religious beliefs whenever he was so moved. [redacted] even went so far as to manually heat water for Mr. Lindh in makeshift vessels so that he could bathe in the hot water."

But assurances that Lindh had been treated well are contradicted in the government's own "Report of Medical Examination and Treatment of American Citizen," which the ACLU also received. The entry on December 2, 2001, read, "The patient appears to be in his twenties or early thirties. He is clad in a pajama-type outfit. Has long unkempt hair and a beard, and bare feet. He is lying on a cot . . . Right thigh: Circular wound, approximately 6 cm diameter on the anteromedial aspect of the thigh." The bullet wound was mentioned again in the December 5 entry, and the surgeon says that "I want the receiving physician to know that if the thigh wound is explored and a bullet is retrieved, a proper chain of custody is essential, as the bullet may be used as forensic evidence." On December 7, the same surgeon would write: "I have repeatedly informed the chain of command here and back in Karachi (through official traffic and telephone calls) of the increasing importance of transferring his care to a higher echelon."

The bullet would not be removed from Lindh's leg until eight days later, on December 15.

When news of the Lindh photographs became public, most Americans thought nothing of it. In retrospect, the photos should have alarmed lawmakers in Washington about the treatment of prisoners captured in the "war on terror." The American public would learn years later that the Bush administration issued a specific direc-tive to find gaps in the Geneva Conventions.

No one in the administration should have been surprised by what happened when the gloves came off and the rules of war were ridi-culed. In December 2001, John Walker Lindh's treatment should have been a warning. Hindsight, of course, is always 20/20.

There were some basic rights that Lindh never enjoyed. He was never given the opportunity to correct errors or misstatements in the FBI interrogation report. It said repeatedly, and incorrectly, that Lindh was part of the "Taliban/al-Qaeda" as if the two organizations were one and the same. They are not. Lindh was a foot soldier in the Af-ghan army. "At present, we have no knowledge that he did anything otherl [sic] than join the Talban [sic]," Radack, the ethics lawyer at the Justice Department, wrote. Conflating al-Qaeda and the Tal-iban publicly, however, was enough to create a groundswell of anger against Lindh, the depths of which his parents never anticipated.

Chapter 7

A WORLD OF PIPE CARRIERS

IN SOUTH DAKOTA, IF VOTERS DON'T LIKE a law passed in the capital of Pierre, they have the right to put it on hold until it can be put to a public referendum. Residents can confirm or kill a law with a simple majority. Opponents need only gather signatures to put it on the ballot. That is how HB 1215, the South Dakota Women's Health and Human Life Protection Act—otherwise known as the "Roe killer"—came to appear on the November 2006 ballot.

The 1973 decision widely referred to as *Roe v. Wade* actually involved two separate abortion cases, not one. *Jane Roe v. Henry Wade* challenged an abortion only-if-the-mother's-life-is-in-danger law in Texas. Its companion case, *Mary Doe v. Arthur Bolton* (argued by ACLU board member Marjorie Pitts Hames), contested a Georgia law that prohibited all abortions except in cases of rape, danger to the woman's life or health, or the likelihood of a serious fetal deformity. In consecutive rulings, the Supreme Court found both the Texas and the Georgia laws to be unconstitutional. *Roe* did away with all existing criminal abortion laws and recognized a woman's constitutional right to choose to terminate a pregnancy. *Doe* established that it is the attending physician who makes the determination whether an abortion is "necessary" for a woman's well-being.

The ACLU has a long history with abortion rights. In 1912, when the New York City police shuttered a lecture by a young nurse named Margaret Sanger, the ACLU's future founder—Roger Baldwin—took up her cause. The lecture was cut short because Sanger was talking about birth control. (Sanger would go on to start America's first birth control clinic in 1916—in Brooklyn—and found what would later become Planned Parenthood.) Sanger's muzzling led to Baldwin's first defense of free speech. He led a protest and spoke out in defense of Sanger's right to discuss issues of reproductive choice. Sanger and a woman named Mary Ware Dennett ended up as two of the first clients represented by the American Civil Liberties Union. In 1920, Baldwin defended Sanger for giving women information about their own bodies and their own reproductive health. Mary Ware Dennett was in the dock for publishing a pamphlet called *The Sex Side of Life: An Explanation for Young People*. It took a jury forty minutes to convict her of obscenity. The ACLU helped overturn the conviction on appeal. In the 1940s, the ACLU led the fight against government prohibitions on the sale and use of birth control devices. Since the 1960s, it has fought for the right to contraception, the right to abortion, and the right to bear children.

On the issue of abortion, the nation has come a long way since the days of Margaret Sanger. Surveys show that many Americans want abortions to be available for victims of rape or incest. Going one step further, an admittedly slim majority of Americans believe that abortion is a personal choice that's best left up to a woman and her physician—not a politician.

In South Dakota, the trend was toward banning abortions altogether. Supporters of the ban would have voters believe that thousands of abortions occurred in South Dakota every year. In 2004, the most recent year for which South Dakota has the statistics, 814 abortions were performed in the state. About 23 of those, according to the figures, were a result of rape or incest. Still, it was South Dakota that would become the battleground for the modern-day battle over the right to choose.

CECELIA FIRE THUNDER WAS born Cecelia Apple and raised on the Pine Ridge Reservation in South Dakota amid a community of people with last names like Featherman, White Plume, Good Crow, and Bear Killer. She went to Red Cloud Catholic Elementary School on the reservation and was sent to Los Angeles on a relocation program from 1963 to 1976—part of the U.S. government's solution to the "Indian problem." (The idea was to fold Indians into the general population in the nation's cities. Fire Thunder said the unspoken assumption was that the Indians would simply disappear, gobbled up by the day-to-day machinations of life outside the reservation. During the 1970s, Los Angeles had the largest Indian population in America.)

Fire Thunder became a nurse, married a man from her tribe, and gave birth to two sons. When she returned to Pine Ridge in 1987, she began working to revive the Lakota language. Concerned about the women of the tribe, she became one of the original founders of the National Organization on Fetal Alcohol Syndrome and started Sacred Circle, which was focused on addressing domestic violence on the reservation.

Fire Thunder might have well decided to focus on her own disability: she was slowly and surely going deaf. Her hearing problem was seen, initially, as a speech impediment. She lisped because, she realizes now, she couldn't hear the higher end of the sound register. The priest who headed her school used to call her in every afternoon to read to him. She didn't realize at the time it was an effort to correct her lisp. Instead she, and the students in her class, assumed she was some kind of teacher's pet. The priest had her read aloud—periodicals and the daily papers mostly—and then asked her to comment on what she read. He gently corrected her soft syllables to diminish her lisp and then allowed her to talk about the issues of the day. "Little did he know he was creating a monster," Fire Thunder says, laughing. Reading the newspaper and commenting on current events at a young age, Fire Thunder says, "I think he made me into a politician."

Fire Thunder is a big woman, tall and round, with the open, wide face typical of an American Indian. Her eyes are black, her hair is pulled back and straight, and her speech merely hints at her disability—hard sounds are faintly distorted or fade before they typically would in the course of normal speech. Fire Thunder lost what was left of her hearing after she had an allergic reaction to an antibiotic in 2002. She had cochlear implants put in and says now she is learning the words to songs she had been mishearing all her life. "I was making up about 60 percent of the lyrics in Patsy Cline songs," she said, laughing. "Now I am learning them all over again." The disability didn't stop Fire Thunder from becoming the first woman to be elected president of the Oglala Sioux tribe. As she saw it, women had always held a place of honor for her tribe and she was merely following Lakota tradition. She won handily.

According to Lakota legend, some 2,000 years ago a white buffalo-calf woman came to earth to bestow ceremonies on the tribe. She appeared to two Lakota warriors who were out hunting for food in the Black Hills of South Dakota. The story says that they saw a figure approaching them from across the prairie and it looked, at first glance, like a white buffalo calf. But as it neared, it changed form and became a beautiful young Indian girl. One of the warriors immediately had lascivious thoughts about her. She beckoned him closer. He took a step forward and a black cloud enveloped his body. When it disappeared there was nothing left of the warrior but a pile of bones. The other warrior knelt before the young girl and prayed. She told him to go to his people and tell them that in four days she would return to present them with a sacred bundle. She turned away and disappeared, and the warrior rushed back to tell the Lakota people of the miracle he had witnessed.

Four days passed, and as the Lakota people awaited their sacred visitor they watched as a cloud formed in the sky. It grew bigger and bigger and seemed to get heavier, dropping lower and lower from the heavens. When it reached the earth, a white buffalo calf emerged. It rolled out of the cloud, shook itself, and then became the same beautiful Indian girl the warrior had seen days before. In her hands she held a small bundle. It was the Lakota people's first sacred peace pipe. Before the heavenly girl gave them her treasure, she taught the Lakota the seven sacred ceremonies of the Sioux Nation. She introduced the purification of the sweat lodge, the naming ceremony for children, the healing ceremony, the adoption ceremony, the marriage ceremony, the vision quest, and the sun dance ceremony. She told the Lakota that as long as they continued to perform these rituals they would remain guardians of their sacred land.

Then she left the very same way she came, on a cloud, promising that one day she would return for the pipe she gave them. The White Buffalo Calf Pipe is kept in a sacred place on the Cheyenne River even today. For Fire Thunder, the legend was applicable to the abortion debate raging in South Dakota. "The Calf Woman's first teaching was about sexual respect," Fire Thunder said quietly, days before South Dakotans were to vote on whether to ban abortions completely from the state. "A man filled with lust was reduced to a pile of bones. And the Lakota people, they worship a goddess and not a god. The pipe carrier was a woman."

In that Lakota legend, Fire Thunder saw the way forward: she called a local journalist and said if the abortion ban was upheld in South Dakota she would be willing to build a Planned Parenthood clinic on the Pine Ridge Reservation. "I will personally establish a Planned Parenthood clinic on my own land, which is within the boundaries of the Pine Ridge Reservation, where the State of South Dakota has absolutely no jurisdiction," she said. "Of course, in our culture, children are sacred, but women are sacred too, and somebody who has been victimized by rape or incest should have options."

As is often the case, people heard what they wanted to hear when she made the announcement. Elders in the tribe were outraged. They believed the clinic was only going to focus on helping Indian women terminate pregnancies. Those outside the reservation saw Fire Thunder as challenging Christian beliefs. Fire Thunder, for her part, described her stand as a simple question of sovereignty. She didn't think lawmakers in Pierre could enact an abortion ban that applied to the Oglala Sioux. Tribal jurisdiction would trump state law. The Oglala Sioux are a nation, as the United States of America is a nation.

"Some people said that what I was doing was against Lakota beliefs but that just isn't true," she said. "We used to have medicines available to terminate a pregnancy. Women like my grandmother were medicine women, and they had medicines one could drink for these kinds of situations. There was even an abortion ceremony. Every culture in the world has ways to take care of itself. And this law was going against that. You can't have people passing laws to control a woman's body. That isn't Lakota." Fire Thunder knew that when it came to abortion, she had to unite her people. "On this issue of a woman's right to choose," she said, "I am the pipe carrier."

ON FEBRUARY 1, 2002, two years to the month after Matthew Limon was escorted from the Lakemary school, a panel of three Kansas judges upheld his conviction and sentence as a sex offender. The decision shocked gay rights and civil liberties groups, since the issue boiled down to this: a young, developmentally disabled man who had just turned 18 was sentenced to 17 years in prison for having consensual oral sex with someone less than 3 years his junior. If that sex had been with a girl, instead of a boy, Limon would probably not have found himself behind bars for that length of time. (If the year had been 1964 instead of 2001, Matthew would have been even worse off. Under a 1913 law repealed in 1965, the state of Kansas forcibly sterilized over 3,000 women and men who had been classified as "insane" or "retarded." At least a quarter of the men were castrated.)

The Kansas court ruled that the state could legally hold homosexuals and heterosexuals to different standards. The court based its ruling on a Supreme Court decision in the 1986 case of *Bowers v. Hardwick*. That case began in 1982, when a police officer saw Michael Hardwick, a bartender at an Atlanta gay club, drinking a beer as he left work. Hardwick threw the bottle into a trash can, but was given a citation for public drinking. According to Hardwick's lawyer, the ticket said that he had to appear in court on Wednesday, but the date was wrong. When he didn't show up at the courthouse on Tuesday, the court issued an arrest warrant. Hardwick paid the fine, but the warrant wasn't retracted.

A police officer arrived at Hardwick's home to serve the papers and the officer found Hardwick and another man having oral sex in a bedroom—a criminal act under Georgia's sodomy law, though it had not been enforced since 1935. "A person commits the offense of sodomy," the statute read, "when he performs or submits to any sexual act involving the sex organs of one person and the mouth or anus of another." It didn't matter that they were in the privacy of one man's bedroom. It didn't matter that they were two adults. It didn't matter that the sex was consensual. In Georgia—just as in plenty of other states—blow jobs were illegal. Both men were arrested.

The case went to the U.S. Supreme Court in 1986, where Hardwick and the ACLU narrowly lost the appeal, five to four. The majority opinion declared that Americans did not "have a fundamental right to engage in homosexual sodomy." *Bowers* provided legal precedent for treating gay people differently. The ACLU had been the one to bring the *Bowers* case to the Supreme Court in 1986 and helped Matthew Limon almost two decades later in his appeal.

Limon and the ACLU appealed his case to the Kansas Supreme Court. On June 13, 2002, the court denied the appeal. By that time, Matthew had already served almost two and a half years behind bars. Matthew's last remaining hope was that the U.S. Supreme Court would agree to hear the case. Matthew Limon had unintentionally become the poster boy for one of the most important issues in the contemporary fight for gay rights—equality under the law. His case also touched two other emotionally charged issues: consensual sexual relationships between teens of the same sex and consensual sexual relationships between developmentally disabled people. His parents could not have been more embarrassed.

The Matthew Limon case was about much more than sex, however. It was about fairness. Why should a straight teenager who has sex with someone who is below the age of consent get a lighter sentence than a gay teenager? It was a simple matter of the 14th Amendment: "No State shall . . . deny to any person within its jurisdiction the equal protection of the laws."

The involvement of the ACLU only made Kansas attorney general Phill Kline more resolute. Kline told reporters at the time that Matthew was sentenced to 17 years in prison because he was a sexual predator. His harsh sentence was a reflection not just of his sexual orientation but also of his repeated "sex offenses against children." Kline was referring to two prior juvenile court convictions Matthew had when he was 14. He had been caught with two other boys his age. It was sexual experimentation in most states and in most people's minds, but in Kansas it was something else: sodomy. As Kline saw it, Matthew would have received a lighter sentence if Lakemary had been the first time that he had been caught having sex with a minor. But Kline considered the Lakemary problem just another in a pattern of Matthew's habitual offenses. Having seen Kline only on television, Matthew described him as a "flat-out racist" and said that he had "some very bad thoughts" about Kline.

MORE THAN A YEAR after the Kansas Supreme Court ruled on Limon's appeal, a ruling by the U.S. Supreme Court in another case offered Matthew some hope. On June 26, 2003, the *Bowers* decision was overturned by the high court's ruling in the case of *Lawrence v. Texas*. It involved John G. Lawrence, a 59-year-old man who was in his apartment with a man named Tyron Garner, 35, when the police, having been told by a neighbor that there was a "weapons disturbance" in Lawrence's Houston home, busted down the door. While the officers didn't find any weapons, they did find the two men having sex. It was eerily reminiscent of the *Bowers* case. Both Lawrence and Garner were arrested, jailed overnight, and fined several hundred dollars. They were convicted under Section 21.06 of the Texas Penal Code, known as the Homosexual Conduct Law, which provided that "a person commits an offense if he engages in deviate sexual intercourse with another individual of the same sex." It was 1998 and Texas was one of only four states that had laws that made sex acts that were perfectly legal for heterosexuals criminal acts for gay people.

Lawrence appealed the conviction on the grounds that the law was discriminatory. A three-judge district appeals court reversed the two men's convictions, a nine-judge appeals court reversed the reversal, and finally the Texas Court of Criminal Appeals demurred about getting involved with the back-and-forth and passed it to the Supreme Court. The *Lawrence* case was about much more than a fine. It went even further than whether the arrest had been right or wrong. The conviction of Lawrence and Garner could have permanently banned them from certain professions, be it school teaching or even bus driving, because they had been found guilty of committing crimes of "moral turpitude." Had the police found a man and a woman having anal sex in Texas, the law would not have applied. This was, Lawrence and Garner felt, enormously unfair. The high court eventually agreed.

The opinion in *Lawrence* was historic because it rolled back many laws that criminalized consensual sexual relations between adults. The Supreme Court expanded the zone of privacy not only around intimacy between adults but around their sexuality as well. Lawrence said that all people—whatever their sexual orientation—were protected by the Due Process Clause of the Fourteenth Amendment to the Constitution.

The problem for Matthew Limon, as he sat in Ellsworth prison, was that the Court didn't include minors in its newly expanded zone of privacy. And the *Lawrence* case was easier to embrace because both defendants were adults.

One day after the landmark *Lawrence* ruling, the high court vacated the decision upholding Matthew's conviction and sentence and remanded his appeal for reconsideration in light of their new ruling. Six months later, in January 2004, the Kansas Court of Appeals ruled against Limon again—thumbing its nose at the high court. According to appeals court judge Henry Green Jr., Matthew's sentence sent a broader message. It encouraged "traditional sexual mores" and the "traditional sexual development of children." The ruling went further, helping protect teenagers from sexually transmitted diseases, he wrote in his decision, which he said were more common among homosexual teens than heterosexual ones.

It was another eight months before lawyers for the ACLU had a second opportunity to argue the case before the Kansas Supreme Court. By then, Matthew had been in prison for four years. A heterosexual teenager, having committed the same offense and having received the maximum sentence, would have been released two years and nine months earlier.

With the legal landscape having been transformed by *Lawrence v. Texas*, the Kansas Supreme Court unanimously sided with Limon. Underage homosexual sex, they said, was not a greater crime than underage heterosexual sex. "The moral disapproval of a group cannot be a legitimate state interest," Justice Marla Luckert wrote in the ruling. Kansas's Romeo and Juliet law was unconstitutional.

Undeterred, Attorney General Phill Kline wrote a brief calling for Limon's continued incarceration. It was his belief that if Matthew Limon was released from prison it would be the beginning of the end for Kansas. He said the case would "begin a toppling of the dominoes which is likely to end with the Kansas marriage law on the scrap heap. Pull a thread on the social fabric that will begin an unseemly process that will end with the State being unable to protect minor children from falling prey to sexual predators while in state institutions, among other deleterious aftershocks."

For Kline, Matthew was the linchpin in the debate over same-sex marriage. "Any court that handed Mr. Limon a win would at the same time (perhaps unwittingly) bring about a court-ordered redefinition of marriage that prohibited all distinctions based on sexual orientation," he warned. Set Matthew Limon free, he added, and before one knew it there would be "three party marriages, incestuous marriages, child brides, and other less-than-desirable couplings."

Kline was seeking to turn Matthew into a symbol of everything that he saw as wrong with America's relationships. This time, the

Kansas Supreme Court disagreed. It ruled that the state could not punish underage sex more harshly simply because it was between two members of the same sex, and as a result, Matthew should be resentenced as if the law treated underage gay sex and underage straight sex identically. The ruling also struck from the law language that would have allowed different treatment of gay and straight teenage couples. "The statute inflicts immediate, continuing, and real injuries that outrun and belie any legitimate claim for it," Luckert wrote, dismissing Kline's argument. The court found that there was no rational basis for a law that limited its application only to members of the opposite sex. M.A.R.'s gender was not relevant to the punishment.

When Matthew first heard of the reversal and imminent release, he was speechless. He couldn't allow himself to believe that soon he would actually be free. He was sent back to the county jail where he had first been detained. "I was dressed up as a pumpkin," Matthew recalled. "I was in an orange jumpsuit on Halloween day, in handcuffs." Going back to the county jail brought back memories from the initial arrest years before. "I wasn't sure if I was getting out or not getting out. I laid back in my bunk and tried to pass out," he said. Then a guard came by Limon's cell and asked, "How would you like to have dinner with your family?" Matthew thought the guard was toying with him.

Matthew was welcomed home like the prodigal son. His mom, dad, sister, three aunts, and a cousin went to the jail to pick him up. The entire family went to a nearby restaurant, where he ate the "best steak in five years." "It took forever to get home," he said. He would take turns riding in one car with his parents, and then in another with his aunts. Everyone wanted to be with Matthew.

THE BROAD STREET OVERPASS rises in an arc—like a bowed concrete frown—over Interstate 10 and the rusting buildings of Mid-

City that run alongside it. It sits just steps away from OPP and was the natural place to evacuate prisoners who had, by the second day of the storm, been standing in their cells, chest deep in water. SWAT teams from the state Department of Corrections arrived to help evacuate nearly 7,000 prisoners. Boats ferried the prisoners from the prison to the overpass, two by two, in almost Noah's ark fashion, skirting downed power lines and floating cars.

Initially, OPP only had five boats and thousands of inmates and civilians to float to safety. Eventually, they were joined by a flotilla of 20 boats from the state Wildlife and Fisheries Department. The boat captains would drop their charges off a short distance from the on-ramp and then they had to wade through the brown oily brew of water to get to the parts of the overpass that were still above the flood level. Greg Davis waded through chest-high water to get out. On his way out, he saw medical supplies floating in the water. Plastic urine-sample bottles, some of them still full. And then he saw the prisoners' food, also floating in the water. "I realized why we didn't eat," he said. During that time, the prisoners shared the chips and cookies they had on hand in their cells. When those ran out, they went hungry. Davis also complained about the heat and smell. "It was so hot, everybody was half naked. . . . And the stench in there . . . no water. We couldn't flush the toilets."

"The House of Detention was the last to get evacuated," Reed recalled. "We brought the inmates through the roof. The maximum security inmates were handcuffed, but everyone else just had these plastic cuffs that linked two people together. There were a few incidents when someone needed to get stunned. I didn't see it, but you could hear it. A couple people were shot with plastic bullets, and a couple were tear-gassed. But it was mostly calm."

Once on the overpass, the prisoners were ordered to sit in rows back to back and weren't allowed to move. Some were there for days as they waited for thousands of their prison mates to be pulled from what was left of Orleans Parish Prison. Some were maced for standing up to go to the bathroom.

Greg Davis considered himself one of the lucky ones. He was on the overpass for only about a day. Many of the other prisoners were there, baking in the hot sun on the blacktop asphalt without food or water, for several days. The evacuation started on Wednesday and went round the clock. Everyone was out of OPP by Friday afternoon in one of the largest prisoner evacuations in U.S. history. Some 8,500 inmates from New Orleans and the surrounding parishes were then bused or flown to 38 facilities around the state. For many of the prisoners, this was only the first chapter in their Katrina ordeal.

When Davis boarded a bus for the Elayn Hunt Correctional Center, he thought: "Things will be better." "But they didn't get no better—because we went to Hunt."

HUNT IS ABOUT 70 miles northwest of New Orleans, in the small town of Saint Gabriel, not far from the Louisiana State University campus in Baton Rouge. It is a 700-acre facility surrounded by new subdivisions and golf courses. From the road, its pale yellow industrial buildings look like some sort of agricultural manufacturing compound. There is a grove of small trees out front, a charming white cattle fence runs along the long driveway, and gray oxen and beef cattle graze in a large pasture between the prison's exercise yard and the road. The only hint that something unusual might be at the end of the winding drive comes from a sign posted on the other side of the two-lane public road outside the prison that warns drivers not to pick up any hitchhikers. Drive up to the prison and the front gate looks uncannily like a toll booth on a bridge. One almost expects to see a banner: "Welcome to Hunt."

The thousands of men from OPP who were transferred to Hunt

after days on the overpass must have felt some sense of relief, as Davis did, as their buses rolled past the white cattle fence toward the front gate. Certainly, now that they were out of New Orleans, away from the floodwaters, conditions would improve. The first evacuees were led into several small yards behind the prison. But there wasn't enough room to hold them. As the rains began anew, the prisoners were ushered out into an exercise yard on the side of the prison. Part of the yard was a slab of concrete that had been a basketball court. The poles, backboards, and nets were gone, but the concrete was still there. The men were not separated by offense but instead, pretrial prisoners were suddenly standing shoulder to shoulder with convicted felons on a broad muddy field. Protective custody inmates were forced into the general population.

Guards established a gun line along the length of the fence and armed guards watched over the prisoners from towers. In a matter of hours, thousands of men were milling around in the yard with nothing between one another but air. The guards remained on the outside of the fence.

Greg Davis's stomach sank as he walked out onto the field. His first meal in three days was "a sandwich and punch." Then he watched as gangs reconstituted themselves. Inmates started to settle scores. "You got enemies out there," Davis explained. An eerie scratching sound permeated the air. It took him a moment to place it: metal scraping on concrete. Prisoners were taking any piece of metal they could find and sharpening them into shivs. "I've never seen anything like it," Davis said. "There was a huge yard and everyone together and all you could hear was everyone making knives on the concrete. People started getting stabbed right away."

Davis wasn't worried about himself. Having been around the system for so long he knew what to expect; he knew how to survive. It was the people on misdemeanor offenses, the ones who didn't know their way around, who worried him. He looked on as a gang set on one inmate, who eventually broke away from the melee and ran toward the guards, bloody and screaming. "They are going to kill me; they are going to kill me. I'm not going back in there." The guards had their guns drawn, aimed at him. He kept coming toward them, begging for their help. They fired a warning shot. Davis recounted: "He refused to move and they took him out on a stretcher."

Ronnie Lee Morgan Jr. was in protective custody when he arrived at Hunt. Before his group stepped down from their bus, the warden came aboard. According to Morgan, he and others on the bus tried to explain that they needed to be put somewhere safe, away from the other prisoners. The warden shook his head. There was no room. He told the protective custody inmates not to tell anyone who they were. The prisoners looked down at their sweatshirts where FEDERAL was spelled out in bold white letters. Blending in wasn't an option. The warden sent them out in the yard with the others anyway. Handing each inmate a sandwich and a bottle of water, guards directed them to go out into the muddy grass. They were sitting ducks. Morgan said he was in the yard less than half an hour before gang members attacked him, stabbing him in the head and back of the neck. When he asked the guards for help, he said, they laughed at him. "I was standing there in the pouring rain," he said, "with blood flowing down my face." (The ACLU has filed a lawsuit against Hunt on behalf of Morgan and some of the other inmates who were injured on the field.)

As the plan was originally envisioned, the visiting prisoners were supposed to get hot meals in the dining hall, but the kitchen couldn't handle the sheer number of new inmates. The warden decided to provide sandwiches instead. Hunt guards began throwing bags of sandwiches over the fence into the crowd, the way that lions are fed at the zoo. Hungry prisoners fought one another for the food. "Guys was fighting, cutting each other," one inmate reported. "The deputies were just looking and laughing. They were throwing sandwiches into the crowd like they were in New Orleans at Mardi Gras."

Davis avoided the food fights. He knew that the biggest prisoners would get the spoils. He looked around the yard and saw one prisoner starting to undress. "This white guy—he just stood in the rain." He had a bar of soap and was lathering himself up, using the rainwater as his makeshift shower. Davis was so tired of being dirty. He smelled of diesel and flood waters and soiled clothing. "What the hell?" Davis muttered to himself. He stripped down to his underwear and tried to find an isolated place on the field. With the rain coming down in sheets, he washed the smell of Katrina from his skin. It felt so good to be clean, he recalled. As he washed he looked at all the men shoulder-to-shoulder on the field facing the fence. Hunt looked like a POW camp, he remembered thinking. But the rain had washed him clean.

Chapter 8

A BREAKDOWN IN COMMUNICATION

On January 3, 2002, Marilyn Walker and Frank Lindh received word through Jim Brosnahan, John's lawyer, that the military authorities now would allow the family to write letters to John as he awaited extradition aboard the USS Peleliu, somewhere in the Indian Ocean. The letters were to go from Brosnahan's office to the Pentagon to John aboard the ship, instead of through the Red Cross.

Dear John,

> *I miss you, sweetie! You have been in my heart and prayers all these many months of "not knowing" where you were. Finding you alive is the answer to all of those prayers. You've been through so much! My friends*

have been sending love and prayers your way as well. James Brosnahan
is the attorney we have retained to represent you and has already been
at work on your case. He is a very good man, John, of great integrity,
knowledge, and wisdom. He will be contacting you as well.

Can't wait to see you, honey.

I love you!
Mama

Frank Lindh wrote a letter the same day:

Dear John,

I am writing to you care of an address we just got from the U.S.
authorities, so I hope this gets to you soon. I have written three other
letters via the Red Cross, but I don't know whether those got through.
We did get the December 3 letter you dictated to the Red Cross and
signed. We all send our love—Mama, Connell, Naomi and myself
(and also Pilgrim [Naomi's pet rabbit]). We are glad you are in safe
hands.

We've hired a really good, trustworthy lawyer to represent you—
James Brosnahan of San Francisco. He has been trying for weeks (since
December 3) to get to visit with you. Please ask the authorities there to
allow Jim and Mama and me to visit with you as soon as possible.

I'm constrained to finish this letter quickly, so just let me close by
saying we all love you unconditionally. You are a very good son and
brother.

Love, Papa

These were the first letters John received from his family. In turn, John Walker Lindh was permitted to write his parents shortly before his return to the United States. He wrote them a quick note.

Dear Mama, Papa, Connell, Naomi, Family and Friends,

I'm dictating this letter to you primarily to tell you I have received your letters and the letter from the lawyer James Brosnaham [sic]. It was very good to hear from you and I would like to hear more of what has been going on from the family and in your lives in the past seven months or so in which I've been unable to keep in contact with you. Also it is comforting to know that you have found a lawyer for me. Obviously there are many things I would like to tell you and many other things I would like to ask you but due to the circumstances I am not able to at the moment. Hopefully soon we will meet in person.

I have been in US custody for more than a month. In this time, I've been completely unaware of my own situation as well as being completely cut off from the outside world, so I don't have much to offer in the way of news. My health has improved generally and I've had the necessary surgery on my leg so there is no need to worry about my physical condition. I'm afraid this whole situation must have caused you more stress and grief than it has myself. I don't know what the future holds but hopefully all of this will come to an end soon.

I love you and I hope to see all of you soon.

Your son, Sulayman/John Lindh.

Attorney General John Ashcroft blinked against the klieg lights of the television cameras. He cleared his throat and began reading from a prepared statement.

"The United States does not casually or capriciously charge one of its citizens with providing support to terrorists," he said on January 15, 2002. In his opinion, John Walker Lindh deserved to be on the receiving end of such charges. "The complaint alleges Walker knowingly and purposely allied himself with certain terrorist organizations, with terror; that he chose to embrace fanatics, and his allegiance to those fanatics never faltered, not even with the knowledge that they had murdered thousands of his countrymen, not with knowledge that they were engaged in war with the United States, and not, finally, in the prison uprising that took the life of CIA Agent Mike Spann."

Lindh, Ashcroft continued, "was given a choice to fight with the Harkat ul-Mujahedeen in Kashmir or join the Taliban to fight in Afghanistan. Walker chose to join the Taliban. He went to Afghanistan and presented himself to a Taliban recruitment center telling the individuals there that—and I'm quoting—quote, 'he was a Muslim who wanted to go to the front lines and fight.'

"The complaint further states that because Walker's language skills were deemed insufficient by Taliban recruiters, he was referred to another group, which he was told was Osama bin Laden's al-Qaeda network. He spent seven weeks in an al-Qaeda camp, training in weapons, explosives and battlefield combat. When his al-Qaeda training was completed, Walker—again by his own admission—chose to go to the front lines of the battle in Afghanistan.

"After he was taken prisoner in Mazar-e Sharif in November, Walker refused to cooperate with U.S. officials and lied about his citizenship.

"Our complaint, based on Walker's own words, is very clear: Terrorists did not compel John Walker Lindh to join them; John Walker Lindh chose terrorists. Walker was blessed to grow up in a country

that cherishes freedom of speech, religious tolerance, political democracy, and equality between men and women. And yet he chose to
reject these values in favor of their antithesis . . .

"We may never know why he turned his back on our country and
our values, but we cannot ignore that he did," Ashcroft told the cameras. "Youth is not absolution for treachery, and personal self-discovery
is not an excuse to take up arms against one's country."

The press conference led all the evening newscasts. John Walker
Lindh was still in Afghanistan and had yet to be indicted. The most
powerful law enforcement official in America had already made his
position clear, however. John Walker Lindh was guilty even though a
formal indictment wouldn't be filed until nearly a month later, in February. Ashcroft held another press conference to announce that development. A week later, John arrived back in the United States, in
chains.

On the issue of John Walker Lindh, even President Bush seemed
more sympathetic than the attorney general. "Obviously, he had been
misled," he told reporters a short time after John Walker Lindh's capture. "It appears to me that he thought he was going to fight for a
great cause when in fact he was going to support a government that
was one of the most repressive governments in the history of man-
kind. Surely he was raised better to know that a government that
suppresses women and women's rights and doesn't educate young
girls is not the kind of government that's worth dying for."

WRITING LETTERS TO JOHN while the maelstrom was unfolding
back home was difficult. The Lindhs were alarmed by the ferocity
with which the media was following the story. The Ashcroft press
conference left them agog. And they were not the only ones who were
taken aback by Ashcroft's presumption of John's guilt. A Michigan
judge, Avern Cohn of the U.S. District Court for the Eastern District,

wrote a letter to the *New York Times* excoriating Ashcroft for violating Justice Department guidelines on the release of information related to criminal proceedings "to ensure that a defendant is not prejudiced when such an announcement is made."

Marilyn Walker knew she couldn't be objective but sensed that the tide was already turning against her son. "I can understand on some level because of 9/11 that emotions were running high when they captured John," she said, recalling the days after her son appeared on the cover of *Newsweek* as the "American Taliban." "It became almost perverse in how much I started to follow these press conferences and news stories. It was as if I needed to see and hear everything to get a sense of the ferocity against him. No one would speak up on John's behalf. Everyone was so quick to judge. He wasn't even back yet and they had already decided. He was guilty."

The Justice Department filed the criminal complaint against John Walker Lindh in the federal district court in Alexandria, Virginia. The Fourth Circuit is arguably the most conservative circuit in the country. Lindh's parents lived in the Ninth Circuit, where he also could have been charged—except that it is commonly known as the most liberal circuit in the country. As with many of the government's high-profile terrorism suspects, the government chose to detain Lindh in the more hospitable Fourth Circuit. Lindh was charged with conspiracy to kill U.S. nationals outside the United States, providing material support and resources to terrorist organizations, and engaging in prohibited transactions with the Taliban. The conspiracy to kill U.S. nationals carried a possible life sentence, while the two counts of providing material support offered 15 years to life.

The most serious count was a charge to commit murder in connection with the death of the CIA agent Mike Spann. The government brought Mike Spann's parents and widow to the courthouse, accompanied by "victim's assistance" representatives from the Department of Justice. In a press conference after John was arraigned, the Spann family denounced Lindh as a traitor and demanded that he be given the death penalty. It led the newspapers the next day.

"The criminal complaint filed today describes a series of crossroads John Walker Lindh encountered on his way to joining not just one, but two terrorist organizations," Ashcroft said. "At each crossroad, Walker faced a choice and with each choice he chose to ally himself with terrorists."

A month later, during his second press conference on the Lindh case, Ashcroft went further. "John Walker Lindh chose to train with al-Qaeda, chose to fight with the Taliban, chose to be led by Osama bin Laden. The reasons for his choice may never be fully known to us, but the fact of those choices is clear. Americans who love their country do not dedicate themselves to killing Americans."

Though there was little public sympathy for Lindh, many saw Ashcroft's statements as excessive or even potentially damaging to the United States's case. William F. Buckley, the conservative columnist, said Ashcroft's comments were "gratuitous." He suggested that Ashcroft just stick to the facts of the indictments and "avoid extra comments which might unintentionally imperil successful prosecutions."

LINDH'S FIRST COURT APPEARANCE was scheduled for the day after he returned to the United States. Frank Lindh and Marilyn Walker met him in the lockup area on the ground floor of the courthouse. He appeared behind a mesh screen and sat down facing his parents. "Hi, Mama. Hi, Papa," he said a bit meekly. It was the first time they had seen their son in two years. Marilyn did her best not to cry. She put her hand up against the mesh and Lindh put his hand up to cover hers. He was wearing a green jumpsuit and looked weary. "We had business that we had to attend to," said Frank Lindh, recalling the visit. "He had to make sure to ask for these lawyers we had retained by name in order to get them assigned." The young Lindh nodded as his father laid out what was going to happen in the courtroom. "Do you trust these guys?" John asked his father. He nodded. "Yes, they are the best."

The preliminary hearing only brought more bad news. The case of *United States of America v. John Philip Walker Lindh* was set before Judge T. S. Ellis. He suggested the proceedings start in August. That meant the jury was likely to start weighing a judgment around the first anniversary of September 11. Lindh's lawyers objected. The judge was firm.

ON APRIL 5, 2002, a military C-130 transport plane carrying another suspected Taliban fighter—a young man named Yaser Hamdi—touched down at Dulles International Airport in Virginia, near Washington, D.C. Hamdi, 22, had arrived from Guantánamo Bay, Cuba, where he had been held since his capture after the prison uprising at Mazar-e Sharif, Afghanistan—the very same uprising that John Walker Lindh experienced.

The western tip of Cuba was probably the last place Hamdi thought he would ever find himself. Guantánamo is one corner of Cuba that Italian, German, and Spanish tourists haven't visited. That's because it's been under U.S. military control since 1934, under a perpetual lease with Cuba that grants the United States "complete jurisdiction and control over and within said areas." Hoping to create a legal black hole where neither international law (like the Geneva Conventions) nor domestic law (like the U.S. Constitution and civil rights statutes) would apply, the American government picked Guantánamo as the site of its prison camp for the "war on terror."

The Guantánamo commissions marked the first time America had established military courts since World War II. With four human rights observers and more than 50 reporters present, the jerry-rigged court in the Caribbean didn't fare well. The rules of evidence were unclear as they departed from established and well-known precedent under the Uniform Code of Military Justice. The translations were garbled at best. Defendants lacked an independent review outside the chain of command. Defense lawyers were hamstrung by lack of resources and by a new set of rules of evidence that greatly favored the prosecution. They were made up specifically for these proceedings. The outcome appeared to have been preordained. The purpose was not to give terrorism suspects a fair trial, but rather to set up a process to convict them.

After leaving Guantánamo and arriving at Dulles, Hamdi was transferred to Naval Station Norfolk, in Virginia, and placed in the brig. He was flown to Dulles for the same reason John Walker Lindh landed there just months earlier—so that his case would be heard in the same federal court—the Fourth Circuit—in Virginia.

American officials were looking into whether his alleged fighting for the Taliban would be sufficient reason to revoke U.S. citizenship. Hamdi's American citizenship was enough to get him out of Guantánamo but not much more—certainly not his 6th Amendment right to a "speedy and public trial." Hamdi ended up spending two years in that naval brig in Norfolk, waiting to be charged. The U.S. had been reluctant to try Hamdi in either civil or military courts and, for over two years of his confinement, refused him access to a lawyer.

Hamdi's case was one of several lawsuits filed by detainees to reach the U.S. Supreme Court. On June 28, 2004, the court ruled that detainees and so-called enemy combatants in American custody have the right to challenge their detention in an American court. In *Hamdi v. Rumsfeld*, Justice Sandra Day O'Connor wrote that "a state of war is not a blank check for the president when it comes to the rights of the nation's citizens."

Ruling on the same day in two separate cases filed on behalf of Guantánamo detainees—*Rasul v. Bush* and *Al Odah v. United States*—

the justices found that the prisoners' status in military custody was immaterial. Justice John Paul Stevens, for the majority, wrote, "What is presently at stake is only whether the federal courts have jurisdiction to determine the legality of the executive's potentially indefinite detention of individuals who claim to be wholly innocent of wrongdoing." The court's ruling allowed the detainees held at Guantánamo the opportunity to press claims of unlawful detention in the lower courts. In 2004, a dim light began to shine into that legal black hole in the Caribbean. At least for a while.

Two terms later, the case of another detainee in U.S. military custody reached the high court. Salim Ahmed Hamdan, a Yemeni citizen, was captured by American forces during the invasion of Afghanistan shortly after September 11. He was sent to Guantánamo Bay and eventually charged with conspiracy to commit terrorism. While he admitted to working as a driver for Osama bin Laden on a Kandahar farm, Hamdan, who had only a fourth-grade education, denied that he had ever supported terrorism or was a member of al-Qaeda.

Represented by his military-appointed lawyer—Lieutenant Commander Charles D. Swift of the U.S. Navy Judge Advocate General's Corps—Hamdan challenged the constitutionality of the system of military tribunals established by President George W. Bush. Two years and a day after the court's rulings in *Hamdi, Rasul,* and *Al Odah,* its decision in *Hamdan v. Rumsfeld* went a step further in rebutting the Bush administration's detention policies. A five-to-three majority of the justices found the military commissions system both unfair and illegal. Congress, they said, would have to fix it.

And Congress fixed it the only way it knew how: by giving President Bush additional discretion and powers. In many respects, the Military Commissions Act of 2006 was even worse than the USA Patriot Act. It granted retroactive immunity to military officers who might have authorized or ordered illegal acts of torture and abuse. It permitted convictions based on evidence that was literally beaten out of a witness. It broadened the president's power to define America's obligations under the Geneva Conventions. But most egregiously, the act undermined a cornerstone of American democracy—habeas corpus, the constitutional right to challenge the lawfulness of one's detention in court. Habeas corpus—Latin for "you should have the body" (so that it may be examined)—was one of the founding principles of our democratic republic. Its lineage could even been traced as far back as the Magna Carta. But after five years of the "war on terror," Congress was unwilling to challenge the administration.

Whether Guantánamo detainees could be stripped of their habeas rights ended up back in the lap of the U.S. Supreme Court in December 2007. Eight months earlier, the Court ducked the habeas issue, allowing the Military Commissions Act to settle the controversy. Then in June 2007, the Court agreed to review the habeas claims of two Guantánamo detainees: *Boumediene v. Bush* and *Al Odah v. United States*. No explanation was offered for its abrupt about-face, but the Court's renewed interest in Gitmo triggered a flurry of speculation that perhaps Justice Kennedy had had a change of heart. And during oral arguments, all eyes were on Justice Kennedy for that reason.

IN 1975, THIRTY YEARS before the *New York Times* would report on the NSA's secret domestic eavesdropping program, congressional investigators discovered that the National Security Agency had been intercepting, without warrants, international communications for more than 20 years. The secret program was called Operation Shamrock, and though Shamrock monitored telegraph communications instead of Internet ones, it was, in many ways, a precursor to the NSA program.

Shamrock started as a World War II military intelligence program but managed to continue well into the 1970s. The government said at the time that Shamrock was intended to monitor only messages that posed a threat to national security. But since the NSA had free access to all wire traffic, it listened to everything it wanted to listen to, not just communications that threatened the nation.

The story behind Operation Shamrock was instructive in that it was strikingly similar to the current state of affairs. In 1939, in the months before the war broke out in Europe, the Army's Signal Intelligence operations asked the three largest wire service companies of the time—ITT World Communications, Western Union International, and RCA Global—for permission to tap their international cables in a bid to look for coded transmissions coming from overseas. The companies, eager to help with the war effort, readily agreed. The program slid down the proverbial slippery slope. The Signal Intelligence Section operation began by concentrating on the overseas transmission but then slowly also began tracking telegraphed messages between the front lines and the home front under the assumption that they might prevent sensitive information—like troop movements or operational details on the battlefield—from getting out. The problem was that Operation Shamrock didn't end with the war. It continued for nearly three decades after that—eventually becoming the NSA's responsibility when Truman created the agency in 1952.

One of the NSA's first responsibilities was to monitor incoming and outgoing wire traffic from a station in New York City. They began transferring the cables to magnetic tape and shifting the program's focus. No longer concerned about wartime secrets slipping out, the program began to focus on the foes of the Cold War. Operation Shamrock hunted for Soviet sympathizers, political muckrakers, spies, and other foes who, in the administration's view, threatened national security. The protests during the Vietnam War provided a new target. Shamrock began tracking antiwar protestors and draft dodgers in an operation code named Minaret. By 1974, intelligence services had information on some 70,000 Americans. It wasn't until after the Watergate scandal in 1975 that the Senate Select Committee to Study Governmental Operations with Respect to Intelligence Activities began to look into the program.

Named after its chairman, Senator Frank Church, the Church Committee began a comprehensive review of American intelligence operations and concluded that the NSA was compiling information on private citizens. Four years later, to ensure that Americans wouldn't need to worry about their own government spying on them, Congress passed the Foreign Intelligence Surveillance Act of 1978.

FISA laid out procedures that the U.S. government must follow to conduct electronic surveillance and physical searches of people believed to be engaged in espionage or international terrorism against the United States. Among other things, it established a FISA court, with seven federal district court judges appointed by the chief justice of the United States (the USA Patriot Act would expand the court from 7 to 11 judges) who were responsible for approving domestic wiretap and eavesdropping requests. To listen in on a domestic call or communication, intelligence officials had to go to the FISA court to seek a warrant within 72 hours of establishing the tap. The idea was to prevent eavesdropping programs from running amok and becoming giant fishing expeditions. The FISA courts worked well enough but were eclipsed by two things: technological advances and the Bush "war on terror."

Since the Vietnam War, NSA code-cracking techniques have continued to improve, keeping pace with the latest technology. Where the NSA had been using satellite transmissions before, now it had modern telecommunications and complicated computer algorithms to help it sift through suspicious phone calls. Pattern analysis allowed it to search for key words and then spit out suspects. That process is known as data mining. It allows intelligence agencies to sift through stacks of information to find patterns, and the buffet of electronic information is endless: every credit card purchase, magazine subscription, Web site visit, and e-mail message could be tracked and categorized.

Advances in technology meant that the NSA could collect a vast array of corporate and public online information—from financial records to news stories—and cross-check it against U.S. intelligence and law-enforcement records. The system could then store it as "entities"—data linking people, places, things, organizations, and events. In its earlier iterations, a person at the NSA decided whether to eavesdrop on someone based on suspicious connections and information. But in the 21st century, the human element was largely eliminated from the program. Suspected "dirty number" phone calls weren't passed through the FISA process. Instead, with the blessing of a sophisticated computer program, taps could go on automatically.

For Joshua Dratel, that meant the research he was doing for his clients in chat rooms and jihadi Web sites or the phone calls he made to potential witnesses or family members were all ripe for the picking. And that, naturally, gave him pause.

"Before the NSA program was disclosed, government officials had to obtain a warrant or a FISA court order to intercept and monitor discussions related to my clients," he said. "Even if the process for obtaining that approval was less rigorous than I would have liked, the process of having to submit an application for a warrant or FISA order provided some sort of protection against federal agents intercepting conversations that should remain confidential—like attorney-client privilege. Now with this program in place, I can't have any substantive conversation or e-mail exchange with my clients. I have to assume that I am being tracked."

As a result, he began having to travel to Israel and to the Middle East to conduct interviews in person. Phone call conversations that followed those meetings took on a *Sopranos* Mafialike quality. "Remember that thing we talked about last time?" one person would say.

"Yes, is that going to go ahead or shall we find another time to talk about that?" It was all vagaries and half sentences. "It is hard to conduct business that way," Dratel said.

ON AUGUST 17, 2006, Judge Anna Diggs Taylor of the United States District Court in Detroit ruled that the NSA program violated the Constitution and federal law. She ordered it shut down. The ruling was the first judicial assessment of the Bush administration's arguments in defense of warrantless spying in this country. "It was never the intent of the framers to give the president such unfettered control, particularly when his actions blatantly disregard the parameters clearly enumerated in the Bill of Rights," Judge Taylor wrote. "The three separate branches of government were developed as a check and balance for one another."

The Republican response to the ruling was predictable. They accused Taylor, 73, of being an activist judge because she had been active in the civil rights movement and had supported Jimmy Carter's presidential campaign. He appointed her to the bench in 1979, making her the first black woman to serve on the Detroit federal trial court. Her opinion was criticized as intellectually shoddy by pundits on both the left and the right with a ferocity unmatched even by criticisms of the dubious legal reasoning in the Supreme Court's opinion in *Bush v. Gore.*

Attorney General Gonzales, for his part, called a news conference after the Taylor decision and said the ruling surprised him. Bush administration officials still believed "very strongly that the program is lawful," he told reporters. The administration had also argued that Judge Taylor should not hear the case at all because it concerned state secrets. She rejected that argument wholeheartedly. The central facts of the case—from the program's existence to its circumvention of the FISA court and the warrant process to its targeting of parties on American soil instead of solely overseas—had all been acknowledged by the Bush administration, Taylor wrote. The president can't claim that something is too secret to discuss in a court of law after already talking about it on television.

She also rejected the government's argument that the plaintiffs, like Joshua Dratel, lacked the legal standing to sue because they had not suffered "concrete harm" from the program. Taylor saw harm in the NSA spying because those named in the suit were "stifled in their ability to vigorously conduct research, interact with sources, talk with clients and, in the case of attorney Plaintiffs, uphold their oath of providing effective and ethical representation of their clients." What was more, Taylor said that the wiretapping violated the guarantees of the separation-of-powers doctrine and the 1st and 4th Amendments of the Constitution. The congressional authorization to use military force after September 11 and the president's powers under the Constitution did not mean that the president was above the law.

"There are no hereditary kings in America and no powers not created by the Constitution," Taylor wrote.

The ACLU offices erupted when Judge Taylor issued her opinion. Staff lawyers gathered in the hallways reading lines from Judge Taylor's opinion aloud. ACLU members called the switchboard just to say "thank you." A victory celebration with staff involved in the case served up South Indian fare and featured the 1998 movie *Enemy of the State,* a fictional account of an NSA turned on the American people in the 21st century. The movie's tagline—*It's not paranoia if they're really after you*—didn't feel so fictional.

Ann Beeson was packing for a family vacation to Costa Rica when the Taylor decision came down. She was folding her six-year-old's swimsuit when the decision popped up on the court's Web site.

"It was a great, great way to start a vacation," she said later. "I remember being in the airport and seeing my case on CNN. It was big news even in Costa Rica."

Chapter 9

THE BEGINNING OF SOMETHING MUCH BIGGER

THE THOMAS MORE LAW CENTER IN ANN Arbor, Michigan, was the brainchild of two men. The first was Thomas Monaghan, the multimillionaire who launched Domino's— the FedEx of pizza delivery. The second, Richard Thompson, was a former Oakland County, Michigan, prosecutor who may be best known for his efforts to prosecute "Dr. Death"—Jack Kevorkian. (He failed several times to convict Kevorkian for physician-assisted suicide.) The center takes its name from Sir Thomas More, the 16th-century lord chancellor whose refusal to accept the power of Parliament to designate King Henry VIII supreme head of the church in England ended, rather predictably, with his beheading.

The center leans unabashedly to the far

right. It has backed a number of pro-life groups, including an organization that created a Web site listing the names and addresses of abortion providers under the heading "Nuremberg Files." It characterizes itself as "Christianity's answer to the ACLU." As if to underscore the point, its Web site has a roster of freebies, including book covers that feature the Ten Commandments. ("Make sure the Ten Commandments are found in your public school!" it says.)

Its cases read like a laundry list of causes backed by the religious right, from opposing same-sex marriage to advocating prayer in public schools. Senator Rick Santorum and conservative presidential candidate Alan Keyes are among those who have sat on the center's advisory board. Bill Buckingham said that he found out about the group from a reporter, though he declined to say which one. But whether Buckingham found Thomas More or Thomas More found him hardly matters. The two were destined for one another.

The center's staff had been traveling around the country looking for a school board willing to play Scopes's role in a test case that would pave the way for teaching intelligent design in the public schools. Four years earlier, one of the center's lawyers, Robert Muise, had been to Charleston, West Virginia, hoping to convince the school board there to use the *Of Pandas and People* textbook in its classrooms. Muise told that school board that they would likely be sued, but he promised that the Thomas More Law Center would provide a legal defense at no cost. Muise would later be a lawyer for the defense in the Dover case.

Richard Thompson, in a phone call with Bill Buckingham, made the identical pledge. "He said that if we wanted to pursue it, we were on firm ground to do that," Buckingham said later. "There is no separation of church and state in the Constitution. Justice Thomas on the Supreme Court agrees with us on this. I felt that if we got a fair shot in court, we could win. And if we had a jury trial, well, I was sure we would win."

Buckingham assured Thompson that Dover could be the test case for which he was searching. The conference report accompanying the 2001 No Child Left Behind Act encouraged teaching alternatives to biological evolution, he said. It was a matter not of religion, Thompson told Buckingham, but of academic freedom.

The legal director of the ACLU's Pittsburgh office, Witold "Vic" Walczak, was also on the case. A small, powerfully built man with short cropped hair who spoke at a breakneck clip, Walczak had been monitoring the unfolding events in Dover through the local papers. "We were aware of the rumblings and what was going on there," Walczak said later. "During that summer there were stories about school board members promoting the *Pandas* book so we knew that the Discovery Institute and the Thomas More Center wouldn't be far behind."

The summer had been one of saber rattling from both sides as the school board went back and forth over how to deal with the issue of new biology books and the specter of providing some sort of alternative to evolutionary theory for students at Dover High School. "There were all kinds of George Bush–like 'bring it on' comments from the other side when we said that we would weigh in if they tried to introduce intelligent design into the classroom," Walczak said. "For the ACLU it was about religious liberty. But from a broader perspective, as we saw it, it was also about scientific integrity. Intelligent design wasn't science and it was wrong to pretend it was."

In Walczak's eyes, the creationists were much more honest than the supporters of intelligent design. "ID says we don't know who created all this, and we won't speculate, wink, wink, nod, nod. And that's not just more disingenuous, it is more dangerous."

Creationism is not the same as intelligent design. Strict creationists believe that the Old Testament and the book of Genesis are not just religious texts but historical ones too. The universe, quite simply, was created in seven days by God, end of story. Intelligent design, by contrast, folds scientific evidence into the mix to provide an explanation for the role of a "designer" in the world's creation. But in Walczak's view, creationism and intelligent design were cut from the same religious cloth and neither had any place in a biology classroom. It wasn't just a legal issue. It was, as Bert Spahr had said, "a question of basic scientific honesty. It turns science on its head."

The ACLU shared many of Spahr's reservations. It wasn't the concept of intelligent design that had ACLU lawyers so upset; it was seeking to insert it into a public school science class that had them up in arms. ID might be appropriate in a comparative religions class where it could be discussed along with other religious creation stories. "We would have been happy with that and I think the Dover parents would have been too," said Walczak later. "But that wasn't going to happen, so we had to take them to court. There was a lot at stake. If we lost, we'd see ID all over this country."

AT A DOVER AREA School Board meeting on October 4, 2004, members said they had a special surprise announcement. The school district had just received an anonymous donation of sixty copies of *Of Pandas and People*. (It was discovered later that the donor of the books was a school board member's father and that Buckingham had helped raise money to pay for them.) It appeared that the financial obstacle to inserting intelligent design into Dover High School's curriculum had fallen. Privately, those behind the scenes had been hoping the issue of money would derail the speeding ID train. Even if school board members wanted to find a way to include *Pandas* in the curriculum, tight budgets were likely to stymie their efforts. That was what Bert Spahr had been counting on. She thought there would be bluster and then ID supporters would retreat from the field of battle when it became clear there was not enough money for both the *Biology* textbook and *Pandas*. Now that *Pandas* had mysteriously appeared, it was harder to argue the book shouldn't be used.

"We knew something was fishy about the way those books just appeared," Spahr said later. "It was just too convenient. Once the argument about money was gone, we had to start arguing about content—what the books actually said—and I had a lot of problems with the Panda books. They were factually inaccurate and really poorly written and I didn't want them in my classroom or muddying the waters for the students."

Among other concerns, Spahr noted that there was not a word in the Panda books regarding the age of the earth. The reason was simple: the age of rocks and fossils support the evolutionary history of life that geologists have embraced for decades. The authors dodged the problem by offering natural history without a time scale. Mentioning it in *Pandas* would have negated its entire reason for being.

The book also misrepresented the nature of the fossil record, Spahr and other Dover science teachers said. "Intelligent design means that various forms of life began abruptly through an intelligent agency," the book reads. "With their distinctive features already intact—fish with fins and scales, birds with feathers, beaks and wings, etc. Some scientists have arrived at this view since fossil forms first appear in the rock record with their distinctive features intact, rather than gradually developing." In fact, the fossil record supplies just the opposite. In stone it shows a roster of adaptations. The earliest known fish, for example, was quite different from today's fishes. Evidence clearly supports the idea that the first land vertebrates evolved from their lobe-finned fish cousins. Early land-dwelling animals had internal gills.

Any doubt about that seemed to be put to rest in 1998. That's when paleontologists Edward Daeschler and Neil Shubin discovered a fossilized fin that was so well preserved that its soft parts could be seen outside its underlying skeleton. The fin had eight well-defined digits—the fish had a fin with fingers. *Pandas*, science teachers complained, pretended those kinds of discoveries didn't exist.

"The absence of the unambiguous transitional fossils is illustrated by the fossil record of whales," the book says. "By and large, Darwinists believe that whales evolved from a land mammal. The problem is that there are no clear transitional fossils linking land mammals to whales. If whales did have land-dwelling ancestors, it is reasonable to expect to find some transitional fossils. Why? Because the anatomical differences between the two are so great that innumerable in-between stages must have paddled and swam the ancient seas."

In fact, three intermediates that link whales to land-dwelling ancestors have been discovered. The actual fossil forms were described in a 1994 article in the journal *Science,* and a less technical account of the finds was published in *Natural History* magazine in April 1994.

There were other things about *Of Pandas and People* that didn't add up, according to the Textbook League, which reviews textbooks for teachers. It carries the imprint of the Haughton Publishing Company, but officials from the Textbook League couldn't find such a publishing house in the *Literary Marketplace,* a comprehensive guide to book publishers operating in the United States. The copyright for the book was held by another entity altogether: the Foundation for Thought and Ethics, out of Richardson, Texas. The Foundation for Thought and Ethics promotes creationism. None of that is apparent in the book. All of that might have been enough to sink the book if the school was going to have to pay for it. But because of the anonymous donation, those arguments lost their impact.

Two weeks later, the school board voted six-to-three that biology teachers must introduce the concept of intelligent design as a viable alternative. "Students should be aware of gaps/problems in Darwin's Theory and of other theories including, but not limited to intelligent design. Note: Origins of life will not be taught," their statement read. For teachers worried about fielding intelligent design questions from students, the board added, there was a statement that needed to be read at the beginning of the evolution unit. "The state standards require students to learn about Darwin and evolution," it said in part, "and to eventually take a standardized test of which evolution is a part. Because Darwin's Theory is a theory, it is still being tested as new things are discovered. The Theory is not a fact. Gaps in the Theory exist for which there is no evidence. A theory is defined as a well-tested explanation that unifies a broad range of observations. Intelligent design is an explanation of the origin of life that differs from Darwin's view. The reference book *Of Pandas and People* is available to students to see if they would like to explore this view in an effort to gain an understanding of what intelligent design actually involves. As is true with any theory, students are encouraged to keep an open mind."

Spahr tried to put herself in her students' shoes. The school board's statement implied that the theory of evolution was a little shaky but intelligent design was on sound footing. You could go home and talk it over with your parents, it suggested, but you will be tested on evolution. Spahr admitted that "to oppose a school board and superintendent took intestinal fortitude." She didn't want to be insubordinate, but she didn't know how she could possibly read the statement. It flew in the face of everything she stood for. It put intelligent design on equal footing with Darwin. "A lot of people in Dover were wondering why I was so stubborn about this," she said later. "Why is it such a big deal to read a statement about intelligent design, they said. For me it was very clear. If we let them get away with this it would be science today, English next and our health education classes tomorrow. We could see this was the beginning of something much bigger."

What Spahr didn't know was that the Thomas More Law Center, whose motto is the "Sword and Shield for People of Faith," thought so too.

No one was really surprised when just two months later, in December 2004, eleven parents led by Tammy Kitzmiller sued the Dover

Area School District. Represented by a roster of civil rights organizations, including the ACLU, the plaintiffs said presenting intelligent design to students in this public school violated their religious
liberty by promoting religious beliefs under the guise of science
education. Spahr and her fellow science teachers were all summoned
to the assistant superintendent's office the day the lawsuit was filed.
The assistant superintendent told the science teachers, "We are all
in this together. And as an employee of the school district, you will
be represented by the Thomas More Law Center." Robert Eshbach,
one of Spahr's protégés, spoke for all of them. "Bullshit," he said, loud
enough to wake the dead. Dover became ground zero for a constitutional test—the first lawsuit against teaching intelligent design in the
public schools.

IN FEBRUARY 2006, the ACLU of Northern California filed a request for information about alleged government spying during
student-led protests at two University of California campuses—
Berkeley and Santa Cruz. The FOIA request sought all the information maintained in the Department of Defense database about the
university groups and the students who belong to them. ACLU affili-
ates in Florida, Georgia, Rhode Island, Maine, and Pennsylvania also
filed similar FOIA requests. "We want to show it's not okay for the
Department of Defense or the Pentagon to spy on its citizens," Kot
Hordynski told reporters at the February press conference.

ACLU lawyer Mark Schlosberg said the group asked the government for an expedited request, which requires a response within 10
days. No response or failure to hand over the information may prompt
legal action by the ACLU, Schlosberg warned. The documents finally
emerged seven months later in October 2006 and, among other things,
explained why the students had been listed as potential threats.

The report specifically mentioned the April 2005 protest at UC

Santa Cruz in which 300 students and community activists "shut down" a career fair attended by military recruiters and vandalized two recruiters' vehicles. It also describes a protest in which activists blocked the entrance to a local recruitment office with two coffins—one draped with an American flag and the other with an Iraqi flag—and chanted, "No more war and occupation, you don't have to die for an education."

While the new information made clear that "no reported incidents have occurred at these protests," it warns that there has been "an intense debate" among antiwar groups over whether to conduct vandalism and civil disobedience. As an example, it mentioned that "at least two members" of the Atlanta-area chapter of Students for Peace and Justice "have expressed interest in doing more than just protesting."

The message that piece of information revealed was clear. "Suddenly we wondered if they had sent people to be among us and report on us," said Hordynski. "It was kind of creepy."

KATRINA LEFT THE PERFECT destruction in her wake. More than a third of the state's lawyers lost their offices. The Orleans Parish Criminal District Court, right next to OPP, sat chest-deep in water for two and a half weeks. Police evidence rooms were a soup of DNA evidence, soaked files, and lost eyewitness accounts. Only about 10 percent of the hundreds of thousands of items in the evidence rooms of New Orleans were in sealed plastic bags. Photo lineup cards used to identify suspects were glued together. The storm not only made it harder to convict the guilty; it also made it more difficult for the innocent to shake the charges against them. That was assuming, of course, that the people who had been evacuated from OPP would get trials at all.

The criminal courts in southern Louisiana, even months after the storm, were still hobbled, struggling just to find functional locations where they could reopen their doors. The Louisiana Supreme Court moved from its New Orleans courthouse to a circuit court in Baton Rouge. The United States Court of Appeals for the Fifth Circuit decamped to Houston. And the local criminal court in New Orleans was still trying to clean up the mess. In the meantime, thousands of detainees languished behind bars. They were in a legal limbo. They had no courts. They had no trials. They didn't even have lawyers. Their families had left and in the haste to get them out of New Orleans, many were lost.

The Department of Corrections started putting advertisements on the Internet and in the local newspapers in Georgia and Texas and Louisiana. "Are you searching for someone who was in prison when Katrina hit?" the ad began. "If you had a family member locked up in Orleans Parish Prison or Jefferson Parish Detention Center when Katrina hit, call the DOC hotline to locate where your loved one is now located. The hotline is taking calls from 7:00 A.M. to 10:00 P.M. No matter where your family member was locked up when Katrina hit, you can also call these numbers to tell your loved one where you are and how you are doing."

A STUDY BY THE DEPARTMENT OF JUSTICE after the hurricane determined that the indigent defense system in New Orleans had essentially ceased to exist. People were in jail without charge. There were no trials. Even defendants who wished to plead guilty didn't have a lawyer who might enter their plea. "New Orleans today lacks a true adversarial process, the process to ensure that even the poorest arrested person will get a fair deal," it concluded.

Pamela Metzger, a law professor at Tulane University, was determined to change all of that. The director of the Tulane Criminal Law Clinic since 2001, she and her third-year law students had been helping the indigent get justice even before Katrina. After the floodwaters subsided, they started fanning out to prisons to interview inmates, seeking to compile a registry of prisoners and lawyers and trying to piece together cases that were lost. It was on one of these trips that Metzger met Greg Davis.

It is hard not to like Pamela Metzger. Smart, personable, and constantly in motion, she was often cited as the favorite professor among the law students at Tulane University. With shoulder-length brown hair and gray-green eyes, Metzger is beautiful. In fact she looks like Jaclyn Smith from *Charlie's Angels*. A graduate of New York University School of Law, Metzger's résumé showed a lifetime of work for the less fortunate, from awards for clinical advocacy to providing legal assistance to incarcerated women as a young law professor at Washington and Lee University School of Law in Virginia. Her published articles focused on constitutional rights, issues of race in Louisiana's justice system, and the plight of battered women.

Metzger and her students at the Tulane Criminal Law Clinic were hunting for lost inmates, prisoners whose paperwork had gone missing and those who had, as the justice system in New Orleans collapsed, been swallowed by the system. The only way to do that, Metzger and her students decided, was to interview the people behind bars—prison by prison, inmate by inmate—and try to match names with charges and, eventually, with lawyers.

Metzger asked officials at the Orleans Parish Prison if they had a list of prisoners who had been sent there. She was met with blank stares. Apparently OPP officials had no idea who had been sent where. There were no lists. Metzger asked for anything they had and offered to do the tracking herself. She ended up matching names on the OPP list with the roster of prisoners at Concordia Correctional Facility, where some OPP prisoners were sent.

"I had intended to keep an arm's distance on this, to run it all administratively," Metzger said more than a year after the storm. "But he's [Davis] the one that hooked me. He ended up being in jail for 10 months because he didn't have a lawyer. He didn't show up to pay fines because he was in prison at the time. If one lawyer, if one clerk, if just one person had taken an interest in him, he wouldn't have been lost for almost a year. It was the profound indifference that got me. It blew my mind."

Metzger also represented a bipolar, homeless, illiterate, schizophrenic man who was caught up in the storm. "He was also toothless," said Metzger with a smile. She quickly added, "If I did this for all of them, it would break my heart and I wouldn't get any fucking work done."

It was another prisoner at Concordia who mentioned that Greg Davis had come in from OPP. He didn't appear on the list Metzger had. Instead he had been awaiting a release order for weeks and the prisoner told her that it never came. Metzger took down Davis's name and promised to investigate. By then Davis had been in jail for seven months for not showing up in court to explain why he hadn't paid his court fees. It was March 2006. In fact, his release order had been signed, but Davis continued to languish behind bars because no one had bothered to fax it to the guards at the prison. Metzger followed up and the fax eventually came, but prison officials said there was no room on a bus that would take Davis to the outtake facility. Metzger offered to drive him herself, but the prison officials wouldn't allow it. Davis was finally released a week later, when there was room on the bus. After seven months in jail, he spent another week behind bars because of a late fax and a lack of buses. "It was so unnecessary, it made me cry," Metzger said later.

Davis was one of many OPP evacuees who spent months in prison without ever seeing a lawyer or a judge. By the time many of these cases were brought to court, the individuals had already served more time in prison than they ever would have, even if they were found guilty. Prisoners called it "doing Katrina time."

From September 2005 until June 2006 there were no criminal trials in New Orleans whatsoever. When the court building reopened, judges couldn't find witnesses or jurors. There weren't enough courtrooms. The ACLU and a group of volunteer criminal defense attorneys started filing *habeas corpus* petitions—the legal instrument or writ by which an individual who has been unlawfully imprisoned can seek release—for inmates who were being held for no valid reason. This was the same right that the Military Commissions Act of 2006 had removed from the detainees at Guantánamo.

Certainly, the Department of Corrections was overwhelmed after Katrina, and that was at least part of the reason why inmates were released so slowly after the storm. But there were also financial considerations. The DOC was receiving money from the Federal Emergency Management Authority (FEMA) for each prisoner it held. The DOC could expect some $13 million for the 4,215 prisoners it held from September 1, 2005, to the end of that year. There was a financial disincentive to emptying the jails as quickly as possible.

It wasn't until May 2006, nine months after the storm hit, that someone managed to ease the backlog. The chief judge of the Orleans Parish Criminal Court, Calvin Johnson, issued an order requiring that everyone charged with municipal or traffic offenses be released. They were to be issued a citation to appear in court at a later date. "New Orleans has a limited number of jail spaces and we can't fill them with people charged with minor offenses such as disturbing the peace, trespassing or spitting on the sidewalk," he said when he issued his order. "I am not exaggerating. There were people in jail for spitting on the sidewalk."

A week later, Judge Arthur Hunter, a former New Orleans police officer, took the next step. He suspended prosecutions put before him in most cases involving public defenders. He felt it was his duty under the Constitution because the defendants had no access to a lawyer. Hunter made the decision, he told the local paper, to focus minds on the problem. Prosecutors convinced him to back down from the order a week later.

Sheriff Gusman, for his part, emerged from the storm denying accusations of prisoner neglect and abuse. Though some people had been detained long past their release dates, courts were moving to take care of those cases first, a prison spokeswoman said, and Gusman could account for all of the prisoners and their safe evacuation. There was plenty of food at the facility to feed everyone during the storm, prison officials said. The problem was one of communication. The public address system was down when the electricity went out, and that caused confusion. If the levees hadn't broken, everything would have been fine at OPP, according to the official line. Because the levees broke, the prison found itself seven feet deep in water. No one could have anticipated that.

Gusman had an evacuation plan, he maintained, and it had worked. But when the ACLU asked for a copy of it under a public records statute, what it received was a paltry two pages long. It didn't mention how OPP would be evacuated. Instead, the double-spaced memo included provisions such as "72 hours before the anticipated arrival of the hurricane in the New Orleans area, all emergency supplies such as flashlights, extra bedding, and emergency rations shall be distributed to the buildings . . ." Essential security personnel would not be given any scheduled days off, it added. It was laughable in light of what had happened. It was a non-plan.

"They blamed everything on the levees or the technology. We've reached the point where technological failures are no longer an excuse for constitutional failures," Metzger said. "The way I see it, this was an example of the State of Louisiana abandoning the Bill of Rights."

Chapter 10

STORM CHASING

It took nearly a year to prepare *Kitzmiller v. Dover* for trial. The night before the September 2005 opening arguments, Vic Walczak gathered the lawyers in his office to go over, once again, what was at stake. "Our job here is to prove to the court what everyone in the world already knows," he told the group. "That ID is a religious theory. People who are in favor of it want to teach religion in the public schools. Those who are opposed don't want to mix religion and science. Either way, it is religion."

Walczak's strategy was to dissect intelligent design from every angle: from a scientific perspective, from a theological and philosophical one, and from a historical perspective. He believed that no matter the lens one looked through, what one saw was the same: intelligent design was not science, it was a religious belief. The focus on the religious aspect was a deliberate one. Walczak thought it was relatively easy to prove that intelligent design was not science or, at best, was bad science. That alone, however, was not a constitutional issue. "It is not unconstitutional to make kids dumb or to have a poor curriculum," he said later. "It was only unconstitutional if we showed that ID was pushing a religious view. If we could prove it wasn't science, then the only argument left standing for the board wanting it in the curriculum was a religious one."

Before *Kitzmiller v. Dover*, the stormy courtroom battles over evolution largely avoided the question of what constituted science. In the Scopes trial, the issue was whether John Scopes had flouted Tennessee law by telling his students "that man has descended from a lower order of animal." The judge in that case didn't allow Clarence Darrow, Scopes's defense attorney, to put evolutionary scientists on the stand. In *Edwards v. Aguillard*, the Supreme Court simply struck down the Louisiana statute that required the teaching of creationism. There was never any testimony. But Judge John Jones III, the George W. Bush appointee who presided over the Dover case in a small ninth-floor Harrisburg, Pennsylvania, courtroom, broke the pattern: his courtroom became a veritable laboratory as witnesses argued about everything from bacteria and blood clotting to molecular biology and dinosaurs.

For that reason, Walczak's first witness was none other than Kenneth Miller, a Brown University biology professor who not only wrote the textbook that Dover High School and others across the country had used for years, but had also written *Finding Darwin's God: A Scientist's Search for Common Ground Between God and Evolution*, a book about Miller's attempts to reconcile his own Catholic faith with his deep love of science.

Miller first began debating creationists in 1981. A young biology teacher at Brown University, he was approached by a handful of students who asked him if he was willing to lock horns with the founder and president of the Institute for Creation Research in California, a man named Henry Morris. The Christian students' association at Brown was bringing him to campus and Morris had dared any scientist on campus to debate him. After much cajoling from the students, Miller accepted the challenge.

The debate, held at Brown University's hockey rink, drew some 3,000 people. Based on reports of a wager between the science writer and the religion writer at the *Providence Journal*, both of whom attended the event, Miller prevailed. He found himself in a number of additional debates with creationists over the years.

"Dr. Miller, isn't evolution just a theory?" Walczak asked at the beginning of his direct examination in September 2005.

"Evolution is just a theory," Miller responded evenly, "in the same way that the atomic theory of matter is just a theory, the Copernican theory of the solar system is just a theory, or the germ theory of disease is just a theory. But theories are not hunches, they're not unproven speculation. Theories are systems of explanations which are strongly supported by factual observations and which explain whole sets of facts and experimental results."

"So is evolution theory or fact?"

"Evolution is, indeed, a theory because it is a powerful, useful, and predictive explanation of a whole range of scientific facts," Miller said. "Facts in science are more susceptible to change than theories, which is one reason why the word 'fact' is not used very much in science. When we say 'theory' in science, we mean a broad, overarching, explanation that's very strongly supported by fact and by factual evidence and that ties all of this together. And if it doesn't do that, it's not a scientific theory."

He smiled. "Religious beliefs," he continued, "are not scientific.

They are philosophical, theological, and deeply personal," he added. "And, as such, they don't belong in a science curriculum and they certainly don't belong in a science textbook."

The statement that the school board wanted teachers to read was inflammatory, he continued. "What it does is put religious conflict into every science classroom in Dover High School," he said. "This is a tremendously dangerous statement in terms of educational effect, in terms of its religious effect, in terms of impeding the educational process in the classrooms of Dover."

To Miller, science was a bridge, not a barrier. He saw science as the closest thing on the planet to a universal culture where the same rules applied everywhere. It was a system for explaining things, and invoking a supernatural force, as he saw it, couldn't be part of science. "I hesitate to beg the patience of the Court with this, but being a Boston Red Sox fan, I can't resist it," Miller said, looking at Judge Jones and trying to suppress a grin. "One might say, for example, that the reason the Boston Red Sox were able to come back from three games down against the New York Yankees was because God was tired of George Steinbrenner and wanted to see the Red Sox win. In my part of the country, you'd be surprised how many people think that's a perfectly reasonable explanation for what happened last year. And you know what, it might be true, but it certainly is not science, it's not scientific, and it's certainly not something we contest."

Judge Jones smiled and nodded from the bench.

Robert Muise, a young, earnest-looking lawyer from the Thomas More Center, couldn't resist starting his cross-examination with a nod to the Boston Red Sox. "Dr. Miller," he began slowly, "as a sympathetic Red Sox fan, I can't help but ask you whether you believe the Red Sox won the World Series because of supernatural causes. And I guess that would be reversing the curse of the Bambino?" he asked, referring to the urban legend that said the failure of the Red Sox to win the World Series for 86 years was directly related to their decision to sell Babe Ruth, the Bambino, to the New York Yankees.

Miller smiled. "I think it's entirely within the realm of possibility, but as I indicated earlier, it's not a scientific hypothesis."

Even though there was so much at stake in the proceedings, baseball and humor were to become recurring themes in *Kitzmiller v. Dover*. At one point, after a long scientific explanation from Miller, the judge wearily called for a break. "My friends in the jury box look like they could use a little caffeine," he said. "That was not a knock on you, Doctor."

Miller grinned and quipped, "I knew I should have shown more slides, Your Honor."

At another point in the trial, Miller noted that 99.9 percent of the organisms that had ever lived on earth were now extinct. "An intelligent designer who designed things, 99.9 percent of which didn't last, certainly wouldn't be very intelligent," he said. The gallery guffawed.

During Muise's cross-examination, Miller alluded to his intelligent design nemesis, Michael Behe. "I'm sure he disagrees with me . . . perhaps he'll get up here in a couple days and say, you know, I listened to everything Dr. Miller said and, by God, he's got it exactly right," Miller said.

Judge Jones couldn't resist. "We'd have a real story then, wouldn't we?" he asked Miller.

The professor nodded. "Exactly."

Muise broke in. "I doubt that will happen."

When a witness for the defense brought up another slide of bacterial flagella, Judge Jones muttered, "We've seen that." The witness nodded. "I kind of feel like Zsa Zsa Gabor's fifth husband," he said. "As the old adage goes, I know what to do, but I just can't make it exciting."

Michael Behe, the man whose name has become synonymous

with intelligent design, testified longer than any other witness. He was on the stand for three days. And for most of that time he seemed authoritative on the structures of microorganisms and the wonders of blood clotting. One of the Kitzmiller lawyers playfully began one cross-examination by saying, "Let's start with bacterial flagellum." The courtroom tittered. "You've made a point about how complicated and intricate it is. But a lot of biological life is pretty remarkable."

Behe narrowed his eyes. "That makes me very suspicious," he said.

"You're suspicious about how remarkable biological life is?" the lawyer asked. His point was to focus on why Behe and intelligent design supporters had focused with such significance on bacterial flagella in a world where there are so many complicated things to choose from. The lawyer suggested the entire human body was a perfect example of a complicated, remarkable thing. "Now that's an amazing biological structure," Behe said, looking upward as if seeing a roster of human bodies dancing in his mind's eye. "I'm thinking of examples."

"Hopefully, not mine!" The lawyer laughed.

"Rest assured," Behe replied. The courtroom erupted, again, in laughter.

While Behe, when questioned by the Thomas More lawyers, was able to talk with ease about the complexities of life that have formed the basis for his belief in intelligent design, he was put on the defensive by the plaintiffs.

How did this intelligent designer do his work? a lawyer for the plaintiffs asked Behe. Did he provide blueprints for someone else to make things? Did he actually make these things himself? Did he make each protein in the flagellum?

"The designer would have to somehow cause the plan to go into effect," Behe said. "There are lots of distinctions to be made. . . ."

The lawyer bored in. Scientists prove their theories with experiments. Had Behe attempted to see if bacterial flagella could actually grow into a complex system without an intelligent designer?

The scientist shook his head no. He preferred, he said, to spend his time on other things.

The trial lasted six weeks. It wrapped up on November 4, just as the members of the Dover Area School Board were up for reelection.

LARNED, KANSAS, IS ANNOUNCED by a public golf course on one side of Highway 56 and a diner on the other. Tourists who follow the two-lane stretch of road through town would naturally find themselves tracking the Santa Fe Trail, the 800-mile route merchant-traders used in the early 19th century to carry goods from the plains to as far west as Colorado. If there was a heyday for Larned, that century was it. Fort Larned—seen as the best of the standing Indian-wars-period forts—sits on the edge of town. It was a base of military operations against the hostile Indians of the central plains who robbed traders along the Santa Fe Trail. Today, Larned is so quiet and so slow, clerks at the Holiday Inn look genuinely surprised when visitors check in. No one, they explain, ever comes to Larned anymore. Scouting groups visit occasionally, but they usually get permission to stay at the fort.

VFW Post 7271 looks like the backbone of the solidly pro-gun, pro-religion city. Bars and liquor stores line the main drag. Signs in front of the Pizza Hut welcome hunters. Fox Liquor Stores advertises, "Sutter Home, Wt. Zin, 750 ml, $3.99 + tax," while Nick's Nasbar on Broadway boasts, "Monday Night Football, $1 draws, $1 chili dogs." The Double "D" Western Store is a one-stop clothes shop for Larned residents. You can get a tuxedo rental for the school prom, a cowboy belt, even a pair of toddler-sized overalls there. The Casey General Store and Tabler Furniture will equip the basics of any

Larned kitchen—from a wooden table to canned goods. You don't even have to leave Larned to go to the movies, as the State Theater is just down the street. And most Larned residents do seem to stay put. Even Matthew Limon.

It was in this sleepy place that Matthew Limon landed after his release from Ellsworth prison. The first thing he wanted to do when he emerged from Ellsworth's administration building, after five and a half years behind bars, was drive. Matthew loved driving so much he could recall each of the cars he had ever driven, in order. His first time behind the wheel was in a 1989 Buick LeSabre. The second time, he was in the driver's seat of a 1988 Dodge Lancer. Someday, Matthew would tell people, he would buy a new Lincoln Town Car with tinted windows. That day is still in the future. For now, he drives a Honda, and has his eye on a new Dodge Ram pickup.

The tension in the Limon household was palpable when Matthew returned. He continued to insist that he was gay. And his parents felt, after all he had been through, that he was just being ornery and stubborn for not renouncing that kind of lifestyle. "I love them to death," Matthew said shortly after his release. "But on this issue I am not sure we'll ever be able to agree." For a time, Matthew went to live with his uncle and work on his sheep farm. But Matthew didn't think that working with smelly animals was the kind of work that he was cut out to do, so he begged his parents to allow him to come home. After hours of conversation, they relented. Mike Limon got his son a job at a local feedlot as a night watchman. Four nights a week, Matthew sat behind the wheel of an old Ford truck and drove the muddy roads around the lot. Cows lowed as he drove past, packed as far as the eye could see. Bales of hay, stacked as tall as buildings, stood on one end of the lot. A mountain of used radial tires sat at the other. Matthew's job was to protect the cattle from potential intruders. "There are never any intruders," he said. "It is kind of a boring job. But at least I get to drive around and listen to the radio and I like that part of it." Now, Matthew and his best friend work at the Larned Wendy's, where he has established a quiet, walk-about authority in the restaurant.

Most people in Larned don't know about Matthew's history, though if they were curious it would be simple enough to find out. They need only visit the Kansas Department of Corrections online registry of sex offenders. Matthew's photo is there, as well as details of his arrest, incarceration, personal characteristics, and more. So far, he said, that hasn't been an issue. His best friend knows what happened and why he was in prison. "She doesn't judge me, she knows about my gay lifestyle, she knows about prison, and none of it seems to matter," he said.

Each week Matthew drives 20 miles to Great Bend, Kansas, where he attends mandatory "sex offender classes." Matthew hates the classes. "They make us feel like pieces of shit," he said. "They think I'm a sick, freak pervert from hell who preys off kids." He added meekly, "I'm not." Matthew is now a 24-year-old gay man. He's no longer a teenager attracted to other teenagers. "I want someone who is grown," he said.

Like any twenty-something, Matthew doesn't have fully formed ideas of what he'll do next. He knows he wants to study music. And if there is a way to do it, he'd like to be a storm chaser—one of those people who jump into a truck to track the violent thunderstorms that roar across the Kansas plains. "I love severe weather, like tornadoes. I like the intensity, the power of it. It's awesome—lightning, thunder—cool," Matthew said. "When I was younger I remember just sitting on the porch and watching the thunderstorms for hours," he added. "You can see them coming from way far off and then the darkness just comes closer and closer to you. I would love to chase storms. If we can get all this other business settled, that's what I am fixing to do: chase storms."

It was something of a perfect storm that sank Phill Kline's 2006 bid for a second term as Kansas attorney general. The voters of Kansas ousted him by a margin of 59 to 41.

WHILE CECELIA FIRE THUNDER saw access to abortion and basic family planning as necessary to the well-being of Pine Ridge, the Oglala Sioux Tribal Council saw it a little differently. In June 2006, three months after Fire Thunder suggested the reservation might have its own clinic, the elders voted to suspend her as president and ban abortions on the reservation. Her crimes, according to the council, included inviting federal and state law onto the sovereign reservation, violating traditional and spiritual laws, misrepresenting to the world that the Oglala supported abortion, and accepting contributions for the clinic.

Anyone who had spent any time at all on Pine Ridge knew that there was much more than abortion behind Fire Thunder's impeachment. There were alliances and family ties and grudges at play. She had been trying to clean up the tribe's finances. She had discovered irregularities and was investigating who might be behind them. Her stand on abortion just provided ammunition for enemies who were gunning for her anyway.

"As a woman, I have to stick up for all women," she told visiting journalists. "My beliefs are grounded in Sioux tradition; it is every woman's sacred choice to determine when to be a mother. My culture encourages me to speak out for what I believe."

"Women of color and poor women have always known that regardless of what happens, women with money will have access to abortion," she told AlterNet columnist Rose Aguilar. "Women with money will have access to contraception. No matter which way you cut it, it's always on the backs of poor women. We're going to go ahead with the clinic no matter what. If nothing else we need to establish a place where women feel comfortable."

The conservative media picked up the story and Fire Thunder's stand became a metachronicle of hysteria. Glenn Beck, a nationally syndicated radio talk show host on the Premiere Radio Network, blasted the tribe. "Indians have found something that can be more profitable than casinos, and that's abortion clinics," he told his listeners. "And then look out, man, exploiting everything illegal for profit."

Fire Thunder's detractors chimed in. They led protests from the powwow grounds in Pine Ridge to the tribal council meeting the same day that abortion rights supporters were to file the 17,000 signatures they needed to temporarily suspend the law and put it to referendum on the November ballot. "The Oglala Sioux do not kill babies, and babies' blood will not flow on our land," said Eileen Janis, one of the organizers of the tribal protest. "Our babies are sacred even in the womb."

Three days later, as the national media looked on, the Oglala Sioux Tribal Council banned abortions on Pine Ridge Indian Reservation and suspended Cecelia Fire Thunder pending impeachment proceedings. Tribal council member Will Peters said that Fire Thunder had improperly used her title and her office. "She acted outside the scope of her duties," he told a packed meeting.

Fire Thunder wasn't at the meeting. She was in Iowa getting a checkup for her cochlear implants. "I guess I got ambushed," she said.

Because she was out of town, she didn't hear the penultimate statement from one of the council members in attendance. "If you were born out of rape or incest," he said to the crowd, "thank you for being here."

THE ORLEANS PARISH PRISON reopened in mid-October 2006, though the storm had so damaged the facility only two of its 12 units were operational. Federal prisoners were among the first to return.

Some said that was because they brought in twice as much money to the prison coffers as local prisoners did. Thousands of local detainees charged with minor offenses languished for months in state facilities as Gusman sought to bring the federal prisoners back to the city. He made clear why in a sheriff's letter written in November 2006. "Our main source of revenue is per diem payments for care, custody, and control of inmates," he wrote. "We have a 90% reduction in revenue, but our fixed costs remain high."

This was the business of incarceration in New Orleans making a comeback. The parish's sheriffs had always thought of prisoners that way. After the number of state prisoners housed at OPP fell between 2002 and 2004, Sheriff Foti remarked: "If you were in the stock market, you would call this a slow-growth period." Foti also once said he wished "there were more high-profit prisoners" at OPP. When the sheriff's office requests payment from the city of New Orleans for housing city prisoners, the invoice refers to the detainees as "units," as if they were cans of soup. The "unit price" is $22.39 a day.

To hear Gusman tell it, prisoners returning to OPP, as destroyed as it was, would be good for New Orleans. Prison labor could help with clean-up. People who were charged with municipal offenses after the storm said that once they pled guilty, they were ordered to complete 40 hours of community service. Their job: cleaning up OPP buildings.

The OPP recruitment effort was so successful it caught the attention of the New Orleans City Council. In November 2006, council members asked Gusman why New Orleans was maintaining one of the highest incarceration rates in the country when its population was just a fraction of the 485,000 it had been before the storm. By that time, Gusman had 2,700 in custody. Some were being held outside of New Orleans but they would come back to the city as soon as temporary jails in high-tech tents were set up near the House of Detention.

As far as locking up people for minor offenses, the council was split. While several council members said they would like to see the department steer away from arresting people for small violations, one councilwoman said she was in favor of a "zero tolerance" policy on littering and public drunkenness. She didn't want those kinds of violators arrested, but advocated that officers, for example, write summonses for people they spot flicking away a cigarette butt.

Chapter 11

TAKING INITIATIVE

JAMIE WOLF (NOT HIS REAL NAME) BEGAN to get an inkling that outside forces were influencing the abortion ban referendum in South Dakota when the radio and television ads before Election Day started getting slick. "I guess I was aware that there was tons of outside money flying at the issue, but it really dawned on me when these polished radio ads started to air," he said. "You could really tell the difference between the Yes on Six ads and those from any other initiative. Initiative 11 was about taxes and those radio ads were just factoids. The Yes on Six ads had music and background noise and professional announcers. It was a night-and-day difference."

Jamie and his wife, Elizabeth, have lived in South Dakota all their lives. He is a successful professional in Sioux Falls. Bearded, and slightly doughy, he has the countenance of an amiable science teacher or good-natured wrestling coach. Elizabeth is a tall, striking redhead. She is shy and her words are measured, but she, like her husband, was worried about how her community was being used by outside groups who had arrived with an anti-choice agenda. As it turns out, Jerry Falwell wrote to his constituents on September 14, 2006, "I will do my best to deliver thousands of people who will financially help to win this historic battle . . . what happens in South Dakota will likely affect the future of America."

"All these outside groups came in and made the issue so divisive," said Elizabeth. "We used to be able to talk about politics for hours. Now we can't. A discussion about politics, about the ban, ends up becoming an argument, so we all avoid the subject. I will be glad when the vote is over—however it turns out."

Both Jamie and his wife planned to vote against the ban. Elizabeth's family, reared as strict Catholics, was supporting the ban. "We've been careful not to talk about it," she said quietly. The concern all their friends shared, however, was what would happen if the ban succeeded. Who would pay for the costs when the ban was challenged in court? Where would the outside groups be then?

"When we're fighting this in court, and everyone knows we'll be fighting it in court, and we are paying for it, I predict South Dakotans will wonder why they ever got involved," Jamie said. "The abortion ban problem is going to become a tax hike problem and no one is going to think it is worth it."

IT WAS UNSEASONABLY WARM in South Dakota in the runup to Election Day. Activists came in from as far as New York in one direction and California in the other. Christian groups bused in young college kids to drum up support for the nation's first outright ban on abortion. The ACLU poured almost $200,000 into a "Vote No on 6!" campaign, and hundreds of volunteers staked out signs and knocked on doors in the days before the election.

There was a spectacle aspect to it. Teenagers in short sleeves lined main thoroughfares waving giant pink-and-blue placards: "Honk if you are voting YES on Six." Front lawns in the suburban developments were littered with "Vote Yes for Life" signs. Neighbors who were against the ban were somewhat more guarded about their view. "We put up a 'No' sign in the yard and it caused some tension with the neighbors so we took it down," one woman said, frankly. "Tempers are running pretty hot."

Leslee Unruh, of the Vote Yes for Life campaign, claimed her volunteers had distributed 42,000 signs. She saw the vote as coming down to three things: what people's churches said, what their families said, and what their neighbors said.

"You can say that about any vote," Kate Looby of Planned Parenthood said in a measured response. "Whatever people are saying publicly, I'm convinced that once people are in the privacy of the voting booth, they will feel empathy and compassion and vote against the ban."

THERE ARE FEW PLACES on earth where one could be impeached as president in the summer and be a viable candidate on the ballot in the fall. Pine Ridge Reservation, it appeared, was one of them. Cecelia Fire Thunder had run in the tribe's presidential primary while she appealed the impeachment decision and was the third-highest vote-getter. Under the tribal bylaws, only the top two finishers could run for the presidency. As far as Fire Thunder was concerned, she could now dispense with politics. But four days before the state's November elections, she got an unusual telephone call. It was a representative from the tribal election committee. "Cecelia, you're on the ballot."

Alex White Plume, the man who had ascended to the presidency after Fire Thunder was impeached, was no longer in the running, the election official explained. A federal background investigation revealed that he had an old felony conviction. Tribal law prohibits anyone convicted of a felony from holding tribal office. White Plume was appealing the election board's decision, a friend of Fire Thunder's told her on the phone, but it was unlikely to go anywhere. Documents at the U.S. District Clerk of Courts office showed that White Plume was charged with assault with a dangerous weapon in 1982. He pleaded guilty to "assault by striking, beating, or wounding" and was sentenced to probation.

Alex White Plume had been the primary's top vote-getter and now, election officials said, he was off the ballot. Fire Thunder would be facing John Yellow Bear Steele instead. "This place is like a soap opera." Fire Thunder laughed as she assigned various relatives to districts in the reservation—two would go to Allen, another would go to Porcupine, three would canvass Pine Ridge. "As Pine Ridge Turns." She smiled.

Fire Thunder pulled out 250 Xeroxed copies of her platform. They were still warm from the copier. Her son was hunting for other reams of paper that might be on the reservation. So far, he had had no luck, she said. "My platform is all about financial security," she told the group as she went over her decisions as president. There was a $38 million loan from another tribe. There were bonds to pay off.

The group listened patiently until one of her nieces spoke up. "Cecelia, you know the first thing that always comes up when people talk about you now is the abortion issue. What do we say about that?"

Fire Thunder pursed her lips. "Tell them that the ball is in another court now. It is out of our hands, it is in the hands of the South Dakota voters now. Tell them that."

Election Day arrived in its full Indian summer glory in South Dakota. It was unseasonably warm—70 degrees—and people were out trying to take advantage of the day. Kate Looby of Planned Parenthood was in the office before 9 A.M. and was slated to help with some last-minute canvassing. Opponents of the ban had managed to knock on 15,000 doors in Sioux Falls and were heading for the rural areas. Young college kids supporting the ban stationed themselves on 41st and Louise, a main thoroughfare in Sioux Falls, with their signs. "Honk if you support Six," they read. There were a lot of honks. Nearly every car that passed sounded its horn. If the cacophony was a poll, it looked like a bleak day for those battling the abortion ban. Looby, for her part, was cautiously optimistic. She thought it would be a squeaker—perhaps 51 percent to 49 percent opposing the ban. In the end, she suspected, the voters of South Dakota would decide that they didn't want to ban abortions in the case of rape or incest, and the Pierre legislature would try again next year with another bill.

Kate Looby was right. South Dakota voters defied the polls and decided that banning abortions for victims of rape and incest went too far. They overturned the ban, 56 percent to 44 percent, even though it appeared to have the best chance at challenging *Roe v. Wade*.

"The battle is a marathon," Vote Yes for Life's Unruh said after the loss. "There are stories and stories and stories of what happens emotionally and physically to those of us who have made that choice. I believe the Supreme Court will listen and overturn *Roe* when they hear about them."

Legislators promised to take another crack at the law in 2007. "This isn't over," one legislator said.

Cecelia Fire Thunder, with only four days to campaign, fared less well. She lost by 1,000 votes. No one could be sure if it was her stand on women's reproductive rights or something else altogether that defeated her.

THE RESULTS OF THE November 2005 school board election in Dover were hardly surprising. But to Robert Eshbach, Spahr's colleague and a son of a minister in Dover who went to high school there before coming back as a science teacher, the win was particularly sweet. He had helped organize the ouster of the eight. "Never in my wildest dreams did I think we would vote them all off," he said. It was a total repudiation of the proponents of intelligent design. Voters swept all eight members up for reelection who had backed the measure out of office and replaced them with a slate of candidates who had campaigned vigorously against it. The people of Dover appeared to be tired of the trial and tired of having intelligent design define their town.

Days later, Dover was back on the national stage, this time in the crosshairs of Christian evangelist Pat Robertson. "I'd like to say to the good citizens of Dover: if there is a disaster in your area, don't turn to God, you just rejected him from your city," Robertson told the broadcast audience of his television program, *The 700 Club.* "And don't wonder why he hasn't helped you when problems begin, if they begin. I'm not saying they will, but if they do, just remember, you just voted God out of your city. And if that's the case, don't ask for his help because he might not be there," he said.

When Bert Spahr heard the attack at school the next day, she scoffed. "It was like the locusts were about to descend," she said later, laughing about it. "It was a totally ridiculous thing to say. I don't hold Mr. Robertson in very high regard."

THE TEACHERS AT DOVER High School were hoping for an early Christmas present. They had been anticipating a verdict in the case before school ended for the holiday break. The librarians in the Audio-Visual Department heard it first—they saw the verdict scroll across the bottom of the screen and started screaming and hugging one another. Someone slipped out to run down to Bert Spahr's classroom.

Spahr, for her part, was in the middle of a chemistry lesson when someone arrived at the classroom door and breathlessly told her to switch on CNN. Judge Jones had found for the plaintiffs. Intelligent design could not be taught in Dover's science classrooms. Spahr couldn't contain herself. She burst out of her classroom right into the arms of another science teacher, Rob Eshbach. Without thinking, he picked up his boss, swung her high in the air, and gave her a hug.

"Now we're two for two," Spahr remembered saying. The fundamentalist members of the school board were gone and now a judge had sounded a death knell for ID. "I remembered thinking that we would not have to deal with intelligent design in January, which was the nicest Christmas present we could ever have."

In a 139-page decision, Judge Jones had ruled that intelligent design was a religious belief, not a valid scientific theory, and teaching it in a public school science classroom would violate the Constitution. "The breathtaking inanity of the Board's decision is evident when considered against the factual backdrop which has not been fully revealed through this trial," the judge wrote in his opinion. "The students, parents and teachers of the Dover Area School District deserved better than to be dragged into this legal maelstrom, with its resulting utter waste of monetary and personal resources."

Kitzmiller v. Dover was a decisive victory for the opponents of intelligent design. Not only did Judge Jones rule that it was unconstitutional to teach intelligent design in a biology class, he said the Dover school district had violated the Constitution by ordering teachers to read a statement challenging Darwin's theory of evolution. Jones was careful to say that he was not an activist judge but had to deal with the issue in response to the actions of the Dover Area School Board. They had tried to conceal their religious motivations for wanting teachers to read a statement against evolution. "We find that the secular purposes claimed by the board amount to pretext for the board's real purpose, which was to promote religion in the public school classroom," Judge Jones wrote. "The evidence at trial demonstrates that intelligent design is nothing less than the progeny of creationism. ID is a religious view, a mere re-labeling of creationism, and not a scientific theory. This tactic is at best disingenuous and at worst a canard. The goal of the [movement] is not to encourage critical thought but to foment a revolution which would supplant evolutionary theory with ID."

Proponents of intelligent design had lost only a battle, not the war, Richard Thompson, the chief counsel for the Thomas More Law Center, told reporters after the verdict. The center was mulling an appeal. It called for teachers to sue for the right to include intelligent design in their classrooms. "We see that as an issue of academic freedom," he said. "Teachers who have specialized education in their fields should be allowed to present the course in accord with the latest scientific information as they see fit."

Spahr celebrated with friends that night. "They will have to call it something else," she said later of intelligent design. "I suspect 'sudden emergence' will be the new term."

Jen Miller, the young biology teacher who had dropped the timeline from her biology lesson plan, agreed. "The movement's not dead. It would be naïve to think it was. But I learned a lot from this. When we danced around the issue, we did the students a disservice," she said. "Next year, I am starting the biology class with evolution."

Intelligent design had been foiled in Dover by a united front of teachers led by Bert Spahr. Clearly she was able, to coin a Spahrism, to take ID out at the knees.

IN JANUARY 2007, GREG DAVIS found himself back in Templeman IV—one of the few functioning buildings in the devastated OPP. His story is a familiar one. Following his release, Davis still had unpaid fines to pay. Then he got picked up again. A resigned Davis says: "I've been in and out of jail my whole life." Pam Metzger, "Miss Pam" as Davis calls her, has a different reaction. She's pissed: "I guess seven months in jail wasn't enough? And they have the unmitigated gall to get their $448 after you serve seven months? Instead of giving this man an apology. Instead of saying we are so sorry. And instead of apologizing for losing seven months, what do we do? We put out an arrest warrant to collect the money from Davis."

Once again, Metzger took Davis's case. But this time, they have 32 full-time public defenders in the office. "We have a public defenders' office today because of sheer force of will. This public defenders' office was willed into existence," Metzger said. "We are not stopping. Nobody is e-v-e-r going to stop us."

Persistence also paid off in the context of domestic government spying. In August 2007, the Department of Defense announced its decision to shut down the TALON database. A Pentagon spokesman, Col. Gary Keck, said that TALON was being shut down not because of public criticism but because "the analytical value had declined." A month later, a federal court in New York struck down the Patriot Act's National Security Letter (NSL) provision. A young ACLU lawyer, Jameel Jaffer, argued that "there must be real, meaningful checks on the exercise of executive power." The NSLs lacked such a check. Judge Victor Marrero agreed: "In light of the seriousness of the potential intrusion in the individual's personal affairs and the significant possibility of a chilling effect on speech and association—particularly of expression that is critical of the government or its policies—a compelling need exists to ensure that the use of NSLs is subject to the safeguards of public accountability, checks and balances, and separation of powers that our Constitution prescribes."

Lindh's attorneys filed seven motions to dismiss the various counts in the indictment. One motion sought dismissal based just on

the statements made by Attorney General Ashcroft. Judge Ellis denied all seven motions. The statements Lindh made while in U.S.
military custody in Afghanistan were never scrutinized in court. Was
he under duress? Was he tortured when he provided all of the information? Rather than open this to debate, the government preferred to
dismiss the most serious charges against Lindh in a plea agreement.
Lindh's lawyers said the government acquiesced because they didn't
want the evidence of military abuse to be introduced in court at the
suppression hearing. On July 15, just as the evidentiary hearing was
about to begin—a hearing that promised to expose the military's treatment of Lindh—the prosecution and Lindh's legal team reached
agreement on a plea.

Michael Chertoff, who later became Secretary of the Department
of Homeland Security, headed the Justice Department's criminal division at the time. He was overseeing all the department's terrorism prosecutions. His team offered Lindh the deal. They said they would drop
the most serious charges—attempted murder, conspiracy to kill Americans, and general terrorism—in exchange for a guilty plea on the
charges of "providing assistance to an enemy of the U.S." and of "carrying a weapon." To Lindh's attorneys, the deal seemed more appealing
than facing a trial in a conservative court around the anniversary of
9/11. The prosecution insisted on three other caveats: Lindh would
have to sign a document that said he had not been tortured (they used
the phrase "intentionally mistreated"); he would have to waive any right
to sue the Defense Department in the future; and he would be sub-
jected to "special administrative measures," unilaterally placed him by
Attorneys General Ashcroft and later Gonzales. The measure included
a gag order: John Walker Lindh could not talk about his experiences in
Afghanistan for the duration of his sentence.

In his plea agreement, John Walker Lindh acknowledged that by
serving as a soldier in Afghanistan he had violated the anti-Taliban
economic sanctions imposed by President Clinton and extended by

President Bush. He also agreed to a weapons charge because he had carried a rifle and two grenades while serving in the Afghan army. All the other counts in the indictment were dropped, including the terrorism charges on which Ashcroft had focused in his January press conference. The agreement also dropped the conspiracy-to-commit-murder charge in connection with the death of Mike Spann. For the two offenses to which he pleaded guilty, John Walker Lindh was sentenced to two consecutive 10-year terms. The prosecutors who negotiated the plea agreement said the White House insisted on a lengthy sentence.

"I have never understood jihad to mean anti-Americanism or terrorism," Lindh said in his address to the court. "I condemn terrorism on every level—unequivocally. My beliefs about jihad are those of mainstream Muslims around the world. I believe that jihad ranges from striving to overcome one's own personal faults to speaking out for the truth in adverse circumstances, to military action in the defense of justice. The type of jihad one practices depends upon one's circumstances. But the essence of any form of jihad lies in the intent."

He acknowledged that he did not have a full understanding of the Taliban's poor human rights record. "I made a mistake by joining the Taliban," he said. "I want the court to know, and I want the American people to know, that had I realized then what I know now about the Taliban, I would never have joined them."

After a brief recess, Mike Spann's father, John Spann, addressed the court. He began by saying that he, his family, and many other people believed that John had played a role in the killing of his son. Judge Ellis interrupted and said, "Let me be clear about that. The government has no evidence of that." Spann responded, "I understand." The judge politely explained that the "suspicions, the inferences you draw from the facts are not enough to warrant a jury conviction." He said that Mike Spann had died a hero, and that among the things he died for was the principle that "we don't convict people in the absence of proof beyond a reasonable doubt."

Spann's father would later continue his campaign. In an "article of appeal," dated February 1, 2006, Johnny Spann rebuts statements made by Lindh's father. He writes that John Walker Lindh "stated that he knew that Al Queda [*sic*] members had been sent to the United States to carry out suicide missions. He stated that he had also been told about the 9/11 attacks on America, but chose to stay and continue to fight with the al-Qaeda terrorists. For all Lindh knew, his own family members could have been victims of the suicide missions." He goes on to argue, "He not only knew about the plans, but also opted—as an American—not to alert anyone about his knowledge. Lindh stated that after training camp he was asked if he like [*sic*] to go to other places to carry out terrorist activities. This proves he was just like the rest of the trainees or he would never have been ask [*sic*] to go."

Judge Ellis sentenced John Walker Lindh to a 20-year term of imprisonment that day, October 4, 2002. He could have reduced the term but said that he found the plea agreement "just and reasonable."

Although the Department of Justice dropped all of the terrorism-related charges against Lindh, Attorney General Gonzales repeatedly made public statements linking him with terrorist activity. In April 2005, Gonzales stated that Lindh was among those who had been "convicted or pled guilty to terrorism-related charges since 9/11." Later that year, in a speech in New York City, Gonzales talked about the prosecution of John Walker Lindh as part of the "fight against terrorists" (lumping him together with Zacarias Moussaoui and Richard Reid—both of whom were convicted on terrorism-related charges). Frank Lindh wrote to Attorney General Gonzales three times. Each time he asked that Gonzales make clear that John was not convicted on any terrorism-related charges. He has never received a response. An exasperated Marilyn said, "John's not a terrorist."

TWO YEARS LATER, IN June 2004, Yaser Hamdi, the Saudi-American who was captured at the same time as Lindh at the Pink Building, got some relief from the Supreme Court. They had agreed to hear his case, along with that of Jose Padilla, a Chicago gang member who was accused of planning to detonate a "dirty bomb" in America. The court remanded the Padilla case on procedural grounds, but they were unequivocal about Hamdi. In an eight-to-one decision, the justices said Hamdi should have had access to a lawyer and should have been either charged or released. Both U.S. citizens and foreign nationals can challenge their detention through the U.S. court system, the court said. In Hamdi's case, they said the government did have the authority to arrest and detain him after his capture, but that his continued detention was unconstitutional.

"Due process demands that a citizen held in the United States as an enemy combatant be given a meaningful opportunity to contest the factual basis for that detention before a neutral decision maker," Justice Sandra Day O'Connor wrote. Only Justice Clarence Thomas dissented from that basic position.

Even the conservative justice Antonin Scalia sided with Hamdi. He wrote, "The very core of liberty secured by our Anglo-Saxon system of separated powers has been freedom from indefinite imprisonment at the will of the Executive."

Less than two months after the verdict, the government announced that Hamdi would be released. In the end, Hamdi's agreement with the government required that his U.S. citizenship be revoked and barred him from suing the government. The *Washington Post* called the government's decision to release him "an adroit backflip." He was reunited with his family in Saudi Arabia.

When the parameters of Lindh's plea agreement were released, few people seemed to notice the fact that Chertoff's team was so determined to avoid any talk of Lindh's treatment in the days after he was turned over to the U.S. military—duct-taping him to a stretcher for days in an unheated shipping container, photographing him in humiliating positions, threatening him with death, waiting weeks to remove a bullet from his thigh—that they required that the plea offer have an expiration date. Lindh's lawyers had to accept the government's terms before the suppression hearing; otherwise, the whole deal was off.

The reason for the reversal is not altogether clear, though it may have had something to do with a secret, presidentially approved program of torture for Afghan captives and those suspected of ties to al-Qaeda. Now, of course, it has been revealed that the program began in late 2001. The Bush administration declared torture "abhorrent" in a December 2004 Justice Department memo. But under the leadership of Attorney General Alberto Gonzales, the Office of Legal Counsel for the Department of Justice issued three classified opinions that were later leaked to the press. The secret memos offered an expansive endorsement of the harshest interrogation techniques. And a year later, Congress further diminished any of the protections once provided by the Geneva Conventions with the Military Commissions Act of 2006.

But at the time of John Walker Lindh's arrest, the American government's policy of torturing terrorism suspects was just a rumor. Lindh's suppression hearing would have confirmed that those rumors were true—years before the Abu Ghraib pictures surfaced. (In an early court filing, government prosecutors wrote that "had Lindh not thrown his lot in with al-Qaeda and the Taliban he would not have suffered the deprivations of low temperatures, 'inadequate' food and water and 'little cover.' ")

What is more puzzling is why these public allegations and photographs didn't raise any red flags. "That may well have been a real danger signal of what was yet to come," said Senator Dianne Feinstein of California. There were early tipoffs but Lindh, human rights officials said later, may have been the earliest one. So close to the 9/11 attacks, however, Americans were not questioning the judgment of government officials. They trusted their leaders to do whatever was necessary to protect the United States.

That trust was misplaced. And when the breach of trust was first revealed through the Abu Ghraib photos and a hundred thousand pages of documents wrangled from the government by the ACLU, no high-ranking official took responsibility. Only low-level soldiers took the fall. Secretary of Defense Rumsfeld himself had authorized aggressive interrogation practices that he later was forced to rescind. But Rumsfeld would play deaf and dumb to the allegations that he knew about the torture. He would do so even though he had visited the Abu Ghraib prison around the time that the torture and abuse were taking place, and even though he received reports of concerns of the International Committee of the Red Cross about conditions at the Iraqi prison. The military doctrine of command responsibility, where a superior takes legal responsibility for the actions of the soldiers on his watch, went out the window with Rumsfeld and the torture scandal. He wasn't there when the torture happened, so it wasn't his fault. Prisoners who had been tortured in Iraq and Afghanistan felt otherwise and, with the help of the ACLU, sued Rumsfeld and three uniformed members of the military chain of command. But Rumsfeld would remain in office throughout the entire torture scandal, only to be sacrificed on the altar of partisan politics after the November 2006 elections.

Most Americans see John Walker Lindh as a traitor, not a harbinger of the government's heavy-handedness in fighting the war on terror. By extension, his mother and father have been reviled for letting him become one. Some blame his upscale rearing in Marin County. Others point to the permissiveness of liberals in northern California. When Frank Lindh looks at his son all he can see is classically American innocence. He was a teenager who found God and followed him, a 19-year-old determined enough to travel to Yemen to learn Arabic, a young man who went to fight for a cause that he believed in, but maybe didn't fully understand.

John is now 26 years old, quietly serving his 20-year sentence in a federal prison. He spends most of his time reading the Koran and books about history and politics. He remains a devout Muslim, though even that is difficult for him: the government imposed another special administrative measure that prohibits him from ever speaking Arabic—even when he is alone, even when he might want to pray. Not only has his freedom of movement and communication been taken from him, his freedom of religion apparently has too.

Rohan Gunaratna, the man who has helped the American government interview more terrorism suspects than anyone else, sees John Walker Lindh as an opportunity lost. "He could have been the poster boy against jihad. Instead now he represents heavy-handedness, America's excesses against Muslims. It's a waste."

Last December, Lindh's attorneys asked President Bush to commute his 20-year sentence, saying that John Walker Lindh and Yaser Hamdi ostensibly committed similar crimes but Lindh was the only one in jail. Hamdi never had to face criminal charges. The Justice Department hasn't responded. When he's called in Saudi Arabia, Hamdi picks up his cell phone in a light, playful way. "Yeah, I can't talk right now, I'm busy with the family, let's talk later," he said. Later, he asked for money to do an interview.

Frank Lindh and Marilyn Walker used to go visit John in Victorville, out in southern California's Mojave Desert, twice a month.

Until last year, Victorville was home to the Roy Rogers Museum—a building shaped like an old cavalry fort with a 24-foot statue of Trigger on his hind legs standing at the lobby entrance. If you narrow your eyes and imagine you are in Afghanistan, it looks eerily like Qala-i-Jhangi, the place where John Walker Lindh's life changed forever. John Walker Lindh was transferred from Victorville to a maximum security prison in Florence, Colorado, in January 2007. His parents were told only afterward. His plea agreement with the government said the government would try its best to house him in a California prison, close to his family. That too has changed for the Lindhs.

MORE THAN A YEAR after President Bush went on national television in December 2005 to acknowledge a secret wiretapping program outside the courts, little had really changed. Though Bush's opponents accused him of breaking the law by circumventing the FISA court, only a couple of lawmakers were calling for impeachment. Attorney General Alberto Gonzales labeled as "myth" the idea that the wiretapping program was "an invasion of privacy and an unlawful eavesdropping tool." The program, he maintained, didn't invade anyone's privacy "unless you are talking to the enemy in a time of war."

The Justice Department, at the end of 2006, appealed Judge Taylor's decision, which held that the program was illegal and needed to be shuttered. Taylor rejected the administration's claims that it had broad executive authority bestowed by Congress in a time of war. After the November 2006 elections swept in a Democratic majority, the White House agreed to limited congressional briefings on the program. The Justice Department's inspector general began a review of the spying program shortly after the midterm elections. It said it would look into the controls in place at the Justice Department for eavesdropping, the way the information it uncovered was used, and the department's "compliance with legal requirements governing the program."

Then on January 17, 2007, the Bush administration changed its mind. It announced that the NSA program would now come under the FISA court's review and authority. The president still retained the power to order NSA spying without FISA, the White House was quick to add. But they decided to go through FISA for now. Details on the scope of the program and the arrangement with the FISA court couldn't be discussed for national security reasons, of course.

The abrupt flipflop on the NSA issue raised more questions than it answered. What if the president decides to secretly bypass FISA again? What about the fact that he had already violated the law? What about the chilling effect on Americans' free speech? For these reasons, the ACLU decided to continue its lawsuit. Ann Beeson, the ACLU's lead attorney on the case, argued the appeal before the sixth circuit on January 31, 2007, in Cincinnati. In July 2007, a three-judge panel of the Sixth Circuit Court of Appeals overturned Judge Taylor's decision and dismissed the case, *ACLU v. NSA*. The court ruled that plaintiffs lacked the legal standing to sue because they could not definitively prove that they were subjects of the government's surveillance. In other words, you can't challenge it in court unless you can prove you were spied on, and you can't prove you were spied on because, of course, it's secret. The only judge on the panel to discuss the merits of the case declared that the warrantless surveillance was illegal. (The ACLU's appeal was pending before the U.S. Supreme Court as this book went to press.)

Notwithstanding the setbacks, Beeson sees the tide starting to turn. "Some judges are starting to react with skepticism and are starting to refuse some claims for government secrecy," she said. "Now a lot of the victims of the government's secret policies and gag orders are refusing to remain silent. They have become very effective and outspoken critics of executive abuses and government claims of secrecy. That is a start."

The Taylor ruling was a harbinger of things to come, Josh Dratel said. "I think people are beginning to realize that 9/11 didn't happen because of inadequate surveillance but it happened because we didn't have the right kind of surveillance. It wasn't because things weren't secret enough, it was because things were too secret. The FBI and the CIA were keeping things from each other."

As he saw it, because of the trauma of the attacks, people had reduced their idea of security to something that was purely physical—whether or not there was an attack. "The idea of thinking about just whether you are physically secure is absurd. That's what you get in a totalitarian state, physical security. We want more than that. We want the security of the institutions that underlie society and it isn't helping terrorists if you demand that. That's what we should expect."

KOT HORDYNSKI SMOOTHED HIS hair with a swipe of his hand and walked to the podium. He couldn't help grinning sheepishly. He stood before a ballroom of over a thousand true believers at the ACLU's membership conference in Washington, D.C. It was the last place he had expected to spend his October.

Hordynski told the story of being a student on the TALON list with a mix of savvy and youthful optimism. Dressed in an Oxford cloth button-down shirt and a V-neck sweater, he looked all Joe College. But when he began to speak there was something more. There was depth that belied his years. He talked about being a child in Poland and of growing up in a household where parents had lived under the fear of martial law. He talked about the mixture of pride and fear when he found out that Students Against War was seen as a "credible threat" by the U.S. government, but mostly he talked about what

America had given him. "This is really important because it goes deeper than activism; it goes to the heart of the matter. If students are on this list, then who isn't being spied on in America?" he said. He talked of learning about the Freedom of Information Act and going through the courts for protection. He talked about the Bill of Rights and freedom of speech. He said all of this without notes, from the heart. And then he stopped, and took a deep breath. "Going through all this made me feel something I didn't really expect, something I had never really felt before . . ." He paused. "It made me feel strangely patriotic. And I hadn't expected that."

The audience exploded into applause. It was, of course, what they all felt after listening to Kot Hordynski's story.

AFTERWORD

Anthony,

Don't shove your way of life down our throats. And if you want to keep on defending terrorists, get the hell out of America and go to Iran. And see if you can get away opening your mouth against a dictator. You phony faggot. The whole civil liberty [sic] union is full of anti-god communists, in-your-face faggots and lesbians.

R. Hudson

Mr. Hudson writes to me almost every day. I have stacks of his messages, which often come on the backs of elegant postcards of pretty New York cityscapes. Sometimes I get a full letter. Then there is radio silence for a while. And just when I think that he's gone away or gotten bored, I find a new missive in my in-box. From the postmark (10022) and return address, it appears that Mr. Hudson also lives in Manhattan. A couple of zip codes from where I live.

I get thousands of pieces of hate mail each year. Some are thoughtful and measured. Many are vitriolic. A couple just make me laugh. My assistant, Scott, has created a bulletin board of "Hate Mail of the Week," and that section of the ACLU headquarters in lower Manhattan sees more pedestrian traffic from staff and volunteers than the cubicle with the perpetually full candy dish outside the Reproductive Freedom Project two floors down.

But it is not just the crazies who say and send hateful things. Bill O'Reilly calls the ACLU the "most dangerous organization in the United States of America right now . . . second to al-Qaeda." And it gets personal. "Romero is leading the charge to change the United States into a secular-progressive (S-P) nation and is an effective and fanatical general for the S-P movement," he says. "He is a first-rate propagandist, unrelenting in his quest to bring down America's Judeo-Christian traditions." Bernard Goldberg, who wrote the book *100 People Who Are Screwing Up America,* ranked me number five. I bested President Jimmy Carter (6), Dan Rather (12), and Howard Dean (20). I am leagues ahead of Barbra Streisand (91). Goldberg writes: "It would help if everyone, starting with Anthony Romero and the ACLU, would be a little more understanding, a little more flexible, a little *less* absolutist. Right now the number one civil right most Americans care about is the one about our ass not getting blown up by some lunatic who thinks he's doing it for Allah. We'll worry about who's looking over our shoulder at the library when things calm down."

American presidents take shots too. President Reagan said that "the ACLU has severely criticized me. . . . Well, I wear their indictment like a badge of honor." The first George Bush ridiculed Michael Dukakis for being a "card-carrying member of the ACLU" and promised that "I haven't joined the ACLU nor do I have any plans to join the ACLU." Each year since 2002, we have invited his son—

George W.—to address the ACLU membership conference. The White House scheduling office sends a polite no.

I make a point of answering serious letters that take issue with a substantive topic. I see engaging the public—and even our critics—as a key part of my job.

Much of the vitriolic mail has to do with religious issues. The ACLU is often seen as anti-Christian, even atheistic. Some people, like Mr. Hudson, just think we are "anti-god communists." We're not against religion. Just the opposite. We work to protect the right of individuals to express their religious beliefs in public. We oppose putting the government in charge of deciding which religious symbols and expressions should be endorsed and financed. Look at any country in the world where the government is involved in the business of deciding which religious symbols to promote, and you will see a country with less religious freedom than the United States. Look at countries like France, Spain, and even northern European countries like Sweden. They all have less religious freedom because the government was directly involved with sponsoring religious beliefs.

My mother asks me a lot of these same questions. I explain to this devoutly Catholic woman who regularly does the first reading in her church and who holds Bible study classes at home that the only way to keep her parish strong and independent is to keep the government as far away from it as possible. "Mami, the minute you have the government deciding what after-school programs your church should run and whether to give programs like it taxpayer money, that's the day your church loses its independence. And it's just too important." She gives it some thought. I also give thought to what she says. Her views reflect those of mainstream America more than mine. Needless to say, the most important institution in my Mom's life is her church. It certainly isn't the ACLU, no matter how much she loves her son.

Religious freedom cuts both ways. The Scopes trial and its

modern-day progeny, Dover, are among the most famous religion cases. There are many other religion cases where the ACLU has defended the rights of religious people—including Christians—and the free exercise of their religious beliefs.

The ACLU came to the aid of a high school senior who wanted to put a quote from the Bible in her high school yearbook. School officials told her that it would violate church-state separation. "Hogwash," said the ACLU. The young girl had a right to free speech—including religious speech. When government officials in Virginia tried to ban baptisms in a state park's river where people were allowed to swim, the ACLU interceded. We maintained that the state couldn't discriminate against religion. And when an elementary school student was barred for singing "Awesome God" in a school talent show, because of its religious overtones, the ACLU joined a lawsuit and the court held that she had the right to go ahead and sing.

In other areas, the ACLU has taken on cases that sometimes shock our critics. When prosecutors were hell-bent on seizing Rush Limbaugh's medical records to prosecute his drug bust, the ACLU stepped in to support his right to privacy. The ACLU stood up for Oliver North's constitutional rights during the Iran-Contra scandal. When Jerry Falwell's church was being denied the right to incorporate in Virginia, the ACLU helped strike down that provision of the Virginia Constitution. The ACLU has sometimes even suffered the ire of its allies when it has argued that anti-abortion protesters have a right to march and express themselves, just as the Saint Patrick's Day parade (a private organization in Boston) has the right to choose its own message and ban a gay contingent from marching in the parade. There was the infamous case in Skokie, Illinois, where Aryeh Neier, the ACLU's director and a survivor and refugee of the anti-Semitic conflagration of World War II, insisted that neo-Nazis had the right to march through Skokie, Illinois—a community with a large population of Holocaust survivors.

Rules and principles must be neutrally applied. Rights attach to each person. Period. And that applies to the "war on terror" as well.

SINCE THE DEVASTATING ATTACKS of September 11, 2001, a national tragedy enabled the Bush administration and apologists on both sides of the political aisle to advance a highly ideological agenda. This agenda challenges some of the most basic underpinnings of our democratic system and the rule of law.

Some on both the right and left have argued that the challenges of modern-day terrorism require America to adapt its rules and restrict rights. John Yoo, a Berkeley law professor, served in the Justice Department's Office of Legal Counsel and argued that there must be a new type of paradigm in this new type of war. A 2002 OLC memorandum defined torture in this way: "Physical pain amounting to torture must be equivalent in intensity to the pain accompanying serious physical injury, such as organ failure, impairment of bodily function, or even death."

In his book *War by Other Means: An Insider's Account,* Yoo squirms on the hot seat, but doesn't give up any ground. "Looking back now, I realize that we did not explain ourselves as clearly as we could have in 2002. I failed to anticipate that the memo would leak and that it would become susceptible to quotations out of context. The definition of severe physical pain or suffering as similar in level to that accompanying organ failure, loss of limb, or death did not do justice to the more complete definition in the memo itself. The environment of war did not give us the luxury to worry about future perceptions of our work.

"But like it or not, the antitorture statute narrowly defined torture as the infliction of *severe* physical or mental pain or suffering. Congress could easily have chosen to broaden this to 'all' or 'any' physical or mental pain or suffering, or the like. It did not." But Yoo does more than snivel apologist statements in his book. Yoo takes the new paradigm a step further and argues that presidential powers need new muscle. A president's commander-in-chief role should necessarily supersede the courts, Congress, and a system of checks and balances. He writes, "The executive branch is always in operation, indeed with much the same personnel from administration to administration regardless of party. It can better react with flexibility to unforeseen events. It is difficult for anyone, Congress or the agencies, to write laws that can anticipate every future emergency. . . . As in any crisis, the administration had to act in the moment, and could not wait for Congress to prescribe detailed rules. Seeking a change in the laws might even tip off al-Qaeda to our intelligence sources and methods. Only the executive branch has the ability to adapt quickly to new emergencies and unforeseen circumstances like 9/11."

Bruce Ackerman, in a less doctrinaire way, grapples with some of the same issues in his book *Before the Next Attack: Preserving Civil Liberties in an Age of Terrorism*. Unlike Yoo, Ackerman has deep-seated concerns about the expansion of presidential powers. He proposes an "emergency constitution" that would allow the government to take necessary and extraordinary actions in the short run to prevent a second strike. Ackerman draws on prior experience, and concedes that civil liberties need to be curtailed under exigent, limited circumstances. Even Lincoln abrogated *habeas* rights during the Civil War, scholars note. Yet others like Geoffrey Stone show what a mistake those abrogations of rights really were. Ackerman struggles with the problem of "how to design an institutionally credible emergency constitution that will permit an effective short-term response without generating insuperable long-term pathologies." But if you grant the executive branch these powers in the short term, the "war on terror" paradigm will quickly provide the perfect laboratory conditions for the cancer of unchecked executive power to metastasize.

In a *New York Times* review of both Yoo's and Ackerman's books, noted and accomplished political commentator Fareed Zakaria says that both authors fail to address the broader political context.

"The United States is fighting a strange war indeed, one that is, in some fundamental ways, an extended campaign of public diplomacy against ideologies of extremism and violence. . . . In its campaign against terror groups, the United States must summon all the strength and skills it can muster. But perhaps our most potent weapons are the sense people around the world have had that the United States is an exemplar of rights and liberties and that it lives by those principles even under storm and stress. When we suspend the writ of habeas corpus, we cast aside these distinctive weapons and trade them for the traditional tools of dictatorships—arbitrary arrests, indefinite imprisonments and aggressive interrogations. Will this trade really help us prevail?"

Zakaria is right, of course.

Ackerman's well-intentioned grope for an "emergency constitution" and Yoo's more cynical "war by other means" fall apart when we consider that this so-called war is unlike other wars the United States has fought. During World War II, the allies rolled into Berlin, the Japanese emperor cried uncle, and then the American government released the 120,000 Japanese-Americans it had interned in detention camps during the hostilities. Even though the ACLU of Northern California failed to stop the internment of the Japanese and lost its lawsuit on their behalf in 1944, the end of the hostilities brought about the internees' release—a return to normalcy. It would take another 40 years to gain reparations from the government under President Reagan. But what would bring a similar end of hostilities in the "war on terror"? The capture of Osama bin Laden? That seems unlikely given the decentralized nature of modern-day terrorist cells. What is clear is that this "war on terror" will never come to a public, decisive end. It is likely, however, to shape the way we think about and experience American democracy as well as its rights and privileges for generations to come.

Many of the Bush administration's post-9/11 strategies have upset the basic system of checks and balances that we learned about in fifth-grade social studies. The genius of Hamilton and Madison was to build a necessary check against abuse of power. They knew that if you concentrated too much power in any one branch, that power would lead to abuse. That's why they designed three coequal branches of government, with each serving as a check on the other two. But that delicate balance has been upset in ways large and small. We had the president's unilateral decision to use the NSA to intercept phone calls and e-mails of Americans without any judicial review or congressional approval, in violation of the Constitution and federal law. We find portions of the USA Patriot Act that allow the FBI to seize a person's Internet records with no judicial review at all. And the Military Commissions Act of 2006 stripped detainees of their *habeas* rights and undermined the Supreme Court's ruling in *Hamdan v. Rumsfeld* that had restored some semblance of checks and balances. The fact that President Bush could climb back on his horse after being thrown by the largely conservative U.S. Supreme Court showed the extent to which this president was able to cudgel a quiescent Congress.

A Democrat-controlled Congress that was ushered in with great fanfare and promises of change in 2006 has proven to be little better. Senate Majority Leader Harry Reid (D-NV) and Speaker of the House Nancy Pelosi (D-CA) failed to restore habeas corpus or end warrantless government surveillance by the end of 2007. Most stunning of all was the Democrats' complete capitulation to the fear-mongering of the Bush Administration when they enacted in August 2007 the so-called "Protect America Act," which essentially gutted FISA and gave President Bush and Attorney General Alberto Gonzales even greater powers to intercept Americans' foreign communications without any substantive judicial review.

I confess a special scorn for a Democrat-controlled Congress that not only ignored civil liberties for the sake of political expediency but responded to the Administration's clear contempt for its constitutional role with a bizarre form of self-emasculation. It's as though they were eager to reward Attorney General Gonzales's own scorn, evasions, and condescension by giving him unchecked power over the FISA regime. It's sad to see what Congress is doing to itself as an institution, apparently because the members fear honorable unemployment more than the dishonorable irrelevance to which they are voluntarily consigning themselves. The fact that Congress is still debating whether to grant immunity to the telecommunications companies that were complicit in the illegal NSA spying program shows how misplaced our faith in civil liberties will be if we place it in the hands of politicians and pundits of any party.

We have a government that has become increasingly closed and secretive—even to our own political leaders. Government programs like the NSA spying program were under wraps for too long and documents were withheld even from senators like Patrick Leahy and Ted Kennedy. The recent disclosure that the CIA destroyed tapes documenting the interrogation of two detainees in its custody is reminiscent of the tape destruction of the Nixon administration. White House officials now appear implicated in the discussion of whether to destroy or retain the tapes. That only complicates the constitutional questions surrounding this administration. Fed up with the our government's legislative branch, which feels perfectly content with its neutered status and knee bent to the "unitary executive," the ACLU filed a contempt motion in federal court challenging the government's destruction of the tapes and failure to disclose them. Prying open this secretive government have been whistle blowers, advocacy groups such as the ACLU, the Center for Constitutional Rights, Human Rights Watch, the Freedom of Information Act (serving as democracy's X-ray), and the press.

(A quick word on the last of these: Nothing is perhaps more important to the functioning of our democracy than having a demanding and exacting press. Information is essential to ensure robust public debate. A more muscular freedom of the press means a healthier body politic. But there have been times when the press seemed to be as quiescent as Congress and the public. In the early days after 9/11, it was almost impossible to get news coverage on civil liberties issues. In October and November 2001, I would hear from members: "Where is the ACLU? Why aren't you out there in the newspapers?" "It's not from lack of trying," I would explain. In fact, there was one reporter from a major national outlet I called every day for a couple of weeks. I stalked him, urging him to write a story about civil liberties after 9/11. Finally, we had a breakthrough when he wrote the first story on civil liberties, the detention of immigrants, and the involvement of foreign embassies in January 2002. The story was a good first start, but it shouldn't have been so hard to get a major outlet to cover the beginnings of the greatest civil liberties crisis since World War II.

In the years since 9/11, the media's initial reticence has changed. The press and media have become the leading forces in cracking open a government with an unprecedented penchant for secrecy. Reporting on torture and illegal spying provide a real public service in exposing the hidden policies and activities of our government. Still, the fact that some of the leading outlets were sufficiently cowed by the administration to delay or even suppress some of their reporting on critical issues underscores the challenges to our democracy.)

As troubling for the future of America is the fact that the Bush administration's "war on terror" has focused on the "enemy within." From the outset, the "enemies within" were immigrants, primarily those of Muslim, Arab, and Asian backgrounds. But the "enemy within" quickly morphed from immigrants to individuals who merely disagreed with the government—individuals like Kot Hordynski. When the government begins to target people based on their political beliefs and not because they have done anything wrong, democratic participation gets the wind kicked out of it.

At its most fundamental level, the erosion of civil liberties in the "war on terror" undermines basic American values. When I made this argument at the conservative Federalist Society, someone came up to me afterward and said: "al-Qaeda doesn't follow the Geneva Conventions. They don't care about the laws of war. They have no trouble beheading people on television. Why should we follow the rules when our enemies won't?"

"Because we're Americans. We're better. We stand for something. We believe in something," I answered. "When we salute the flag or sing the 'Star Spangled Banner' at a baseball game, or go to the ground zero site and feel patriotic, what is it we feel?" I asked him. In a country with no unifying language, no unifying religion, no unifying culture, what binds us as Americans is our belief in the rule of law and the basic rights that the Constitution affords to everyone. Values like innocent until proven guilty; equality under the law; the right to due process; the right to talk to one's lawyer; the right to confront one's accuser; the right to rebut the evidence when charged with a crime. Those are what define us as Americans. The "war on terror" isn't about the guys in orange jumpsuits; it's about who we are as Americans. It's about what we see as a people when we look in the mirror. It's about the aspirations we set for ourselves. The land of the free and the home of the brave . . . brave enough to hold on to our freedoms even during the most difficult of times.

The "war on terror" has curbed our freedoms in areas and contexts that have nothing to do with national security. When the government uses the rationale "Trust us, we're the government," prisoners almost drown in a New Orleans jail. The "prisoners will stay where they belong," says the sheriff, and we are expected to blindly trust the people in charge. We are also supposed to blindly trust the president when he unilaterally seizes additional law enforcement powers without judicial review or congressional oversight. When we accept the mind-set that the government can strip detainees in Guantánamo of their habeas rights, it becomes a little easier to imagine stripping women of access to reproductive health services, or sentencing an 18-year-old boy to serve 17 years in prison for having oral sex with a boy three years his junior.

As the old civil liberties adage goes, "When the rights of any are sacrificed, the rights of none are safe."

"Civil liberties in the age of terror" is more than just a series of national security cases that affect a handful of people. It's about where we draw the line between government power and government restraint. It's about the ability of a people to question its government and demand accountability. It's about the transparency of a democratic decision-making process that fulfills the mandate of the majority while protecting the rights of the minority. As John Stuart Mill wrote in *On Liberty,* "The aim . . . of patriots was to set limits to the power which the ruler should be suffered to exercise over the community; and this limitation was what they meant by liberty."

IF YOU WERE EXPECTING a legal or historical analysis of the Bush "war on terror" and its impact on civil liberties, I apologize for disappointing you. If you were expecting a liberal screed with a heavy-handed, pedantic tone, I actually hope you are disappointed.

This is a book of stories—stories of real Americans who struggle to live life with dignity. The right to live with dignity is what the entire human rights struggle is all about. And that right attaches to everyone—regardless of race, creed, or gender.

This is a book about an America we may not see or experience directly. An America we may not always consciously understand, but an America we carry in our hearts. An America based on fairness, on equality, on respect for the dignity of all people.

In writing this book, I found that American spirit alive and kicking in nooks and crannies I had never imagined.

In Great Bend, Kansas, on my way to meet Matthew Limon, the car rental agent asked me if a Dodge Ram pickup truck was OK. I said it couldn't be that much different from my MINI Cooper. His eyes twinkled. He took a closer look at the car rental form and said, "New York . . . ACLU, huh? You a long way from home, boy. Welcome to Kansas." Later that night at the Page Bar, eating my supper, I struck up a conversation with Andre, a truck driver. I had guessed that he was named after a once-famous wrestler. My father used to watch professional wrestling on television and loved "Andre the Giant." I would watch it with him. This trucker wasn't a giant, but he was the Giant's namesake. I had sworn to myself that I wouldn't bring up politics in the bar or tip my liberal hand to Andre the trucker or the other hunters who were eating steaks and drinking beer. No need to ruin everyone's good time—including my own. But unable to control myself and having enjoyed two lagers and a nice chat with Andre, into the conversation about George Bush I finally plunged. I had a hard time reading him at first, since I really couldn't make eye contact. The brim of his cowboy hat often got in the way. But when he broke his long silence and thanked me for "fighting for America on a different front," I almost fell off my bar stool. I'd been bracing myself for a fight.

I also found America later the next day, sitting for hours and talking to Matt Limon in the Wendy's where he works. When I got back to my Best Western hotel, my clothes and hair smelled of the french fry grease that invisibly clung to the air inside the fast-food joint. My mind was still locked on the coming-out story of this young Latino. I heard him describe his struggle with his father's disappointment in his being gay. I saw his quiet resolve to be who he is. I remembered the same emotions coursing through my young body when I came out to my Spanish-speaking, Catholic, Puerto Rican parents. I told Matt how my father and I had reconciled our differences after he was diagnosed with lung cancer. "Sometimes it takes the strangest things," I said. "But in America, you have the right to be who you are." "Even in Larned?" Matt asked. "Even in Larned," I reassured him.

I found America in a moonlight dip in the waters of Guantánamo

Bay. When I packed for the first week of military commission proceedings in August 2004, I didn't imagine that we would go swimming at Gitmo. I brought lots of suits and ties but no swimming trunks. This was the first week of the proceedings, and I was finally granted access to Gitmo after pestering the government for years. After a long week, you couldn't help but think, "America is better than this, this is awful. It's downright embarrassing." The Australians were ribbing the Americans with, "So this is American justice?" The patriotic impulse was to argue back, but we couldn't muster up the arguments. As Americans, we were embarrassed and disillusioned.

On our last night, a bunch of us just left the Uniform Code of Military Justice, the rules of evidence, the Combatant Status Review Tribunals, and the Geneva Conventions behind and just stripped down to our underwear and plunged into the Caribbean for a respite from what we'd seen. Treading water on my back, looking at the moon, I was trying to tune out the soldiers and reporters. Then I heard a whispered, "Hey, Anthony." I looked over and treading water next to me was Bob, an army enlistee from somewhere in the South. Mississippi, I think. He spoke with a quiet earnestness. "You know I believe in our president. I believe we are doing the right thing holding these guys here. But I'm really glad you are here. You have a job to do." And then he extended a wet hand and a bone-crusher handshake as we both flailed to keep from going under the salty and balmy water.

I found America sitting in the highly ordered and perfectly sterilized science lab of Bert Spahr. I immediately sat up straighter, paid closer attention, and gave her the respect that she has demanded from generations of students who sat in the same room. I thanked Bert for having the courage to stand up for her beliefs. "We have the easy job. The hard part is finding people who have the courage to stand up." Her eyes looked like they were getting moist. And then in a blink, the moisture was gone. I must have imagined it.

And I found a sadder part of America and its seeming indifference to the plight of poor people of color when I visited New Orleans. I drove around the Lower Nines with ACLU lawyer Katie Schwartz-mann. She's young and dynamic. A fighter. New Orleans native. She shows me the devastation, but it pains her to do so. Block after block in the Lower Nines. The signs are handmade, put up by local folks so that they would know which street was which. The familiar land-marks or official street signs were long gone.

Katie's Toyota hatchback smells of cigarette smoke. We listen to brass band music—from the Social Aid and Pleasure Clubs—that is played at New Orleans jazz funerals. Oddly appropriate. Sad but up-lifting. Enjoyable. A little eerie.

Eighteen months after the storm, life has yet to come back to the Lower Nines. There are a lot of front steps to houses that are no lon-ger there. The steps look like tombstones in a graveyard. One house has the word "Baghdad" scrawled on it. Our own American city is bombed out. And you wonder if the Lower Nines will ever be re-built.

Sure, politicians make promises. Bush in New Orleans. I remem-ber President Carter coming to my native South Bronx when I was a kid, making a similar promise. But little changes for poor people of color in America.

Katrina thrust poverty and race back into America's face. It hap-pens every so often in our America. Years ago it was Newark and Detroit in flames. Now it may be Latino janitors stopping Los Ange-les traffic, demanding dignity. America looks long enough to see the reflection of its broken aspirations in the faces of poor people of color, only to recoil or flinch at what they see. The fury of Katrina should have made it harder to recoil and look away. But look away we did. Think about how we were all glued to our television sets watching the storm and fury of Katrina hit our fellow Americans with biblical venom. Compare that to our passive indifference and the prevailing view that "it's a shame what happened down there. But what can you do?" I found America, her broken promises, and her still unrealized greatness in the Lower Nines.

I smoked my first cigarette in a long while with Katie driving around the Lower Nines. It was an American Spirit. Regular. And while Bert Spahr may be too tough to cry, a tear did well up in my eye.

I BELIEVE IN THE GREATNESS of our America. In any other country the world over, the son of a waiter with a fourth-grade education would probably be a waiter with a fourth-grade education. In most countries, gay men still live in fear for their physical safety, and many never experience the openness and love that I often take for granted. The images of the two young men hanged in Iran because they were caught in a gay liaison made me further appreciate the luck of my birth. It also made me think of Matt Limon. I have been fortunate enough to offer this country the best of my talents and energies. And for that opportunity to contribute, I am eternally grateful.

I am also unapologetically patriotic. That patriotism doesn't conflict with my day job. In fact, it *is* my day job. With all of its imperfections, and broken promises, and unrealized potential, America is unlike any other place on earth. A melding of people from the world over. A history of lofty ideals. And a commitment to realizing those ideals, even if it is through lurching progress and intermittent setbacks. I believe in the goodness and fairness of the American people, from South Dakota to Dover to the Lower Nines to Larned. Progress will come only when we demand it and when we refuse to allow America's reality to fall short of its ideals. Upholding American values—in defense of our America. That is both our birthright and our responsibility.

My grandmother used to say, "*La luz de enfrente es la que alumbra.*" The light in front is the one that shines the way. That light is America.

NOTES ON SOURCES

In addition to multiple interviews with the players in these cases, we also wish to acknowledge the use of the following sources. The notes on sources below are categorized by case rather than specific chapter to help facilitate further reading on each particular issue.

WARRANTLESS WIRETAPS AND THE NSA

Leila Abboud, "Missed Signals: The Roadmap to 9/11," master's project, Graduate School of Journalism at Columbia University.

Bruce Ackerman, *Before the Next Attack: Preserving Civil Liberties in an Age of Terrorism* (New Haven: Yale University Press, 2006).

ACLU, "Comments of the American Civil Liberties Union Before the Federal Communications Commission on the Application for Consent to Transfer of Control Filed by AT&T Inc. and BellSouth Corporation," June 5, 2006.

American Civil Liberties Union et al. v. National Security Agency et al., United States District Court, Eastern District of Michigan, Southern

Division, Case No. 2:06-cv-10204, Complaint for Declaratory and Injunctive Relief. See brief on Behalf of Amici Curiae Business Leaders in Support of Plaintiffs' Motion for Partial Summary Motion; Declaration of Joshua L. Dratel; Declaration of Leonard Niehoff; Plaintiffs' Motion for Partial Summary Judgment; Statement of Undisputed Facts in Support of Plaintiffs' Motion for Partial Summary Judgment; Memorandum of Law of *Amici Curiae* National Association for the Advancement of Colored People, American-Arab Anti-Discrimination Committee, Asian American Legal Defense and Education Fund, Japanese American Citizens Defense League, the League of United Latin American Citizens, and United for Peace and Justice in Support of Plaintiffs' Motion for Partial Summary Judgment, Plaintiff's Reply Memorandum in Support of Plaintiffs' Motion for Partial Summary Judgment, Order Denying Defendant's Motion to Stay Consideration of Plaintiffs' Motion for Partial Summary Judgment.

James Bamford, *Body of Secrets* (New York: Anchor Books, 2002).

———, "Private Lives: The Agency That Could Be Big Brother," *New York Times*, December 25, 2005.

———, *The Puzzle Palace: Anatomy of the Ultra-Secret National Security Agency* (New York: Anchor Books, 2001; revised 2002).

Ann Beeson, "The Secrecy Trump," in *Liberty Under Attack* (New York: Public Affairs, forthcoming, 2007).

Joel Brinkley, "A Father Waits as the U.S. and the Saudis Discuss His Son's Release," *New York Times*, October 10, 2004.

———, "From Afghanistan to Saudi Arabia, via Guantánamo," *New York Times*, October 16, 2004.

Lowell Bergman, Eric Lichtblau, Scott Shane, and Don Van Natta Jr., "Spy Agency Data After Sept. 11 Led F.B.I. to Dead Ends," *New York Times*, January 17, 2006.

Joel Brinkley and Eric Lichtblau, "U.S. Releases Saudi-American It Had Captured in Afghanistan," *New York Times*, October 12, 2004.

Elaine Cassel, "Why Citizens Should Be Concerned When Their Government Mistreats Aliens: A Review of David Cole's *Enemy Aliens*," Findlaw .com, October 31, 2003.

Leslie Cauley, "NSA Has Massive Database of Americans' Phone Calls," *USA Today*, May 11, 2006.

Joshua L. Dratel, "A Legal Narrative: The Torture Memos," *Counterpunch*, February 1, 2005.

———, "Client Statement on *ACLU v. NSA*," retrieved September 19, 2006, from http://www.aclu.org/safefree/nsaspying/23481res20060116 .html.

Noah Feldman, "Our Presidential Era: Who Can Check the President?" *New York Times Magazine*, January 8, 2006.

Tim Golden and Don Van Natta Jr., "U.S. Said to Overstate Value of Guantánamo Detainees," *New York Times*, June 21, 2004.

Suzanne Goldenberg, "US Phone Firms Gave Spy Agency Records of Billions of Calls," *Guardian* (London), May 12, 2006.

Alberto R. Gonzales, "Prepared Statement at the Senate Judiciary Hearing on the National Security Agency's Domestic Surveillance Program," February 6, 2006.

Karen Greenberg and Joshua L. Dratel, "Interrogating Donald Rumsfeld," MotherJones.com, January 10, 2005.

———, "The Torture Papers," Washington Post Online discussion, February 15, 2005.

Eric Lichtblau, "Despite a Year of Ire and Angst, Little Has Changed on Wiretaps," *New York Times*, November 24, 2006.

———, "Justice Official Opens Spying Inquiry," *New York Times*, November 28, 2006.

Eric Lichtblau and James Risen, "Eavesdropping Effort Began Soon After Sept. 11 Attacks," *New York Times*, December 18, 2005.

———, "The Program: Spy Agency Mined Vast Data Trove, Officials Report," *New York Times*, December 24, 2005.

———, "Justice Deputy Resisted Parts of Spy Program," *New York Times*, January 1, 2006.

———, "Legal Rationale by Justice Dept. on Spying Report," *New York Times*, January 20, 2006.

———, "The Hearings: Top Aide Defends Domestic Spying," *New York Times*, February 7, 2006.

Adam Liptak, "Many Experts Fault Reasoning of Judge in Surveillance Ruling," *New York Times*, August 18, 2006.

———, "Panel Dismisses Suit Challenging Secret Wiretaps," *New York Times*, July 7, 2007.

———, "Judge Voids F.B.I. Tool Granted by Patriot Act," *New York Times*, September 7, 2007.

Adam Liptak and Eric Lichtblau, "Judge Finds Wiretap Actions Violate the Law," *New York Times*, August 18, 2006.

Jerry Markon, "Hamdi Returned to Saudi Arabia," *Washington Post*, October 12, 2004.

————, "Father Denounces Hamdi's Imprisonment," *Washington Post*, October 13, 2004.

Jane Mayer, "Annals of Justice: Outsourcing Torture," *New Yorker*, February 14 and 21, 2005.

"National Security Agency Hall of Honor: Herbert O. Yardley," retrieved December 29, 2006, from http://www.nsa.gov/honor/honor00006.cfm.

"National Security Agency Museum: American Black Chamber Exhibit," retrieved December 29, 2006, from http://www.nsa.gov/honor/honor 00006.cfm.

James Risen, "The War on Terror, Under New Scrutiny," *New York Times*, November 28, 2006.

————, *State of War: The Secret History of the CIA and the Bush Administration* (Free Press, 2006).

————, "Bush Signs Law to Widen Reach for Wiretapping," *New York Times*, August 6, 2007.

Anthony D. Romero, "A Little Straight Talk, Please, on the NSA Scandal," *Salt Lake Tribune*, May 20, 2006.

Don Rothwell, "David Hicks and the US Military Commissions Process: Next Steps," *Jurist Legal News and Research*, October 11, 2006.

David Savage, "No Trials for Key Players: Government Prefers to Interrogate Bigger Fish in Terrorism Cases Rather Than Charge Them," *Los Angeles Times*, May 4, 2006.

John Shovelan, "Guantanamo Detainees Win Right to Appeal Their Detention," ABC Online, June 29, 2004.

TheTalkingDog.com, blog interview with Joshua Dratel, May 8, 2005.

Time, "A Verdict Against Richard Nixon," December 27, 1976.

White House, Office of the Press Secretary, Press Briefing by Scott McClellan, January 17, 2006.

"With Democrats Like These . . ." [Editorial] *New York Times,* October 20, 2007.

TORTURE, DETENTION, AND THE CASE OF JOHN WALKER LINDH

ACLU Fact Sheet, "El-Masri v. Tenet: Background on the State Secrets Privilege."

American Civil Liberties Union, "America's Disappeared: Seeking International Justice for Immigrants Detained After September 11," January 2004.

————, "Enduring Abuse: Torture and Cruel Treatment by the United States at Home and Abroad," April 2006.

————, Washington Legislative Office, "Conduct Unbecoming: Pitfalls in the President's Military Commissions," March 2004.

Associated Press, "Yaser Esam Hamdi: Saudi-American Speaks Out on Confinement," October 16, 2004.

James Best, "Black Like Me: John Walker Lindh's Hip-Hop Daze," *East Bay Express,* September 3, 2003.

Joel Brinkley, "A Father Waits as the U.S. and the Saudis Discuss His Son's Release," *New York Times,* October 10, 2004.

————, "U.S. Releases Saudi-American It Had Captured In Afghanistan," *New York Times*, October 11, 2004.

————, "From Afghanistan to Saudi Arabia, via Guantánamo," *New York Times*, October 16, 2004.

James Brosnahan (attorney for John Walker Lindh), Commutation Petition, December 20, 2005.

CNN.com, "Second American Taliban on U.S. Soil," April 5, 2002.

David Cole, "Why the Court Said No," *New York Review of Books*, August 10, 2006.

Lawrence Donegan, "Doubts Cloud US Taliban Case," *Observer*, February 17, 2002.

Khaled El-Masri, press statement, November 28, 2006.

————, "I am not a state secret," *Los Angeles Times*, March 3, 2007.

William Glaberson, "In Shift, Justices Agree to Review Detainees' Case," *New York Times*, June 30, 2007.

Tim Golden, "The Battle for Guantánamo," *New York Times Magazine*, September 17, 2006.

Jack Goldsmith, *The Terror Presidency: Law and Judgment Inside the Bush Administration* (New York: W.W. Norton & Company, 2007).

Alberto R. Gonzales, "Memorandum for the President. Subject: Decision Re Application of the Geneva Convention on Prisoners of War to the Conflict with Al-Qaeda and the Taliban," January 25, 2002.

————, prepared remarks at the Council on Foreign Relations, December 1, 2005.

Linda Greenhouse, "Legal Battles Resuming on Guantánamo Detainees," *New York Times*, September 1, 2007.

————, "Supreme Court Refuses to Hear Torture Appeal," *New York Times*, October 10, 2007.

Human Rights Watch, "Afghanistan, Humanity Denied: Systemic Violations of Women's Rights in Afghanistan," October 2001.

————, "Military Assistance to the Afghan Opposition: Human Rights Watch Backgrounder," October 2001.

————, "The Road to Abu Ghraib," June 2004.

Tom Junod, "Innocent: The State of the American Man," *Esquire*, July 1, 2006.

————, "The Reach of War: Legal Advice; Author of '02 Memo on Torture: 'Gentle' Soul for a Harsh Topic," *New York Times*, June 24, 2004.

Lakhdar Boumediene, et al., v. George W. Bush, et al., and *Khaled A. F. Al Odah, et al., v. United States, et al.*, Brief *Amicus Curiae* of the American Civil Liberties Union and Public Justice in Support of Petitioners, August 24, 2007.

Frank Lindh, "The Crimeless Crime: The Prosecution of John Walker Lindh," *Washington Lawyer*, May 2005.

————, "John Lindh: Constitutional and Human Rights Dimensions of an Extraordinary Case," Speech at the Commonwealth Club, San Francisco, January 19, 2006.

John Walker Lindh, "Thoughts on the Legitimacy of Suicide Bombings," *Coastal Post*, March 2003.

Adam Lisberg, "An Exclusive Look at Lindh's Life Behind Bars," *New York Daily News*, November 2, 2006.

Joseph Margulies, *Guantánamo and the Abuse of Presidential Power* (New York: Simon & Schuster, 2007).

Jerry Markson, "Hamdi Returned to Saudi Arabia," *Washington Post*, October 12, 2004.

———, "Father Denounces Hamdi's Imprisonment; Son Posed No Threat to U.S., He Says," *Washington Post*, October 13, 2004.

Mark Mazzetti, "C.I.A. Destroyed 2 Tapes Showing Interrogations," *New York Times*, December 6, 2007.

Mark Mazzetti and Scott Shane, "Bush Lawyers Discussed Fate of C.I.A. Tapes," *New York Times*, December 19, 2007.

Jane Mayer, "Lost in the Jihad," *New Yorker*, March 10, 2003.

———, "Measuring Betrayal, Q & A," New Yorker Online, March 10, 2003.

Alfred W. McCoy, *A Question of Torture: CIA Interrogation from the Cold War to the War on Terror* (New York: Metropolitan Books, 2006).

Tara McKelvey, *Monstering: Inside America's Policy of Secret Interrogations and Torture in the War on Terror* (New York: Carroll & Graf, 2007).

Barbara D. Metcalf, " 'Traditionalist' Islamic Activism: Deoband, Tablighis, and Talibs," *Social Science Research Council*, retrieved January 22, 2007, from http://www.ssrc.org/sept11/essays/metcalf.htm.

Minnesota Daily, "Justice for the American Taliban," editorial, April 17, 2006.

Newsweek Web exclusive, "Examining the E-mail," June 15, 2002.

Jim Puzzanghera, "Abuse Foreshadowed in Lindh Case," *San Jose Mercury News*, May 15, 2004.

Jonathan Raban, "The Prisoners Speak," *New York Review of Books*, October 5, 2006.

James Risen and Eric Lichtblau, "Bush Lets U.S. Spy on Callers Without Courts," *New York Times*, December 16, 2005.

———, "Rice Defends Domestic Eavesdropping," *New York Times*, December 19, 2005.

———, "Spying Program Snared U.S. Calls," *New York Times*, December 21, 2005.

Nic Robertson, CNN interview with Yaser Hamdi, CNN.com, October 14, 2004.

Timothy Roche, Brian Bennett, Anne Berryman, Hilary Hylton, Siobhan Morrissey, and Amany Radwan, "The Making Of John Walker Lindh," *Time*, October 7, 2002.

Kenneth Roth, Minky Worden, and Amy D. Bernstein, eds., *Torture: Does It Make Us Safer? Is It Ever OK?* (New York: New Press, 2005).

Charlie Savage, "Moussaoui Pleads Guilty to Conspiracy but Denies Role in 9/11 Attacks," *Boston Globe*, April 23, 2005.

Scott Shane, David Johnston, and James Risen, "Secret U.S. Endorsement of Severe Interrogations," *New York Times*, October 3, 2007.

Tamara Sonn, Report to James Brosnahan, George Harris, Tony West, and Raj Chatterjee Regarding John Lindh, August 22, 2002.

Johnny Spann, "False and Misleading Statements by Mr. Frank Lindh: Article of Appeal," February 1, 2006, from http://www.honor mike/ spann.org/pdfs/flindh_retort_feb2006.pdf.

J. Stevens, opinion, *Hamdan v. Rumsfeld*, 126 U.S. 2749 (2006).

———, opinion, *Rasul v. Bush*, 542 U.S. 466 (2004).

"Supreme Disgrace" [Editorial] *New York Times*, October 11, 2007.

U.S. Department of Justice, Office of Legal Counsel, "Memorandum for Alberto R. Gonzales, Counsel to the President," August 1, 2002.

Jennifer Van Bergen, "Methods Questioned in Investigation Leading Up to the Sears Tower Arrests," TheRawStory.com, June 29, 2006.

Margaret Warner, "Plea Bargain," Online NewsHour, July 15, 2002.

Pete Williams, "High Profile Terror Arrests Yield Small Sentences," NBC News.com June 27, 2006.

Yaser Esam Hamdi v. Donald Rumsfeld, Brief Submitted on Behalf of the American Civil Liberties Union and American Civil Liberties Union of Virginia as Amici Curiae, United States Court of Appeals for the Fourth Circuit, No. 02-7338; O'Connor, J., opinion, *Hamdi v. Rumsfeld*; Scalia, J., dissent, *Hamdi v. Rumsfeld*.

John Yoo, *War by Other Means: An Insider's Account of the War on Terror* (Atlantic Monthly Press, 2006).

Fareed Zakaria, "The Enemy Within: Does the War on Terror Require Completely New Laws?" *New York Times Book Review*, December 17, 2006.

United States of America v. John Phillip Walker Lindh, Proffer of Facts in Support
of Defendant's Suppression Motions, June 13, 2002; Grand Jury Indictment,
February 2002; Memorandum of Points and Authorities in Support of Defendant's Motion to Suppress the Interrogation by US Agents at Qala-i-Janghi and
the Defendant's Responsive Silence, June 17, 2002; Defendant's Memorandum
of Points and Authorities in Support of Motion to Suppress Statements for
Violation of His Fifth Amendment Rights, June 14, 2002; Defendant's Memorandum of Points and Authorities in Support of Motion to Suppress Statements
Made on December 1, 2001, to US Special Forces and Robert Pelton, June 17,
2002; Defendant's Sentencing Memorandum, September 26, 2002; Prepared
Statement of John Walker Lindh to the Court, October 4, 2002.

DOCUMENTS RELEASED PURSUANT TO ACLU FREEDOM OF INFORMATION ACT REQUEST

"ARCENT CAAT Initial Impressions Report (IIR)," chapters 3–9.

Documents relating to charges against (partially redacted by U.S.
government), from http://action.aclu.org/torturefoia/released/050206.

Memorandum from AOSO-DCG re: Findings and Recommendations
Regarding 15-6 Investigation of Photographs Taken of John Walker Lindh
by 5th Special Forces Group (Airborne), aclu.org/projects/foiasearch/pdf/
DoD 016246.pdf.

Memorandum for Commander, United States Army Special Forces Command
(Airborne), Fort Bragg, North Carolina 28310. Subject: Review of Informal 15-
6 Investigation, aclu.org/projects/foiasearch/pdf/DoD 016261.pdf.

Memorandum for Col. David Buford, United States Army Special Forces
Command (Airborne), Fort Bragg, North Carolina 28310. Subject:
Appointment as Investigating Officer. From Geoffrey C. Lambert, Major
General, USA, Commanding General, aclu.org/projects/foiasearch/pdf/
DoD 016273.pdf.

Report of Proceedings by Investigating Officer AR 15-6, aclu.org/projects/foiasearch/pdf/DoD 016291.pdf.

Letter re John Walker Lindh from his attorney, James Brosnahan, to Powell, Ashcroft, Rumsfeld, Tenet, McNamara.

"Detention of American Citizens as Enemy Combatants," Congressional Research Service Report to Congress.

SCOPES IN REVERSE: THE DOVER CASE

Kurt Anderson, "Backward, Christian Soldiers! Why Must Intelligent Design Be Stopped?" *New York*, January 9, 2006.

Peter Applebome, "70 Years after Scopes Trial, Creation Debate Lives," *New York Times*, March 10, 1996.

Mike Argento, "Scientists, Sex Mark Day 10," *York Daily Record*, October 18, 2005.

———, "Behe's 15th Century Science," *York Daily Record*, October 19, 2005.

———, "The Makings of a Bad Defense," *York Daily Record*, October 21, 2005.

Larry Brumley, "Dembski Relieved of Duties as Polanyi Center Director," Baylor University Press Release, October 19, 2000.

John Angus Campbell and Stephen Meyer, "Evolution: Debate It," *USA Today*, August 15, 2005.

Paul Chesser, "Big Mouth Pat," *American Spectator*, January 10, 2006.

Percival Davis and Dean H. Kenyon, *Of Pandas and People: The Central Question of Biological Origins,* 2nd ed. (Dallas: Haughton Publishing Co., 2004).

David DeWolf, John West, Casey Luskin, and Jonathan Witt, *Traipsing into Evolution: Intelligent Design and the Kitzmiller v. Dover Decision* (Discovery Institute Press, 2006).

Discovery Institute, Center for Science and Culture, "Santorum Language on Evolution," retrieved January 22, 2007 from http://www.discovery.org/scripts/viewDB/index.php?command=view&id=1109.

Economist, "Intelligent Design Rears Its Head," July 30, 2005.

M. J. Ellington, "The Pledge of Allegiance's Surprising Past," *Decatur Daily,* July 3, 2005.

Hudson Institute, "Hudson Institute History," retrieved January 17, 2007, from http://www.hudson.org/learn/index.cfm?fuseaction=history.

Woody Klein, *Liberties Lost: The Endangered Legacy of the ACLU* (Westport, Conn.: Praeger, 2006).

Marquis James, "Dayton, Tennessee: A Summary," *New Yorker,* July 11, 1925.

Al Kamen, "Supreme Court Voids Creationism Law," *Washington Post,* June 20, 1987.

Christina Kauffman, "New Criticism for Dover Intelligent Design Ruling," *The York Dispatch,* December 12, 2006.

Edward J. Larson, "The Biology Wars: The Religion, Science and Education Controversy," transcribed remarks at Pew Forum's Faith Angle Conference on Religion, Politics and Public life, Key West, Florida, December 5, 2005.

Lauri Lebo, "Some Allies Question Dover Board's Policy," *York Daily Record*, December 19, 2004.

———, "Dover Area in Spotlight," *York Daily Record*, November 23, 2004.

———, "Intelligent Design Lawsuit Coming," *York Daily Record*, December 14, 2004.

———, "She Hopes for Change," *York Daily Record*, December 15, 2004.

———, "Dover Figures Deny Remarks on Creationism," *York Daily Record*, January 16, 2005.

———, "Experts Won't Back Dover," *York Daily Record*, November 15, 2005.

———, "Dover Leads Fake Report on Evolution," *York Daily Record*, September 14, 2005.

———, "Scientist: Design Is Science," *York Daily Record*, October 18, 2005.

Rick Lee, "Judges' Wording Often Borrowed," *York Daily Record*, December 13, 2006.

Dwight MacDonald, "Profiles: The Defense of Everybody," *New Yorker*, July 11, 1953.

———, "Profiles: The Defense of Everybody—II," *New Yorker*, July 18, 1953.

Joseph Maldonado, "Dover Schools Still Debating Biology Text," *York Daily Record*, June 9, 2004.

———, "Residents Join Creation Debate," *York Daily Record*, June 10, 2004.

———, "Book Is Focus of More Debate," *York Daily Record*, June 15, 2004.

———, "Bio Book Might Be Approved," *York Daily Record*, July 14, 2004.

———, "Biology Book Squeaked By," *York Daily Record*, August 4, 2004.

———, "Controversial Bio Book Allowed," *York Daily Record*, October 5, 2004.

———, "Pandas Book Prompts Concerns," *York Daily Record*, October 7, 2004.

———, "Parents React to Decision," *York Daily Record*, October 20, 2004.

———, "Dover Curriculum Move Likely a First," *York Daily Record*, October 20, 2004.

———, "Creation Debate Draws in Teachers," *York Daily Record*, October 24, 2004.

———, "Union Says Intelligent Design Questions Still Unanswered," *York Daily Record*, December 3, 2004.

———, "Dover Science Faculty Uneasy," *York Daily Record*, December 4, 2004.

———, "Dover Area Loses Official, Again," *York Daily Record*, December 7, 2004.

———, "Board Member Says the Worst Is Coming," *York Daily Record*, December 8, 2004.

————, "District Officials Consider Suit, Ponder Response," *York Daily Record*, December 19, 2004.

Steven C. Meyer and John Angus Campbell, "Controversy over Life's Origins: Students Should Learn to Assess Competing Theories," *San Francisco Chronicle*, December 10, 2004.

New York Times, "Justices Hear 2 Views on Creation Law," December 11, 1986.

H. Allen Orr, "Annals of Science: Devolution," *New Yorker*, May 30, 2005.

"The Pandas Scam," from the *Textbook Letter,* March–April 1990.

Michael Specter, "Political Science: The Bush Administration War on the Laboratory," *New Yorker*, March 13, 2006.

Michelle Starr, "Debate over Statement Perplexes Students," *York Daily Record*, October 13, 2005.

————, "Nilsen Doesn't Recall Details," *York Daily Record*, October 21, 2005.

————, "Origin of Board Decision Probed," *York Daily Record*, November 3, 2005.

————, "Dover Trial Witnesses Treated Like Royalty," *York Daily Record*, May 16, 2006.

Margaret Talbot, "Darwin in the Dock: Intelligent Design Has Its Day in Court," *New Yorker*, December 5, 2005.

Margaret Graham Tebo, "An Evolving Conflict: Intelligent Design Proponents May Have Lost a Battle but They'll Continue the Fight," *ABA Journal*, March 2006.

Bill Toland, "Intelligent Design: Is It Just Creationism Lite?" *Pittsburgh Post Gazette*, January 9, 2005.

Shanker Vedantam, "Eden and Evolution," *Washington Post*, February 5, 2006.

Samuel Walker, *In Defense of American Liberties: A History of the ACLU*, 2nd edition (Carbondale and Edwardsville: Southern Illinois University Press, 1999), chapter four, "The First Victories 1925–1932."

Jonathan Wells, "Survival of the Fakest," *American Spectator*, December 2000.

Jodi Wilgoren, "Politicized Scholars Put Evolution on the Defensive," *New York Times*, August, 21, 2005.

TRANSCRIPTS

Transcripts of Proceedings of Bench Trial Before Honorable John E. Jones III, Courtroom Number 2, Federal Building, Harrisburg, Pa.

Plaintiff's Pretrial Memorandum, *Kitzmiller v. Dover.*

Complaint, *Kitzmiller v. Dover.*

Defendants' Statement of Material Facts Pursuant to LR 56.1, *Kitzmiller v. Dover.*

Plaintiffs' Response to Defendants' Statement of Material Facts Pursuant to LR 56.1, *Kitzmiller v. Dover.*

Opposition to Defendants' Motion for Summary Judgment.

Memorandum Opinion, *Kitzmiller v. Dover.*

THE PERFECT STORM:
NEW ORLEANS PARISH PRISON

American Civil Liberties Union, National Prison Project, "Abandoned & Abused: Orleans Parish Prisoners in the Wake of Hurricane Katrina," August 2006.

Peter Applebome and Jonathan Glater, "The Lawyers; Storm Leaves Legal System a Shambles," *New York Times*, September 9, 2005.

Dan Baum, "Letter from New Orleans: The Lost Year. Behind the Failure to Rebuild," *New Yorker*, August 21, 2006.

Pearl Bland, OPP Prisoners Questionnaire, ACLU National Project.

Peter J. Boyer, "Letter from Mississippi: Gone with the Surge," *New Yorker*, September 26, 2005.

Michelle Chen, "Investigation Details Abuse, Endangerment of Prisoners After Katrina," *New Standard*, November 18, 2005.

Ceci Connolly, "9th Ward: History, Yes, but a Future?" *Washington Post*, October 3, 2005.

Christopher Drew, "In New Orleans, Rust in the Wheels of Justice," *New York Times*, November 21, 2006.

Leslie Eaton, "Judge Steps in for Poor Inmates Without Justice Since Hurricane," NOLA.com, May 23, 2006.

Olenka Frenkiel, "Prisoners of Katrina," BBC News, August 10, 2006, http.//www.news:bbc.co.uk/1/tri/programmes/this-world/52-11988.stm.

Barry Gerharz and Seung Hong, "Down by Law: Orleans Parish Prison Before and After Katrina, Dollars and Sense," *Magazine of Economic Justice*, March/April 2006.

Matt Gnalzda, "Katrina Exposes Orleans Parish Prison's Flaws," *Epoch Times*, October 16, 2006.

Human Rights Watch, "New Orleans: Prisoners Abandoned to Floodwaters. Officers Deserted a Jail Building, Leaving Inmates Locked in Cells," September 22, 2006.

Laura Maggi, "N.O. Prison Critics Grill Sheriff," *New Orleans Times-Picayune*, November 15, 2006.

David Morton, "The Rise and Decline of the New Orleans Jail: Empire Falls," *New Republic*, August 14 and 21, 2006.

Laura Parker, "Louisiana Judge Might Free Some Held Since Storm," *USA Today*, August 21, 2006.

Michael Perlstein, "Katrina: Prisoners and Guards," *Times-Picayune*, September 23, 2005.

T. J. Scott, "8,200 Prisoners Evacuated After Katrina," TheNewstar.com, September 8, 2005.

Samuel Walker, "An Uncertain Defense: Presidents and Civil Liberties" (in preparation), chapter 3.

Richard A. Webster, "Prisoners Evacuated for Katrina and Scattered in Jails Throughout Louisiana," Dolan Media Newswires, 2006.

SOUND OF THUNDER:
ABORTION IN SOUTH DAKOTA

Susan Ager, "Strong Woman, in the City and on the Plains," *Detroit Free Press*, April 14, 2006.

Rose Aguilar, "The Power of Thunder," AlterNet, April 4, 2006.

Doe v. Bolton, 410 U.S. 179 (1973).

Steve Cartwright, "Fire Thunder Challenges Ban," *American Indian Report*, May 2006.

Cecelia Fire Thunder v. Oglala Sioux Tribal Council, Complaint for Injunctive and Declaratory Relief, Oglala Sioux Tribal court documents; Affidavit in Support of Temporary Restraining Order; Oglala Sioux Tribal Court documents; Motion for Temporary Restraining Order; Oglala Sioux Tribal Court documents; Order Vacating in Part Order Issued July 17, 2006; Motion to Vacate; Application for Writ of Mandamus; Order of Recusal.

Monica Davey, "National Battle over Abortion Focuses on South Dakota Vote," *New York Times*, November 1, 2006.

By-Laws of the Oglala Sioux Tribe of the Pine Ridge Indian Reservation of South Dakota.

Steven Ertelt, "South Dakota Indian Tribe Bans Abortions," LifeNews.com, May 31, 2006.

Cecelia Fire Thunder, Response to Removal Complaint, June 29, 2006, Oglala Sioux Tribal Court documents.

Tim Giago, "Oglala Sioux President on State Abortion Law," Indianz.com, March 21, 2006.

Cynthia Gorney, "Letter from South Dakota, Reversing Roe," *New Yorker*, June 26, 2006.

Bill Harlan, "Tribal Leader Rallies for Abortion Clinic on Reservation," *Rapid City Journal*, October 23, 2006.

———, "Oglala Tribe Bans Abortions," *Rapid City Journal*, June 1, 2006.

Jill Lawrence, "Some Abortion Foes Balk at South Dakota Law," *USA Today*, October 23, 2006.

Bob Mercer, "Abortion Clinic Idea Dividing Line on Pine Ridge," *Aberdeen American News*, May 27, 2006.

Megan Myers, "S.D. Rejects Abortion Ban," *Argus Leader*, November 8, 2006.

Theda New Breast, "To Lead a Nation: The Life of Cecelia Fire Thunder," *Well Nations Magazine*, May 26, 2006.

Evelyn Nieves, "S.D. Abortion Bill Takes Aim at 'Roe,'" *Washington Post*, February 23, 2006.

————, "S.D. Makes Abortion Rare Through Laws and Stigma," *Washington Post*, December 27, 2005.

Ordinance to Establish Procedure for Impeachment, Oglala Sioux.

Amanda Paulson, "South Dakota's Stark Abortion Choice," *Christian Science Monitor*, October 12, 2006.

Roe v. Wade, 410 U.S. 113 (1973).

Kathleen Sweeney, "South Dakota Indians Unanimously Vote to Ban Abortions on Reservation, Impeach Council President," *National Right to Life News*, July 2006.

Nadine Strossen, "Medical Privacy—Minors' Rights, and Other Assaults on Reproductive Freedom," prepared remarks at Planned Parenthood of Greater Cleveland 70th Anniversary Fall Forum, Cleveland, Ohio, November 4, 1999.

Shirley Velasquez, "A Woman's Health Crusader," *Glamour*, July 2006.

Samuel Walker, *In Defense of American Liberties: A History of the ACLU*, 2nd ed. (Carbondale and Edwardsville: Southern Illinois University Press, 1999), chapter four, "The First Victories 1925–1932."

KANSAS V. LIMON

Michael Bronski, "The Other Matthew," The Phoenix.com, April 25, 2006.

"Discovering New Pathways to Learning," Lakemary Center pamphlet, Paola, Kansas.

Laura Douglas-Brown, "*Bowers v. Hardwick* at 15," *Southern Voice*, July 12, 2001.

Chris Grenz, "Kline Appears on National Talk Show," *Capital Journal*, October 1, 2003.

John Hanna, "Supreme Court Rejects Harsher Treatment of Illegal Gay Sex," Associated Press, October 21, 2005.

———, "Kline Says Marriage, Consent Laws in Danger; ACLU Disputes Claim," Associated Press, September 15, 2003.

Denise Hollinshed, "Group Collects Old Wheelchairs, Has Them Fixed Up to Aid Needy Overseas," *St. Louis Post-Dispatch*, May 22, 2003.

Al Knight, "The Case of Romeo and Romeo," *Denver Post*, October 26, 2005.

Lawrence Journal-World, "Morrison Defeats Attorney General Kline," November 7, 2006.

Lawrence v. Texas, 539 U.S. 558 (2003).

Dahlia Lithwik, "What 'Is' Is: More Fun with the Kansas Teen-Sex Trial," *Slate*, August 10, 2006.

Carl Manning, "Matthew Limon Back in Court on a New Charge," Associated Press, November 18, 2005.

Allie Martin, "Kansas AG Fears Sexual Offender's Appeal May Become Homosexual Rights Test Case," *Agape Press*, September 22, 2003.

Nadia Pflaum, "A Body's Life: The Supreme Court Effectively Threw Out the Kansas Sodomy Law, but State Attorney General Phill Kline Won't Let Matthew Limon Out of Jail," *Pitch*, January 22, 2004.

State of Kansas v. Matthew R. Limon, Supreme Court of the State of Kansas, No. 00-85898-S, Syllabus by the Court; Defendant-Appellant's Supplemental Brief on Review; Brief of Amici Curiae of the National Association of Social Workers and the Kansas Chapter of the National Association of Social Workers in Support of Defendant/Appellant Matthew Limon; Supplemental Brief of Appellee; Defendant-Appellant's Response to State's Supplemental Brief on Review; Court of Appeals of the State of Kansas, No. 00-85898-A, Appellant's Opening Brief on Rehearing; Brief of Amici Curiae of the Kansas Public Health Association, American Public Health Association, American Academy of HIV Medicine, American Foundation for AIDS Research, HIV Medicine Association, International Association of Physicians in AIDS Care, National Alliance of State and Territorial Directors, National Minority AIDS Council; Petition for Writ of *Certiorari*; Appellant's Reply Brief on Rehearing; Appellant's Response to Amicus Curiae Brief of Kansas Legislators.

Ayelet Waldman, "Raped by Statute," *Salon*, May 13, 2006.

KOT HORDYNSKI AND THE TALON LIST

Editorial: "Spying on Civilians," *Time*, March 9, 1970.

Sarah Kershaw, "A Protest, a Spy Program, and a Campus in an Uproar," *New York Times*, January 14, 2006.

Mark Mazzetti, "Pentagon Intelligence Chief Proposes Ending a Database," *New York Times*, April 25, 2007.

MSNBC.com, "Department of Defense Database Listing Domestic 'Threats,'" December 13, 2005.

MSNBC.com, "Senator Demands Investigation of Spy Database," December 14, 2005.

Lisa Myers, Douglas Pasternak, Rich Gardella, and the NBC Investigative Unit, "Is the Pentagon Spying on Americans?" MSNBC.com, December 14, 2005.

Walter Pincus, "Defense Facilities Pass Along Reports of Suspicious Activity," *Washington Post*, December 11, 2005.

"UCSC Chief Alleges Spying," *San Jose Mercury News*, December 29, 2005.

GENERAL REFERENCES

Bruce Ackerman, *Before the Next Attack: Preserving Civil Liberties in an Age of Terrorism* (New Haven: Yale University Press, 2006).

Steven Brill, *After: How America Confronted the September 12 Era* (New York: Simon & Schuster, 2003).

Cynthia Brown, ed., *Lost Liberties: Ashcroft and the Assault on Personal Freedom* (New York: New Press, 2003).

Center for Constitutional Rights, *Articles of Impeachment Against George W. Bush* (Hoboken, N.J.: Melville House Publishing, 2006).

Nancy Chang and the Center for Constitutional Rights, *Silencing Political Dissent* (New York: Seven Stories Press, 2002).

David Cole and James X. Dempsey, *Terrorism and the Constitution* (New York: New Press, 2002).

David Cole and Jules Lobel, *Less Safe, Less Free: The Failure of Preemption in the War on Terror* (New York: New Press, 2007).

Diane Garey, *Defending Everybody: A History of the American Civil Liberties Union* (New York: TV Books, 1998).

Robert P. George, *Making Men Moral: Civil Liberties and Public Morality* (Oxford: Clarendon Press, 1993; reprinted 2002).

Danny Goldberg, Victor Goldberg, and Robert Greenwald, eds., *It's a Free Country: Personal Freedom in America After September 11* (New York: RDV Books, 2002).

Senator Edward M. Kennedy, *America Back on Track* (New York: Viking, 2006).

Richard C. Leone and Greg Anrig Jr., *Liberty Under Attack: Reclaiming Our Freedoms in an Age of Terror* (New York: Public Affairs, 2007).

C. William Michaels, *No Greater Threat: America After September 11 and the Rise of a National Security State* (New York: Algora Publishing, 2002).

Dina Temple-Raston, *The Jihad Next Door: The Lackawanna Six and Rough Justice in an Age of Terror* (New York: Public Affairs, 2007).

John Stuart Mill, *On Liberty* (New York: Penguin Books, 1974).

Aryeh Neier, *Taking Liberties: Four Decades in the Struggle for Rights* (New York: Public Affairs, 2003).

Bill O'Reilly, *Culture Warrior* (New York: Broadway Books, 2006).

David Rose, *Guantánamo: The War on Human Rights* (New York: New Press, 2004).

Frederick A. O. Schwarz Jr. and Aziz Z. Huq, *Unchecked and Unbalanced: Presidential Power in a Time of Terror* (New York: New Press, 2007).

Mark Sidel, *More Secure, Less Free? Antiterrorism Policy & Civil Liberties after September 11* (Ann Arbor: University of Michigan Press, 2004).

George Soros, *The Age of Fallibility: The Consequences of the War on Terror* (New York: Public Affairs, 2006).

Richard W. Steele, *Free Speech in the Good War* (New York: St. Martin's Press, 1999).

Geoffrey Stone, *Perilous Times: Free Speech in Wartime from the Sedition Act of 1798 to the War on Terrorism* (New York: W. W. Norton & Company, 2004).

John Yoo, *War by Any Other Means: An Insider's Account of the War on Terror* (New York: Atlantic Monthly Press, 2006).

INDEX